1991 Walpa Repr

The New River Early Settlement

by

Patricia Givens Johnson

Other Books by the Author
James Patton and The Appalachian Colonists
William Preston and The Allegheny Patriots
General Andrew Lewis of Roanoke and Greenbrier
Elder Jacob Miller Founder of Dunkard Churches,
Virginia, Ohio, Indiana and Descendents

Special acknowledgement is due the Great Britain Public Records Office for all references to the Great Britain Public Records, Colonial Papers, from transcripts in the Library of Congress. These transcripts of Crown-copyright records in the Public Record Office in London appear by permission of the Controller of H.M. Stationery Office.

Printed in the United States of America by
Edmonds Printing Inc.
Pulaski, Virginia

Dedicated to
The People of the New

Table of Contents

Page

Introduction 1

Chapters
I   The New River 5
II   New River Named 23
III   Flowering of the New 26
IV   Teays River and The Prehistoric New 31
V   Mondongachete... 35
VI   Curious Rising Hills and Brave Meadows 42
VII   Wood's River.. 49
VIII   Pallatia 55
IX   A Trip Through Pallatia 61
X   Patton's "Great Grant"... 66
XI   Hunters and Mahanaim.. 73
XII   The Warwick Road 86
XIII   Dr. Thomas Walker and Christopher
        Gist Go Exploring.. 94
XIV   Moravians on the New 100
XV   Patton's Law on the New 104
XVI   Frenchmen on the New... 110
XVII   The Massacres — 1755 115
XVIII   Cherokees Defend the New 123
XIX   Strange Land by the Sinking Sun 132
XX   Halifax and Bedford Defend the New 136
XVI   Cherokee War 141
XVII   The Long Hunters 152
XVIII   Pontiac's War 157
XIX   The Welsh Mines 165
XX   Treaties Place the New in Botetourt 175
XXI   First Settlement on the Upper New in Virginia 183
XXII   First Settlement on the Upper New
        in North Carolina 189
XXIII   First Settlement on the Lower New in
        West Virginia 198
XXIV   Epilogue 205
        Index 217

The New River
Early Settlement

by
Patricia Givens Johnson

Introduction

The New River is not new at all. Geologists say that it is the second oldest river in the world. Only the Nile is older. The New River's age is over 100 million years according to geologists. The New, a remnant of the prehistoric Teays River, predecessor of the Mississippi, is the oldest river in the western hemisphere. The land masses where the New rises are the oldest land masses in North America.

Just as the name New is a misnomer the theories as to how it got its name are incorrect. Not always called New River the river has had numerous names. For one hundred years it was called Wood's River.

The New has the best white water in the eastern United States. Its West Virginia Gorge called the "Grand Canyon of the East" is now the New River Gorge National River. North Carolina's New is part of the National Wild and Scenic Rivers System.

Always noted for its treacherous current, the Indians of West Virginia called it "The River of Death". A 1781 traveler along the river noted, "The New River is broad, deep and rapid, frequently impassable and always dangerous."

The New was discovered by Europeans nearly one hundred years before they actually settled along its banks. Though further west and deeper in the Virginia mountains than the Shenandoah the English had gone further west on New River than any other place in Virginia — all by 1671. Charles II sat on the throne of England when explorers Batts and Fallam crossed the Allegheny divide and walked along New River. This was forty-five years before Governor Spotswood's more famous "Knights of the Golden Horseshoe" crested the Blue Ridge and glimpsed the Shenandoah Valley. The Shenandoah Valley filled with settlers before the New River Valley but the New River had been explored first.

Batts and Fallam camped on the banks of the New, a branch of the Mississippi, two years before the famed French explorers Marquette and Joliet penetrated the Mississippi Valley. They were on the New, a branch of the Ohio, before the French explored it. Historians today question whether La Salle ever discovered the Ohio, so when Batts and Fallam walked along the New they were in the Ohio drainage basin before the French knew of it. Marquette's map of the Mississippi Valley made in the 1670's, for example, shows no Ohio Valley or New River. Batts and Fallam were not the first Europeans on the New. Others had preceded them but made no record. They are the first to record their passage through the Appalachian Mountains in Virginia into the Mississippi watershed.

England's claim to the Mississippi Valley was initially based upon the 1671 explorations by Batts and Fallam on New River. This was a fact known in England at the time, nearly forgotten by the mid-1700's, but quickly remembered when France made its bid for North America in 1754.

Since prehistoric times the New River has been a corridor between the southeastern American continent and the Mississippi and Great Lakes region. In historic times it was a warpath for the Iroquois to travel to their southern enemies. The first white settlers also used it as a pathway into the southwest, Kentucky and the midwest.

These first settlers were from such diverse places as Northern Ireland, Wales, Africa, Czechoslovakia, Alsace-Lorraine, the Rhine Valley, the cantons of Switzerland, the parishes of England and the Scottish Highlands. They came to New River from other places in America such as New England, New Jersey, North and South Carolina and Pennsylvania.

The New has always been a pathway for exploration further west. The Salling-Howard party followed it to the Mississippi. The Long Hunters followed it to Tennessee and Kentucky, Daniel Boone being first guided across the New by an African named Burrell. Following the hunters came settlers and then came Indian war, one after another for fifty years along the New.

For twenty-five years the New River was the western frontier and boundary between the Indian nations and Virginia. It was the "wild west" before the American Revolution. During that war it was a battleground for Patriots and Tories. Afterwards it was a gateway for thousands following the Wilderness Road westward.

Noted for periodic flooding the waters of the New have been tamed in the twentieth-century by numerous hydro-electric dams.

But the scenic beauty has not been destroyed due to a recent battle between the people and the largest American hydro-electric company.

Today the New River Valley is noted as a cultural and recreational center in Appalachia. Many state parks nestle along the New and several national parks touch its banks. At home in its valley are three state universities, Appalachian State University, Radford University and Virginia Polytechnic Institute and State University. Wythe Community College is in the valley as is New River Community College named for the old river. As in prehistoric times when it was a cultural corridor the New River Valley still serves the same purpose for permanent residents as well as thousands passing through to a new life.

A New River "birthing place" Blowing Rock, North Carolina

Stuart Dam on New River near the
North Carolina line

Byllesby Dam of New River

Iron Furnace on Cripple Creek

Chapter I

The New River

The New River rises in the mountains of western North Carolina crosses the entire width of the Appalachians from the Blue Ridge in North Carolina through Virginia to West Virginia where it joins the Gauley to form the Kanawha which flows into the Ohio. The waters of the New coursing to the Mississippi pass some of the most scenic and unspoiled terrain of the eastern United States.

The New is 320 miles in length. Unlike nearly every other northeastern river in the United States the New flows from south to north. Unlike every other Appalachian river it crosses the mountains from east to west cutting through every ridge of the Alleghenies.

The New does not flow along mountain ridges as most rivers do but across them. This leads geologists to theorize that the New was there before the mountains cutting its channel as the mountains rose. Parts of Ashe County where it rises are acclaimed as the oldest land masses in North America.

Many places in North Carolina are claimed as its head. The famous places, Grandfather Mountain and Blowing Rock compete with the less famous, Dog Creek, Whitetop and Silverstone, as the headwaters of New River. One tributary can be seen at Green Park Inn golf course in Blowing Rock. There in a stone niche a fine trickle of water shows us one "birthing place" of New River.

The New heads in Ashe, Watauga and Allegheny Counties, North Carolina with a North and South Fork lying at 36 degrees latitude. North Fork rises in the Stone Mountains at Whitetop, Grayson and Tolliver with tributaries of Laurel, Horse and Helton Creeks. It's 55 miles is entirely contained in Ashe County having elevations of 2800 to 5200 feet. The river plentiful with trout flows pass West Jefferson to join the South Fork.

The South Fork of New River is nearly 85 miles long, contained in Ashe and Watauga Counties. The oldest maps of the region, the

Fry-Jefferson 1751 **Map of Virginia,** published in 1753, Robert De Vaugondy's 1755 map, Collett's 1770 **Map of North Carolina,** calls South Fork, Fulcarson River. The meandering course of South Fork in a wide shallow basin indicates the eozoic age of the river. South Fork tributaries nearly touch Yadkin tributaries draining to the east. Forests cover the area. Boone, Todd and West Jefferson are the towns on South Fork. Three small streams come together near Boone known as Three Forks where the oldest church (1790) was built on the upper New. At Boone the New passes Howard Knob where stands the largest wind generator in the world.

The confluence of the North and South Forks occurs about four miles before the New enters Virginia near Sparta, North Carolina. In this area the New has numerous excellent rapids flowing through deep gaps and past high steep hills. It has excellent whitewater and unspoiled scenery of great beauty. Sheer 500-foot bluffs enclose the river and interesting rapids run over a rocky bed. The high peaks of Buck and Point Lookout Mountain form an impressive skyline. This portion of the New including 26.5 miles of both North and South Forks has been made a National Wild and Scenic River.

The New enters Virginia near the town Mouth of Wilson. About three miles downstream lies Stuart Dam. The river follows the state line here through rugged ravines, passing the Peach Bottom where once stood a colonial fort. In this area are Molly Osborne Shoals and Buzzard's Roost where the Appalachian Power Company planned their Blue Ridge Project, a pumped-storage dam backed by immense reservoirs. Independence lies just off the river here. A U.S. Highway parallels the river and travelers can see rugged shores and wooded hills. Here near Galax was the scene of the fabled Indian quarrel with an Osborne. When Osborne shot a squaw the Indians retaliated by skinning him alive.

Fries Dam next appears on the New after which we see whitewater falling fast. The next three miles are swift and end in two miles of whitewater dropping over a 45-foot gradient. This impressive stretch is funneled between 400-foot bluffs. The river then flows swiftly toward APCO'S Byllesby Dam built in 1913 in Carroll County.

To reach Byllesby travelers leave the main road, cross a spur of the Iron Mountains and go down again approaching the New winding through laurel thickets and pine forests. The devastating flood of 1916 forced the operators of Byllesby to flee for their lives leaving the generators to run submerged until the river went down.

Below Byllesby Dam is one of the most dramatic scenes along the New. After passing a mile long island of near tropical beauty reminding one of river islands far to the south the river makes a bend past an 800-foot abruptly rising precipice. The coloring of the rocks, dark gray-green, give an eerie effect to this stretch of the river leading us to believe the great eozoic age of the river. Grey-green cliffs towering dramatically above rocky rapids inspires one with a sense of great age.

Below the Byllesby Dam is another small APCO Dam, Buck Dam. Continuing on the New winds pass Ivanhoe, Cripple Creek and Austinville where once were the most productive lead mines in Virginia. Upon the product of these mines depended the destiny of General Nathanael Greene's Continental Army when he was harassed by Lord Cornwallis in the race to the Dan. George Rogers Clark's western troops also depended upon the New River Lead Mines.

Austinville is named for Moses Austin who operated the Lead Mines after the Revolution and went from there "down the New River in a large boat" to Illinois. [1]

The highway runs parallel to the river here as the New flows on past the old Shot Tower and Jackson's Ferry in use until 1930. It is now dwarfed by the I-77 bridge with its giant girders spanning the river.

Downstream from the Shot Tower are fine rapids at Foster's Falls named for William Foster who bought land in the forks of Cripple Creek in the 1750's. On the right bank is a ghost town and the remains of an old iron foundry. Below the falls the New makes a sharp bend between sheer rock cliffs. Rapids are located here making exciting runs. About three miles east of the Bakers Island, rapids rush around a promotory. The river passes Lone Ash, Carter Island, Barren Springs, gradually approaching the backwater of Claytor Lake near Hiwassee.

The river from Fries to this point is inaccessible, with cultivated fields in bottom land. This unspoiled region has been considered for the National Wild and Scenic River system. The river between Fries and Austinville has a number of impressive fast water stretches. The Double Shoal Rapids about three miles below Fries are the "best on the river" according to the National Park Service. Tributaries here are Big Reed Island Creek, offering great white water canoeing and Cripple Creek with good trout fishing. There once were many iron furnaces in this area, Boom Furnace being one.

Then the river comes to Claytor Lake State Park and Dam built by APCO in the late 1930's. This is the first of three large dams on

New River, the others being Bluestone built by the Army Corps of Engineers and Hawk's Nest built by Union Carbide. Claytor Lake inundated the old ferry crossings of Lowman, Linkous, Towes and Smith. Submerged were the buildings of old Dunkard's Bottom, the chimney of only one now visible above the lake's surface.

From Claytor Dam to Glen Lyn where the headwaters of the Bluestone Reservior begin is a 56-mile stretch of the New. It is scenic and largely undeveloped. The wide flood plains in this area are used for row crops or pasture.

After passing Claytor Lake and the mouth of Little River the New flows under I-81 bridge, majestically on past the city of Radford, the first city on its banks. Along this stretch can be seen ancient Indian fishtraps on the river's bottom.

Beyond Radford the river makes a dramatic northwest turn cutting across the Alleghenies, thus becoming the only river to cross the Appalachian chain from east to west. The gradient is 20 feet with numerous rapids, the river making great loops or horseshoes passing the "Big Horseshoe". There are other "horseshoes" on New River but this is the most noted, for it is the earliest settled and the site of Radford Arsenal.

During the spring when flood flows are moderated by the operation of Claytor Dam, the river offers excellent canoeing in this stretch where the New makes a 180° turn passing Tom's Creek, Whitethorne, and Adam Harman's colonial ford, the earliest known ford on the New.

The New curves again running past Belspring and Parrott widening to 350 yards. Downstream from Parrott the river makes a spectacular run through the ridges. The New is very impressive seen from the air at this point for it is clearly visible how it cuts through the Allegheny divide.

Flowing past Big Walker Mountain (Cloyd's Mountain), Gap Mountain, Spruce Run and Buckeye Mountains past Burton and Goodwin's Ferry, the river produces thrilling whitewater. The two miles from McCoy to Big Falls, having a 20-foot gradient, ends in a great rapid. The current here is very dangerous.

The dangerous current in this region is illustrated by a heliocopter pilot's experiences flying an Aero Jet Ranger April 3, 1981 in a forest fire fight. He had a 50-gallon bucket attached to the heliocopter which he repeatedly dipped into New River and dumped on the fire. He related that each time he scooped water from the New the strong current nearly dragged the helicopter into the river.

WARNING:

The New River *Is* Dangerous!

1. Undertow is strong and deadly.
2. Water levels change quickly and radically.
3. Rocks are slippery.
4. Alcohol and tubing don't mix.

EXERCISE EXTREME CAUTION!

Castle Rock, Pembroke, Va.
The families of Elizabeth
Snidow and Thomas Burk
settled here circa 1770
(Courtesy Ethel Lucas Walters
and Alice Porterfield Thorn)

Eggleston Palisades, Here Mary
Draper Ingles was found on her
return from the Shawnee
Villages in 1755.
(Photo by Clarence Hunter)

The New tortureously passes Eggleston Palisades 280 feet high overhanging a bottomless pool. When the river is high logs and driftwood are sucked under the palisades and come out again downstream. The highest point is "Anvil Rock." Opposite are "Pompey's Pillar" and "Caesar's Arch". Sinking Creek sinks into the ground and finds its way into the pool at "Anvil Rock."[2]

Passing Pearisburg the New drops over a rapid, heads toward Turnhole Knob, turns sharply to the southwest, passes the town of Narrows, loops around a promontory and flows north into a gap between Peters and East River mountains, known as the Narrows. Along this dramatically beautiful stretch the New cuts through another Allegheny Ridge exposing crinoid and tribolite fossils of interest to paleontologists. The unbelievable exposure of rock strata is a geologist's paradise.[3]

Along the left bank 1700-foot slopes tower above the course while 1800-foot slopes adorn the opposite shore. The New in this region is very reminiscent of the Rhine in Germany.

About 2½ miles north of the Narrows, the straight course once again begins a series of meanders. Dramatic bluffs rise precipitously above the river. At an elevation of 1500 feet the high point of the flood control waters of Bluestone Reservoir can be felt here especially during floods. From Glen Lyn, Virginia into West Virginia there is a long stretch of flat water interspersed by ledges. Water levels fluctuate here. These low ledges are called "falls" and do demand respect due to the volume of water. Martin's 1836 **Gazetteer of Virginia** is aptly descriptive. "The New River is borne down with so much force as to render its crossing hazardous . . . the falls being so rapidly successive as to resemble artificial steps."

Shumate Falls is the most difficult rapids to handle if in a boat or raft. Four miles below is Wylie Falls on the West Virginia State line. Other falls are Sandbar, Anderson, Harvey and Harmon. Passing Wylie Falls, a short, steep drop over eroded ledges and Wylie Island, the New is now in West Virginia and enters a picturesque gorge, enclosed by 600-foot walls. The river bends around a mountain spur of Crump's Bottom and approaches the backwater of Bluestone Reservoir in the vicinity of Indian Creek junction. The New from this point can be seen only by white water paddlers.

The Bluestone River whose Indian name was Momongoseneka or Big Stone enters the New from the west through a splendid gorge with entrancing waterfalls.[4] From the east the Greenbrier joins the New draining some of the most fertile farmland in West Virginia. The Bluestone and Greenbrier add a great volume to the New increasing

Bluestone Dam

(Photo by Gerald S. Ratcliff, West Virginia Governor's Office of E.C.D.)

its flow to 7,531 cubic feet per second making it one of the higher volume white water streams in the United States. To control this mighty thrust of water the Army Corps of Engineers began building the Bluestone Dam in the 1930's. This dam completed in 1947 intended to protect the Kanawha Valley from devastating floods. It uprooted many families such as the Meadors whose Baptist minister ancestor Josiah had settled there in 1797. Even at that Meadors was a late-comer for Andrew Culbertson had settled here in 1753.[5] Pipestem State Park is located here.

Below the dam the New passes Hinton the only major town on its banks in West Virginia. Here begins the rough mining country where it was said, "No Sunday west of Clifton Forge, No God west of Hinton."

Below Hinton the New widens to almost a half mile but gradually narrows again into what is known as the New River Gorge where the river cuts through 2,000-foot walls. This sixty-six mile segment of New River was included in 1975 in West Virginia's Natural Streams Preservation System. The 94th Congress of the United States named this segment of New River a component of the National Wild and Scenic Rivers System. In 1978 the New from Hinton to Fayetteville was designated New River Gorge National River as part of the National Park System. The area from Fayetteville to Gauley Bridge is also being considered as part of this park. Two state parks, Babcock and Grandview, are already in the area. Areas needing protection are Keeney's Creek, Piney Creek, Gauley River, Falls Branch, and Mann Creek.[6]

From Hinton down river to Thurmond the New is generally broad with powerful current. The twenty-three mile section from Hinton to Prince has fairly calm water ideal for canoeing. The twelve mile stretch from Prince to Thurmond provides swifter water conditions to be undertaken only by experienced raftists. Brooks and Sandstone Falls interrupt many long flatwater pools. Sandstone Falls, a visual wonder. attracts trout fishermen and nearby is a place called Ramp named for that "pungent-enough-to-drive-you-wild" mountain onion.

Brooks Falls is a vigorous drop over the complete width of the river. Below Brooks are dangerous rapids. Whitewater experts recommend caution saying "an upset on such a wide powerful river would make rescue very difficult."

Below Sandstone is the fishery at Meadow Creek. Glade Creek and Sewell Branch are near. Then comes Quinimont, Grandview State Park and McCreery Beach, Stretcher Neck, Army Camp and

The Grand Canyon of the East, Grandview State Park of West Virginia
(Photo by Gerald S. Ratcliff, West Virginia Governor's Office of E.C.D.)

Terry. Prince Bridge is an outstanding landmark where Highway 41 crosses the New. Below Terry are Dowdy Bluff and Dowdy Creek, places of great beauty.

Between Sandstone and McCreery are long expanses of flat water. The rapids are generally long chutes dropping over ledges. However there are several dangerous spots where canoes might swamp so use caution.

The New passes Thurmond the once famous mining town in the Gorge, now a ghost of its former brawling self. Gambling, women and whiskey centered around numerous hotels. The 100-room Dunglen Hotel was host to the longest continuous poker game in history, fourteen years. Brawls and murders were frequent. Bodies were seen next morning floating in the New. The only way into town was by rail and many men rode into Thurmond that never rode out. Sheriff Harrison Ash was imported from Kentucky and in several years shot twelve men and killed seven. It was said of Thurmond, "The only difference between Hell and Thurmond was a river ran through Thurmond."[7]

Below Thurmond the river narrows to one third of its upstream width and the water becomes as rambunctious as wild Thurmond. The channeling of water into this narrow gorge results in the best white water that can be run year around in the eastern United States. The New's whitewater here is second only to the Colorado. People come from over the nation to run the New River Gorge from Thurmond downstream. By 1981 there were twenty groups licensed to run the New River Gorge rapids, most operating out of Thurmond. The challenge in this type of water is remaining upright while bobbing among six to eight foot waves.

If you have time to look you will note that the gorge is immense with extremely rugged mountains and cliffs in view all the way. The part of of the gorge that is in Fayette County is of strikingly similar proportions of height and width of the Inner Gorge of the Grand Canyon and led the naturalist John Burroughs to name it the "Grand Canyon of the East."

Massive rocks lie strewn in the gorge. Waterfalls and springs rush into the river making the New River Gorge picturesque beyond belief. Only the railroad follows the river through the gorge to Gauley Bridge. There the Gauley and New merge to form the Kanawha.

Between Thurmond and Fayetteville are Dunlop and Arbuckle Creeks and the old mining towns of Rush Run, Beury, Sewell, Caperton, Nuttall and Kaymoor. Stonecliff Bridge is near here. One

The New near Fayette Station
(Photo by Gerald S. Ratliff, West Virginia Governor's Office of E.C.D.)

Classification of Rapids:

The number appearing beside the name of each rapid indicates its classification:

Class 1—Open canoe, small waves. Some skill required.

Class 2—Open canoe & small raft. 2' waves, few large rocks. Skilled canoeist or beginner rafter.

Class 3—Rafts and closed boats. 3' waves, some small hydraulics, scouting a good idea.

Class 4—Rafts and closed boats. 3' to 5' waves, hydraulics. Scouting necessary. Skill in closed boats and rafts required.

Class 5—Rafts and closed boats. 5' to 7' waves, strong currents and hydraulics, scouting absolutely necessary guiderafting only.

Class 6—Rafts and closed boats. For expert kayakist or expert raft guides only, very dangerous.

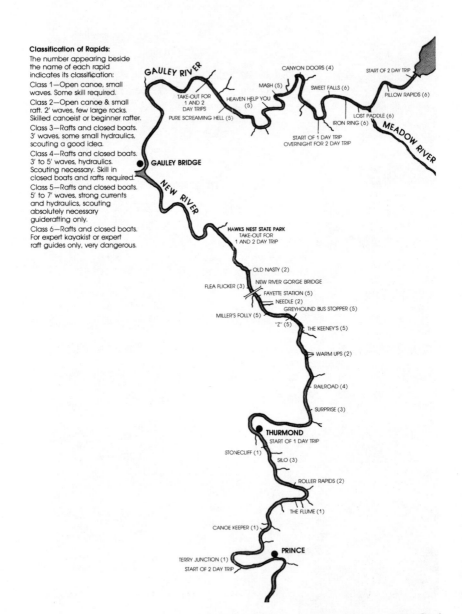

GAULEY RIVER

CANYON DOORS (4)

START OF 2 DAY TRIP

MASH (5)

SWEET FALLS (6)

PILLOW RAPIDS (6)

TAKE-OUT FOR 1 AND 2 DAY TRIPS

HEAVEN HELP YOU (5)

LOST PADDLE (6)

PURE SCREAMING HELL (5)

IRON RING (6)

MEADOW RIVER

GAULEY BRIDGE

START OF 1 DAY TRIP
OVERNIGHT FOR 2 DAY TRIP

NEW RIVER

HAWKS NEST STATE PARK
TAKE-OUT FOR
1 AND 2 DAY TRIP

OLD NASTY (2)

NEW RIVER GORGE BRIDGE

FLEA FLICKER (3)

FAYETTE STATION (5)

NEEDLE (2)

GREYHOUND BUS STOPPER (5)

MILLER'S FOLLY (5)

"Z" (5)

THE KEENEY'S (5)

WARM UPS (2)

RAILROAD (4)

SURPRISE (3)

THURMOND

START OF 1 DAY TRIP

STONECLIFF (1)

SILO (3)

ROLLER RAPIDS (2)

THE FLUME (1)

CANOE KEEPER (1)

PRINCE

TERRY JUNCTION (1)
START OF 2 DAY TRIP

(Map Courtesy Mountain River Tours, Inc.)

—16—

of the roughest rapids in this gorge is called Greyhound Bus Stopper alias "Titlow's Folly" named for an English journalist who took a spill here.[8]

The big rapids for white water enthusiasts begin at the Three Kenney Brothers rapids, Upper Keeney, Middle Keeney and Lower Keeney. Concerning Lower Keeney whitewater experts say, "It cannot be snuck, it cannot be lined, and it is one hell of a carry over the house-sized boulders, so you may as well make up your mind to run it. The current surges from the right to left bombarding the huge boulder on the left. If you are following somebody closely, do not be disheartened when he drops from view because you will look the same to the paddlers behind you."[9]

Whitewater experts advise scouting Lower Keeney before attempting it. "Lower Keeney is scouted everytime even by those very familiar with the river" is a rule-of-thumb for anyone attempting it. The river at this point has narrowed to the size of a

New River Overlook, Hawk's Nest State Park
(Photo by Peggy Powell, West Virginia Governor's Office of E.C.D.)

small trout stream thus concentrating a tremendous volume of water in a narrow passage.

After Keeney's comes the Sunset or Double Z rapids. This is a Class 5 rapid, exceedingly difficult to negotiate even by expert white water people. Following Double Z are three more rapids, Old 99 Hook, Greyhound Bus Stopper, and Tipple Rapids - a little easier to manuever than Double Z.[10] Next is the Undercut Rock Rapids. Here you encounter enormous waves. The New continues its tumultous way past Ames Heights, Hico and Ansted. In its passage it has passed Grandview and Babcock State Parks. Now it rushes on by Beauty Mountain and Hawk's Nest State Park at Ansted.

The Hawk's Nest is a towering stack of rocks 585 feet high overlooking the New. Hawk's Nest Dam and the infamous tunnel built by Union Carbide divert the New five miles to a power plant owned by Union Carbide. When there is more water than the tunnel can handle the excess is released back into the old riverbed. This section is referred to by paddlers as the Dries. The tunnel demands so much the river is usually empty until the New's flow exceeds 3.5' at Hinton or 4' at Fayette.[11] This part of the New is full of huge boulders.

The construction of the Hawk's Nest Dam is one of the saddest chapters in New River history. The tunnel built by New-Kanawha Power Company to divert the New's water for power production was drilled through solid silica rock under conditions, according to one report, "that resembled the Dark Ages." The workers were practically slaves. At least 476 men were known to have died from contracting silicois and many were quietly buried in unmarked graves. Attempts to investigage were suppressed for years. The power from Hawk's Nest Dam runs Union Carbide's smeltering plant.[12]

The most recent addition to New River scenery in this area is the New River Gorge Bridge on U.S. 19 52 miles southeast of Charleston. From Charleston take U.S. 60 to Hico, then turn right on U.S. 19, continue three miles to the bridge overlook. This New bridge opened in October 1977 eases travel across West Virginia and the New. Previously there had been only three roads that crossed the New in a thirty mile stretch of gorge. One was Fayette Station Road (State 82) a one-lane path that hairpinned down one side and up the other.

The New River Gorge Bridge is an architectural and engineering feat noted as the world's longest steel-arch bridge, (1,700 feet) the highest east of the Rocky Mountains and standing 325 feet taller than the Washington Monument.

While building the bridge workers teetered 876 feet above the raging New attempting to span 3,030 feet from canyon rim to canyon rim. To move massive steel into place a 230-foot-high tower was built on each side of the canyon. Workmen then strung trolleys on 3,500 foot cableways between the towers to place the steel beams into position. People from over the nation come to look at the bridge and some still travel the old Fayette Station Road to the bottom to get a river level view of the new bridge.[13]

As most rivers do the New floods on occasion. Claytor Dam and Bluestone Dam have controlled its rampages in recent years. Previously it was a different story. In the days before the dams were built observers say the New flooded periodically.

"For some meteorological reason about every quarter of a century an abnormal amount of rain is dumped on the mountains of

New River Gorge Bridge
(Photo by Gerald S. Ratcliff, West Virginia Governor's Office of E.C.D.)

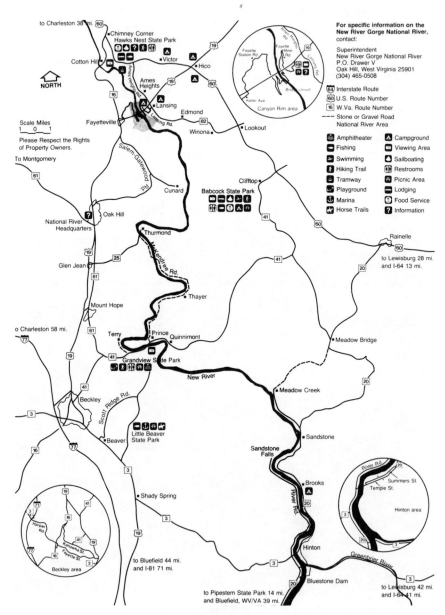

—20—

North Carolina," says one student of the New, "sending a torrent down river which takes out railroads and highway bridges and floods out most of the plant sites."[14]

Old farmers in the Galax area say the New floods more frequently, about every seventeen years. They call this a "fresh" or "freshening". Many have seen the New do this, widening at these times to more than three times its width between Carolina and Fries. In historic times we know floods occurred August 25, 1749; October 5, 1861; 1878; 1916 and August 13-14, 1940.

The first observer to record a flood on the New was a Sabbatarian writing from Dunkard's Bottom in 1749. He wrote, "On the 25th of August our river as well as Little River were very high but nobody here suffered mentionable damage."[15]

On October 5, 1861 the rain fell so incessantly it raised the New to the highest point in history and hampered plans of the warring Union and Confederates.

In 1878 the flood was more damaging in the New-Kanawha Basin than on the upper New.

The 1916 flood originated on the upper New in North Carolina completely destroying the Wilkesboro-Jefferson Turnpike laboriously built by convict labor in Ashe County. Water at Galax rose to 25 feet above normal.

One man writes of this flood, "In the summer of 1916 as I crossed the New River on a ferry boat at Pembroke, I saw a man high on a bridge pier using a tripod instrument. A short time later that pier was laying on the edge of the river. The same flood carried away the Narrows Bridge and left its skeleton in the middle of the river. The same fate was experienced by other bridges on the river."[16]

By the time of the August 1940 flood the U.S. Geological Survey Office was operating 200 measurement stations over the area. They record heaviest rainfall on August 13 and 14, the highest known to that time on the New. Ten inches of rainfall fell in North Carolina in less than twenty-four hours. The most seriously damaged towns were Narrows, Eggleston and Hinton. Houses at Parrott and Burton were washed downstream and lodged against Eggleston Bridge.[17] Twentieth-century dams have tamed the rampaging New and it is unlikely these floods of the past will ever reoccur.

FOOTNOTES—Chapter I

1. Fries, Adelaide L., ed., "Report of the Brethren Abraham Steiner and Fredrich c. von Schweinitz Journey to the Cherokees," North Carolina Historical Review, v. 21, pp. 330-333 hereafter cited as Fries, Steiner Journey, and Hugh P. Givens, Letter to author, August 1970.

2. CS, I, p. 347; Pulaski County Historical Map, Clarita Morgan and Lloyd Matthews; W.F. Burmeister, Appalachian Waters as quoted in United States Department of the Interior, South Fork New River National Wild and Scenic Rivers North Carolina (Washington: G.P.O., 1976) hereafter cited as South Fork New River pp. 236 and John P. Hale, Trans-Allegheny Pioneers Historical Sketches of the First White Settlers West of the Alleghenies 1748, reprint, (Charleston, W. Va.: The Kanawha Valley Publishing Company, 1931) hereafter cited as Hale, Trans-Allegheny Pioneers, p. 73.

3. Elizabeth Watson, "Wild and Scenic New River", The Environmental Journal hereafter cited as Watson, February 1975, p. 10 and Maurice Brooks, "The Very Old New River," Wonderful West Virginia, hereafter cited as Brooks, Old New, March 1970, p. 7.

4. Bob Burrell and Paul Davidson, Wild Water West Virginia (Parsons, W.Va.; McClain Printing Company, 1975) hereafter cited as Wildwater West Virginia pp. 131-135.

5. Watson, p. 10 and Michael Meador, "Aunt Nannie Meador and the Bluestone Dam", Goldenseal, January 1980, p. 26.

6. Draft Land Acquisition Plan, New River Gorge National River (West Virginia: U.S. National Park Service, 1980) p. 6.

7. Wildwater West Virginia, p. 131, 136-137 and Otis Rice, History of the New River Gorge Area (Montgomery, West Va.: Institute of Technology, n.d.) hereafter cited as Rice, Gorge.

8. Watson, ibid.; Wildwater West Virginia p. 199 and Author's conversation with Wildwater Unlimited guide.

9. Wildwater West Virginia, pp. 139-140.

10. George Laycock, "New River Old Problem," Audubon, November 1975, pp. 58-63.

11. Wildwater West Virignia pp. 140-141.

12. Laycock, ibid.

13. "Bridging the Canyon Walls," Southern Living, April 1979, p. 74.

14. Hugh P. Givens, letter to author, August 1970.

15. Klaus Wust, "The Great Flood of 1749", Journal of the Roanoke Historical Society cited hereafter as Wust, Flood, VII, pp. 1-4.

16. Rice, Gorge, p. 4; Mark A. Mathis, ed., North Carolina Statewide Archaeological Survey (n.p. North Carolina Archaeological Council, 1979) hereafter p. 186 and Hugh P. Givens, Letter to author, August 1970. cited as Mathis North Carolina Archaelogy.

17. U.S. Geological Survey, Southern Appalachian Floods of mid-August 1940 in the New-Kanawha River Valley, 1940 and U.S. Army Corps of Engineers, Flood Conditions (Washington: Government Printing Office, 1940) pp. 1-10.

Chapter II

New River Named

The New River has had many names in the memory of the white man. These are Teays, Mondongachate, River of Death, Sault, Chinondacheta or Chinondaichio, Wood, Conway, Great Conhaway or Kahaway, Conoy, Kanawha, Allegheny and New. South Fork was once called Fulcarson River.

Geologists call the New, Teays, Indians called it Mondongachete, River of Death or Chinodacheta and the French called it Sault River all the way to its Carolina headwaters and Chinodacheta along the Kanawha portion. De Vaugondy's 1755 map calls it "Grand Cohaway nominee Wood or R. Neuve." Virginia land jobbers called it Wood or Allegheny and Virginia colonial officials called it Great Kanawha for the Algonquian tribe. Generally this name applied to the lower portion below the gorge while that east of the gorge was called Wood or New.

Current theories about how the New got it's name are varied and confusing. From discovery by the English until about 1745 it was called Wood River supposedly for Abraham Wood who sent out the exploring party that recorded their discovery. Thomas Wood, possibly Abraham's son, died in an attempt to reach the river in 1671. It was a colonial custom to name a stream after a person who gave their life exploring a stream. The two names, Wood's and New were used interchangeably in records and on maps until about 1770.

Suggestions have been made that it was named for ranger Francis New; for an early ferryman; named by North Carolina's governor in 1750; by Fry-Jefferson on their 1751 map or Peter Fontaine surveying in 1752 or Captain Byrd in 1775; named by the settlers hearing the Indian word for Kanawha or for a Charles City County family. [1]

The suggestion that it was named for Francis New in Captain Robert Wade's ranging party in 1758 is false since the river was called

New years before 1758. The suggestion by Jedediah Hotchkiss, Stonewall Jackson's topographical engineer, that it was named for Mr. New who ran a ferry is untrue since the river was called New before ferries ran upon it. The suggestion that Governor Johnston named it when the boundary surveyors found a river "nobody ever dreamt of before" is wrong. Johnston might not have known of it but Pennsylvanians had been calling it New River for years before 1749.

Suggestions that Peter Jefferson and Joshua Fry named it New on their 1751 **Map of Virginia** is ruled out by the river already having that name before 1751. They simply placed on the map the name the river was already being called.

The claim that it was named by Major Peter Fontaine surveying along it in 1752 is ruled out for the same reason as is the notion that in 1775 a Captain Byrd constructing a road came to the river and not knowing what to call it, named it the New River.

The theory that it was a translation of the Shawnee word Kanawha which means New Water cannot be disproved yet is not plausible. It assumes that white settlers were well enough acquainted with the Shawnee language to translate and call the river by a name given it by the Indian tribe they most hated. This seems doubtful.

The suggestion that after the exploration of the Batts-Fallam party from Charles City County, that other families from the county, the News, Blands and Laceys, interested in peltry came to the river, naming it New. Although the Blands, formerly of the Skinner's Guild in London, had an interest in peltry, there is no actual proof they came to New River nor changed its name from Wood's to New.

Two decades of research by the present author into the history of the New River Valley has revealed a more logical explanation. Locally in Virginia the river was called Wood's but further afield was called New. There is an explanation for this.

In 1742 John Peter Salling made his trip down the river and upon returning called it **Wood's River.** In September 1745 when Colonel John Buchanan made a land selling trip to the river his entry book for buyers had written upon it, **Wood's River Land Entry Book.** The people already settled on the river petitioned Augusta court for a road in 1749 asking that a road be built for them on **Wood's River.** James Patton writing from New River in January 1753 says, "I have a just claim for 100,000 acres of land on **Wood's River."** [2]

John Peter Salling, John Buchanan, James Patton and the river petitioners were all local people.

Further afield, the name was changing. In May 1745 the Court of Orange County, Virginia, could not decide what to call it. So, a court order for a road to Adam Harman's Ford calls it "the road to Wood's or New River."[3]

Far from the river, in Pennsylvania, the German newspapers by 1745 were calling the river, New River. Religious groups like the Sabbatarians (Dunkards), Moravians and Lutherans all called the river New River. In September 1745 while John Buchanan was at the river carrying along his **Wood's River Land Entry Book**, a German newspaper in Lancaster County, Pennsylvania, mentioned "a river 400 miles distant, running into the Mississippi - New River, by name." In 1748 a Moravian missionary in Pennsylvania said "a few German families live on **New River**."[4]

Certainly the Pennsylvanians were basing their knowledge of a river 400 miles distant on something other than local tradition. They were basing their knowledge upon maps and official reports coming from London which in turn were based upon earlier reports sent from America. Thus we come to how the New got its name.

In 1651 Edward Bland sent a pamphlet to London describing the western territory of the Carolinas and Virginia within the latitude where the New heads in Carolina as New Brittaine. From that time designating the western tramontane territory of this latitude as **New Brittaine or New Virginia** was the practice in official reports to London from America. They called the area of western Virginia drained by the New - **New Brittaine or New Virginia**. This was true from the time of Bland's 1651 pamphlet to 1766 when New Jersey Governor Thomas Pownall's **A Topographical Description of such parts of North America as are contained in the annexed map of the Middle British Colonies in North America Based on Lewis Evans 1755 Map** was sent to London. It said, "New River, and Greenbrier are fine large branches of Canhawa, which in Future Times will be of service for the Inland Transportation of New Virginia."

Pownall also said that the Kanawha would provide "a passage to the **New Virginia**, a very great advantage."[5]

Since this area was known in England as **New Virginia** it seems logical that the river that drained it, the first travelers came to when they crossed the Allegheny divide, flowing in a new direction, should be called **New River** after **New Virginia**. We see this clearly when a Lutheran minister writing of the Ephrata Cloister Sabbatarians remarks, "They have one society in **New Virginia** upon **New River**."

Another of the ministers speaking of the Sabbatarians says: "The mother cloister began a number of daughters in several places in Pennsylvania and New Virginia but they were sickly from their birth."[6]

Most maps of the New River area from 1751 show it as New River. One exception is Mitchell's Map of the British Dominions 1755 which shows the river as Wood's or New River. This is easily explained since Mitchell said he was guided by John Peter Salling's Journal and Salling calls the river Wood's River.[7] Jeffery's American Atlas of 1776 shows the New River head in North Carolina and calls it New River.

FOOTNOTES—Chapter II

1. H.H. Hardesty, Excerpts from Hardesty's Historical and Geographical Encyclopedia (New York: H.H. Hardesty & Co. Publisher 1884) hereafter cited as Hardesty; p.4. Raymond E. Janssen, "The Teays River," The Scientific Monthly hereafter cited as Janssen, Teays River, December 1953 pp. 306-314; VMHB, XXX, p. 213; CS, I, p. 434; Hamil Kenny, West Virginia Place Names, Their Origin and Meaning (Piedmont, W. Va: 1945) .... p. 342; Herman Moll, 1720, New Map of the North Part of America claimed by France Library of Congress, Map Division, Washington, D.C. Hale, Trans-Allegheny Pioneers, p. 54; DU, James Patton, Letter, 1750; Marion Tingling, ed., The Correspondence of the Three William Byrds of Westover, Virginia, 1684-1776 (Charlottesville: The University Press of Virginia, 1977) hereafter cited as Tingling, Three Byrds, II, p. 703; David E. Johnston, A History of the Middle New River Settlements and Contiguous Territory (Huntington, West Virginia: Standard Publishing and Printing Company, 1906) hereafter cited as Johnston, Middle New, p. 8; NCCR, IV, p. xiii: James Adair, The History of the American Indians (London: 1755) reprint, ed. Samuel C. Williams (New York: Argonaut Press. 1966) hereafter cited as Adair, American Indians map opposite p. xxx; DP, I, p. 282; CVS, I, p. 255; John Manahan, "New Light on Charles City County", VMHB, v. 64, p. 473; Father Bonnecamp's 1749 Map of the Ohio River, Charles Hanna. The Wilderness Trail or the Ventures and Adventures of the Pennsylvania Traders on the Allegheny Path, (New York: G.P. Putnam's Sons, 1911) hereafter cited as Hanna, Wilderness Trail, p. 360.

2. Colonel James Patton to President John Blair, January 1753, WH, I QQ p. 78.

3. Orange County, Virginia, Order Book IV, pp. 331-332.

4. Gottschalk, Report, 1748, VHMB, v. 11, p. 234; J. F. Sachse, The German Sectarians of Pennsylvania, 1742-1800 A Critical and Legendary History of the Ephrata Cloister and the Dunkers (Philadelphia: P.C. Stockhausen, 1900) hereafter cited as Sachse, German Sectarians.

5. Hugh T. Lefler, ed., North Carolina History told by Contemporaries (Chapel Hill: The University of North Carolina Press, 1965) hereafter cited as Lefler, Carolina History, pp. 12-13 and Thomas Pownall, A Topographical Description of the Dominions of the United States of America ed. Lois Mulkearn, (Pittsburgh: University of Pittsburgh Press, 1949) hereafter cited as Pownall, Description, pp. 137, 144.

6. Felix Reichmann and Eugene E. Doll, Ephrata as Seen by Contemporaries (Allentown, Pennsylvania: The Pennsylvania German Folklore Society 1953) hereafter cited as Reichman, Ephrata, p. 75 and Klaus Wust, The Saint-Adventurers on the Virginia Frontier (Edinburg, Va.: Shenandoah History Publishers, 1977) hereafter cited as Wust, Saint, p. 118.

7. Clarence W. Alvord and Lee Bidgood, The First Explorations of the Trans-Allegheny Region by the Virginians (Cleveland: The Arthur H. Clark Company, 1912) hereafter cited as Alvord-Bidgood, Explorations, p. 204.

Chapter III

Flowering of the New

The New River is unique in a biological sense. There are many species of plants and animals found along it that are not found together any place else. Plants from the far north grow beside near-tropic types. The ancient Teays River and more recently the New have acted as carriers for spores, seeds and germinal materials from the southern Appalachians and Piedmont areas into West Virginia. West Virginia botany includes a long list of plants with great horticultural value which arrived by way of New River.

The Catawba rhododendron is a vivid example of a plant whose natural habitat is in North Carolina and Tennessee but by the beneficence of the New appears now in West Virginia. There are showy stands in the New River Gorge along U.S. 21 in Fayette County, at Hawk's Nest State Park and the canyon below Grandview State Park. It is estimated one million of these flowers are in bloom in New River Gorge in May.

Another beautiful plant that usually grows far south but has been carried north by the New is the Carolina silverbell or Halesia Carolina. In New River Gorge country there is a great show of these trees growing from seeds brought from the Carolinas. These trees grow to 80 feet in the Smokies but are smaller other places. In late April or early May before leaves are full on every twig there are paired clusters of these blossoms, each one an inch or more in length, having a white bell-shaped flower, with a fringe of delicate pink. These grow in great profusion. Appalachian naturalist Maurice Brooks has said, "I do not know of another Appalachian tree that presents an equal display."

The silverbell likes well-watered slopes so does not grow too far up New River's banks. These can be seen where U.S. 21 crosses New River at the Cotton Hill Bridge and along U.S. 19 west of Prince railroad station before the highway climbs the gorge up to Beckley.

The New brings to West Virginia two southern hardwoods, the Spanish oak and the red or sweet gum. The Spanish oak has made itself just as at home in Charleston, West Virginia as in Charleston, South Carolina.

The red gum or liquidamber is an ornamental and member of an ancient plant group destroyed by the glaciers. Yet sweet gums grow today in the alluvial soil of the New-Kanawha valley brought there by New River. Because of its five-pointed leaf, the sweet gum is incorrectly called "star maple" though it is not a maple.[1]

The cup plant, the water willow, goldenrod, McDowell's sunflower as well as others are southern imports into West Virginia. Goldenrod has been found in only two places in West Virginia. McDowell Sunflower occurs only along the New. Other small plants not common to West Virginia may be seen along the New.

Goldenseal or hydrastis is found in the New corridor. Goldenseal, also known as puccoon, orange-root, eye-balm or Indian paint is a plant type whose only other known species is found in Japan.

Alabama lipfern grows along the cliffs of New River near Mountain Lake its known northeastern limit. At this locale in a wooded limestone plateau area Robert P. Carroll found Engelmann's adder's tongue fern, a plant of the warm lowlands.

Botanists have studied the gorge area since 1849 when Isaac Holton collected from Gauley Bridge to Hawk's Nest. In 1877 James Jones investigated at Hawks Nest. Loup Creek was studied also. Edward Lyman Morris curator of Brooklyn Institute Museum collected plants south of New River in Summers and Mercer counties in 1900. His collection is in the National Herbarium. Mine-operator Lawrence Nuttall from 1890 to 1897 collected 1000 species of flowering plants. As results of study from 1967 to 1975 Bill Grafton and Claude McGraw have published "The Vascular Flora of New River Gorge West Virginia" listing 1,067 species of which ten were new. There are also twenty-three species of plants and animals found in the New River ecosystem along the Gorge that are unique to this region. These species are believed to have migrated by way of New River from the Virginia Piedmont.[2]

Other native New River plants are Virginia bluebells, sweet william, aster, Queen Anne's Lace, Joe Pye Weed, pinks, pink azalea, flame azalea, dogwood, redbud, parvis, tulip trees, arbutus, ginsing, sassafras, persimmon, chinqapins, rosebay, trillium, wild iris, dogtooth violets and mountain laurel.

Just as southern plants are found far out of their latitude along the New so are plants of the far north found there. The glaciers that buried the ancient Teays River and cut off the New River Valley also produced special conditions for plant and animal life along the New. Many northern plants and animals forced southward by the advancing ice were unable to compete with similar forms already present in the south. They vanished. But some found bits of territory suited to their needs and survived. One important habitat of this sort is the southern mountain bog or "islands in the sky" where typically northern plants and animals are able to survive in areas far removed from their normal range.

Mountain bogs are found in shallow poorly drained upland valleys surrounded by ridges of higher land. Usually they have a small stream draining them. These upper bogs are characteristic of the Allegheny ridges which the New River transects. Cranberry Glades in West Virginia and Burke's Garden on Big Walker Creek of New River are outstanding examples of mountain bogs. The cranberry bogs behind Mountain Lake in Giles County, Virginia, is another example. The bogs at Mountain Lake overlooking New River are natural refrigerators which resisted the glaciers and kept their remnants. Cranberries were "in plenty" on the upper New in Ashe County, North Carolina, wrote a settler in 1811.

Slopes around these bogs are generally forested with maple, beech, birch and other hardwoods of the region but also resemble misplaced Canadian landscape. Fringed by balsams, fir, red spruce, and tamarack, trees of the north, the bogs also have quaking aspen, largetooth aspen and black ash. The bogs are covered with shrubs such as Canadian yew, chokeberry, serviceberry, and St. John's wort. Nine-inch high bunchberry which looks like flowering dogwood is found in the bogs as well as north to Alaska. Bog orchids, cranberries, goldthread, dwarf dogwood, sundew, purple pitcher plant thrive in the Allegheny highlands though their natural habitat is Ontario and New England. Remnants of pre-glacier Northern spruce forests still live on Mount Rogers.[3]

The Mountain Lake Biological Station of the University of Virginia has long been a center for the study of Appalachian plants. Overlooking New River Valley from the 4,000 foot summit of Salt Pond Mountain, the station was founded by Dr. Ivey F. Lewis, a student of ferns. Here 2,000 feet above New River are rare ferns and many northern plants. Hardwood forests, hemlock and spruce are present. Cranberry bogs are present. The valley below has oak-hickory and oak-pine forests with southern hardwoods brought in by New River. However local ferns including grape ferns, wood-ferns and clubmosses are the most exciting thing to botanists.

Many of them are of northern affliations and at the southern limits of their range. New ferns are constantly being discovered leading botanists to believe that any eastern fern except Floridian types may be found in the Mountain Lake area.

Other botanical peculiarities of the New valley are laurel slicks, heath balds and rhododendron thickets. Balds are interesting since they are natural and not man-made.

Animals of the far north are found along the New in the bogs. Northern flying squirrels, which the author's father saw as a child along Sinking Creek, as well as water shrews, star-nosed moles and an occasional snowshoe hare are found in the bogs.

White-throated sparrows, among the finest singers of the Canadian forests are found in West Virginia. Winter wrens, brown creepers, red-breasted nuthatches, golden-crowned kinglets and common snipe hang around the bogs. These water soaked hollows in the southern mountains would look like a Canadian forest if it were not for the presence of so many southern birds and mammals. The bogs are a naturalist's delight because they have a mixture of species not normally found together.[4]

There are evidences of fish life in the New River that indicate a former connection with the Great Lakes. Small mouth black bass, muskellunge, walleyed pike, and lake sturgeon are Great Lakes fish found in the New as well as members of the catfish, sucker and minnow families. North Carolina's best small mouth bass and rock bass are found on the South Fork of the New. Sixteen rare animals including salamanders, reptiles and birds are along South Fork. Everything from bog turtles and golden eagles to the Indiana Bat make the upper New their home.

Endangered fish found only on South Fork are the New River shiner, Kanawha minnow and darter, big-mouth chub and blunt--nosed minnow. In all the U.S. Fish and Wildlife Service had identified eleven species of aquatic life in the New that exist nowhere else in the world.[5]

FOOTNOTES—Chapter III

1. Maurice Brooks, The Appalachians (Boston: Houghton Mifflin Company, 1965) hereafter cited as Brooks, Appalachians, p. 177 and Brooks, Old New, p. 8.

2. New River Gorge Newspaper (Oak Hill, W.Va.: U.S. National Park Service, 1982) v. 1, no. 1, p. 1 and v. 2, no. 1, p. 4 and Brooks, Appalachians, p. 201.

3. Maurice Brooks, The Life of the Mountains (New York: Mc-Graw-Hill Book Company, 1967) pp. 119-120; Brooks, Appalachians, p. 202; A.R. Newsome, "Twelve North Carolina Counties, 1810-1811,"North Carolina Historical Review V hereafter cited as Newsome, Carolina Counties pp. 419-420, Harry Piper, 1977 Test Excavations in the Corrider of the Proposed Scenic Highway in Mount Rogers National Recreation Area, Virginia (N.P. 1977) p. 12.

4. Brooks, Appalachians, pp. 121, 202, 225.

5. Brooks, Old New p. 7 and South Fork New River, pp. 119, 126, 138-139.476.

Chapter IV

Teays River and the Prehistoric New

According to geologists, the New River, a remnant of the great prehistoric Teays River, was born over 100,000,000 years ago. The Teays drained the area now drained by the Mississippi and Ohio extending from North Carolina across Virginia, West Virginia, Ohio, Indiana and Illinois where it turned southward toward St. Louis, Missouri, to enter the Gulf of Mexico which at that time extended to southern Illinois. The waters of what are today the Great Lakes intermingled with those of the Teays, in this paleozoic time. The Teays cut through the ancestral Appalachians, a vastly higher system that preceded the present ranges. These mountains were eroded to an almost level plain during the Mesozoic era, the Teays being one stream that eroded them. Later this plain was elevated to a high plateau and the Teays was carried upward by the rising land. The Teays cut through the bedrock, keeping the same course it had on the low plain. Evidence of this can be seen in the New River Gorge. The canyon with its rising walls, marks the extent of the river's erosion since the uplift.

The sediment carried by this mighty Teays was enormous helping it to build the great Mississippi Valley from Illinois to the lower delta, thus molding a vast part of our continent. The New played its part in this development and can be called a continent builder.

Then came the glaciers pushing down from Canada a million years ago, a recent event, geologically speaking. The last ice age glaciers spread farthest south in Illinois. The ice moved over the lower half of the Teays burying it and filling its valley with glacier debris. The front of the glacier standing as a wall of ice across the river's path blocking the flow of water, converted the river into a long narrow lake filling present Kanawha Valley. Our present New River, an untouched remnant of the Teays, was thus a tributary into this glacial lake.

As glacial ice receded, the Ohio River was established, Teays Lake drained away and the Teays did not return to its former valley. Nearly all the river systems which are tributaries of the Mississippi were formed at this time. Only the part of the Teays that is present New River was undisturbed flowing along in its old channel. From Blowing Rock, North Carolina to Gauley, West Virginia the New occupied the bed of the preglacial Teays River. Some of the plant and animal life associated with the Teays remained on the New, especially the fish. Many of them are Great Lakes species trapped on the New behind the glacial wall. [1]

Anthropologists say that man appeared a million years ago in North America while the glaciers were moving. However, the first clearly defined cultural tradition dates only from 10,000 B.C. and is called the big-game hunting or Paleo-Indian culture. Scholars report that New River Valley was inhabited from that time.

Dr. Harvard Ayers, anthropology professor at Appalachian State University in 1965 conducted the first official archaelogical survey of the upper New. In two weeks he located 20 sites of Paleo-Indian habitation, one a rock shelter at Galax, one at Oldtown and another in Little River's Valley where he found a highly polished stone axe.

Another survey was done in 1969 by Dr. C.C. Holland revealing a "very large Indian village" and evidence that New River Valley had been occupied ten thousand years. The Clovis fluted projectile point is a distinctive tool from this era and is found in the New River Valley. Other surveys have uncovered 24 Indian sites on South Fork in Watauga County.

The Thunderbird Research Corporation led by Dr. William Gardner of Catholic University, Washington, D.C., was hired by Appalachian Power Company to make an archaelogical survey in Grayson County, Virginia, at Molly Osborne Shoals where the company planned to build a dam. This 1976 study revealed heavy Indian habitation dating back ten thousand years. [2]

Scattered archaelogical investigations have been made at Austinville, Radford and Eggleston in the middle New River Valley. Two Paleo-Indian sites have been located in New River Gorge area in West Virginia dating thousands of years, and another near Pearisburg, Virginia.

The Paleo-Indian culture died out when the bison, mastodon and other large animals became extinct and man turned to smaller game, fish, seeds, berries and wild plants for sustenance. The tools used in hunting became smaller. This era is the Archaic Era and many tools developed including awls, harpoons, needles, pestles and mortars.

The Archaic people were more sedentary and more numerous but not farmers. They moved camp frequently but it was not haphazard wandering. They knew the seasons when the wild foods were most abundant. From spring through summer they lived in the river bottom where they could hunt, fish, collect shell fish and bottomland plants. In fall they moved into the hills to collect nuts. The Wakeman site at Ellison Mountain below Tater Hill, excavated by Appalachian State University is an example of a Archaic hill site. During winter they lived in rock shelters. [3]

The New River Valley was extensively occupied during this era. Sites on the flood plain as well as the ridges show the valley as highly inhabited and serving as a passageway through the Appalachians.

About 1000 B.C. another culture began to appear in the New River Valley. Clay pottery was introduced as were burial mounds over the dead. In Watauga County, North Carolina, a prehistoric trash pit on the property of Bob Rosaco near Valle Cruis has been found with thick crude pottery fragments radio-carbon dated at 405 B.C. one of the earliest dates for pottery in North Carolina. This culture is called the Eastern Woodland or Burial Mound culture.

The Adena-Hopewell, two cultures which overlapped, moved from the Ohio Valley with the Eastern Woodland culture. The Adena culture was established about 800 B.C. and the two cultures extended to 1000 A.D. The Adena people lived in the lower New River Gorge area though their principal concentration was in the Ohio—Kentucky area.

Pottery of the Adenas and Hopewells was cord or fabric marked with designs in the pottery made with a small paddle wrapped in fabric and pressed in the soft clay before firing. This pottery has been found in the New River Valley. Both cultures lived in small villages of round houses made of saplings, the Adenas being the first house builders in America. But the most evident remains of these people are their conical burial mounds constructed over log pits in which the bodies were interred.

The Hopewell culture built larger conical burial mounds and had a widespread trading network. Their settlements spread over the eastern United States and since the New River is a natural corridor from east to west we can be sure it played an important part in this trading system.

By 1000 A.D. this natural corridor was bringing to the New River people the new advances in America — maize cultivation and ceramics manufacture. The cultivation of maize came out of Mexico, spread up the Mississippi Valley and was widespread at the coming of the white man. Slash-burn techniques of clearing ground accompanied the growing of maize. The first white explorers along New River found many cleared fields.

Ceramics appearing in the valley about 1000 A.D. were soapstone developing to crushed stone tempered by 1200 A.D. and crushed limestone by 1300 A.D. The Dan River series (sand tempered, fabric impressed, incomplete firing) seems the dominant ceramic type found so far.

By 1000 A.D. the prehistoric ancestors of the Cherokees known as the Pisgah people were in Watauga County along Watauga River a few miles from the New. Similar but as yet unknown sites of the Pisgah were certainly on the New. One Pisgah site on Watauga River at the mouth of Cave Creek has remains radio-carbon dated at 1390 A.D.[4] These Indians had left the area before the arrival of the white man.

In summary the New River in recent prehistory was a route of contact and diffusion between the East Tennessee Dallas culture, the Appalachian Summit Pisgah culture and the Ohio Fort Ancient Culture. Actually very little archaelogical research has been done, so Dr. Holland and other anthropologists believe extensive research will show successive levels of development of mankind in the New River Valley from Paleo-Indian times to the fifteenth century. "It is one of the few areas left where scientists can study every level of human development on the continent," claims Dr. Holland.[5]

FOOTNOTES—Chapter IV

1. Janssen, **Teays River**, pp. 306-311; Raymond E. Janssen, "Blue Ridge Dams: The Pollution Dilution Approach," **National Parks and Conservation Magazine**, v. 45, pp. 14-16 and Brooks, **Old New**, p. 7.

2. Ayers, **Archaelogical Resources**, pp. 34-36 quoting the **Congressional Record** September 24, 1975; **New River Gorge Newspaper**, v. I, no. 1, p. 3; and Mathis, **North Carolina Archaelogy**, pp. 178, 199 quoting North Carolina vs. FPC and APCO, October 1975; William M. Gardner, **An Archaelogical Survey of the Proposed Dam Sites Along the Upper New** (Washington: Thunderbird Research Corporation, 1976) pp. 5-6, 28, 70, 135, 138.

3. Ibid. pp. 180-181; Harvard G. Ayers, **An Appraisal of the Archaelogical Resources of the Blue Ridge Project Grayson County, Virginia and Allegheny and Ashe Counties, North Carolina** (Washington: Smithsonian Institute River Basin Surveys, 1965) hereafter cited as Ayers, **Archaelogical Resources**, p. 3.

4. John R. Swanton, **The Indians of the Southeastern United States** (Washington: Government Printing Office, 1946) p. 2, map; Virgil Lewis, **West Virginia Its History** (Charleston: The Tribune Printing Company, 1904) hereafter cited as Lewis, **West Virginia**, p. 29; Robert F. Spencer and Jesse D. Jennings, **The Native Americans** (New York: Harper & Row, Publishers, 1965) pp. 60, 64 and Ayers, **Archaelogical Resources**, pp. 7-20.

5. Dr. Charlton G. Holland, "Testimony," **Congressional Record**, September 24, 1975 and Gardner, ibid.

Chapter V

Mondongachete

Since so little archaelogical research has been done writing of New River Indians in the centuries before the white man's arrival is like confronting several puzzles lacking pieces. Attempting to accurately picture these swarthy inhabitants resembles assembling the puzzles in a darkened room. Any description of the Pre-Columbian Indian will be fragmented and afford only a glimpse of them.

In prehistoric times the New River Valley was heavily inhabited but at the white man's arrival was a great emptiness, a no-man's land, where only the roving hunter dared stray. Mondongachete was the name some Indians were calling the New. The Bluestone was called Momongoseneka and the Roanoke, Hocomawanach. Upon these rivers the headwaters of which intermingled lived many Americans hundreds of years before the white man's coming. But something happened shortly before the Jamestown settlement in 1607 that changed this and explains why West Virginia Indians called the New River, "The River of Death."

On the Great Lakes about 1570 was formed the Iroquois Confederacy or Five Nations of Onondagas, Cayugas, Mohawks, Senecas, and Oneidas, later Six Nations when the Tuscaroras joined them. Though their headquarters was on the Great Lakes they exerted an unbelievable influence upon the New River Valley using it as a warpath from the Ohio Valley. In 1607 the Monocan Indians at Jamestown begged Captain John Smith to free them from their enemies the Massosomacks, their name for the Iroquois "who had so many men they did war on all the world." In 1630 the Dutch began selling them firearms with which by 1656 they had nearly exterminated their Algonquian neighbors, the Eries. In 1662 they began driving another Algonquian tribe, the Shawnees, into the southern Ohio Valley to the Kanawha and Cumberland Rivers. By 1671 the Shawnees engaged in this "hot and bloody war with the Iroquois" were near extermination because they had no firearms. Finally they were grudgingly incorporated into the Iroquois League but not a standing equal to the other nations. [1]

Cadwalleder Jones, commander of the Rappahannock River fort in Virginia, writing in 1681 said all summer the Senecas had "so oppressed the Virginia Indians that they have made no corn this year."[2] The Senecas raided so regularly through the New River Valley that today their path is called the Seneca Trail.

In 1751 the Virginia Government ordered Joshua Fry to make a **Report on the Back Settlements** to accompany his and Peter Jefferson's **Map of Virginia** being sent to London. Fry said, "The Ohio Indians live on the river of that name, above the mouth of New River, for below or anywhere on the New River there are no Indians seated, and they must be subject to or in alliance with the Six Nations."

Of the Iroquois Fry said, "They would hardly suffer a nation of Indians to live within a thousand miles of them unmolested" and traveled south every year "making incursions on the Catawbas meerly for the sake of killing them, traveling on foot for this purpose a country of the extent of eight or nine degrees of latitude."[3]

The warlike indomitable Iroquois undefeated by any Indians and conquerors of all, whose most noted modern descendant is Winston Churchill, exerted the greatest influence of any Indian group upon the New River Valley.

By 1755 most of the Siouan tribes of Virginia including the Saponey, Totelo (Toteras), Occoneechee and others who had lived south of New River and east of the Blue Ridge had moved further south "in order to protect themselves against the Iroquois who have overrun those parts."[4]

It is significant that several New River area Indian villages dating from recent prehistoric times and excavated by archaelogists have palisades and are "fortified" villages.

Thus the Iroquois had begun one hundred and fifty years before white settlement to make New River Valley a no-man's land. When the whites arrived it was a buffer zone fit only for a hunting ground. Yet we know it was inhabited before the Iroquois drove everyone out and figures prominently in legends of many tribes as having once been their home.

An Indian village on the south bank of the New at Radford dating from 1600 was uncovered by Colonel Howard McCord, Virginia State archaelogist, in 1974. McCord estimated the Indians lived at Radford from 1600 to 1620. Wooden poles outline the large palisade that encircled the village and 35 dwellings. A handful of blue glass beads made in Italy found at the site similar to ones found at Jamestown reveal that Jamestown settlers traded indirectly with New River Indians 250 miles inland.

"That's a first for southwest Virginia," says McCord, who claims this site is most important for New River Valley. The beads were made by Venetian artisans about 1600. From the time settlers traded the beads to Indians until they reached New River would have taken about ten years, estimates McCord, who believes the Indians were at Radford until 1617. After that they disappeared. From whence the Radford Indians came, to what larger Indian family they belonged, or where they went are unknown. [5]

In view of the trading beads found at Radford it is interesting to read a letter sent from Virginia to King Charles I in 1628. "There is a great hope of the richness of the mountains," reads the letter. "There

The Radford Indian Village was similar to this eastern Virginia Village.

(Drawing by John White)

—37—

was a discovery made formally 19 years since (1609) in which some of us were, and about four days journey above the falls of James River as we are informed certain assurance of a silver mine."[6]

Four days journey above the falls of James River would place a traveler near New River. Not far upstream from the Radford village were the lead deposits which yield silver. Is it possible that Europeans had touched the New by 1609?

There is evidence that European influence was felt even in the lower Kanawha Valley by the early 1600's. An iron hatchet has been found in a tree at Charleston, West Virginia. The tree had grown around the hatchet and from the tree's rings observers estimate it had been there since before 1620. Some people think this is evidence of French explorers in the area.[7] However, the French by their own accounts did not explore the Ohio Valley until late 1600. The iron hatchet may have arrived on the Kanawha by way of a Jamestown-New-Kanawha trade route.

An Indian village known as the Shannon site on the headwaters of Roanoke River about 20 miles from the Radford settlement was excavated in the 1960's. Though not a New River settlement yet it is only about ten miles from the New and gives insight to the life style of New River Indians before 1607. The Shannon site in Ellett Valley at the golf course, inhabited from 1550-1600 is believed abandoned before the Radford site and before whites came into the region since there is no evidence of European trade goods. The Shannon village had an ellipical palisade of posts rammed in the ground at one foot intervals. Repairs had been made with a double row of posts. There were two entrances, one funnel-like. All houses were circular dome-shaped dwellings close to the palisade. They were made of saplings bent over, tied together, forming a frame then covered with matting or animal skins. The larger houses had fire pits. Burials were near the palisade, bodies in flexed position. Burial customs are important in showing tribal origin. Neither these Indians nor the Radford Indians were Shawnee, the tribe that was moving into the New River Valley at this time for Shawnee bury their dead inside their dwellings.

The bones in the Shannon burial sites reveal the prevalent diseases as congenital syphilis and arthritis. Ends of the bones were completely eaten away by these diseases. The oldest inhabitants were about fifty. The burial artifacts reveal a trade with far-flung tribes. Copper artifacts show an Ohio Fort Ancient cultural influence while Siouan pottery indicates trade with the North Carolina Piedmont and

Tennessee. It is most plausible that these people received their artifacts by way of the Kanawha-New route.[8]

When Virginia Route 100 was being modernized at Draper Valley in 1958 the "Draper Valley Indian Village" was unearthed. Local tradition had said there was a "pow-wow" site here and it yielded hundreds of artifacts including an English coin of 1746, a kaolin pipe with "P O S E" on it, bear's tooth pendants, pipes and stem fragments. One burial Christian fashion was found as well as burials in the flexed Indian position, resembling Conner's Island, Halifax, Virginia burials. There were no beads at Draper's site but at Eggleston beads were found with adult burials, thus Eggleston Indians may be a different group than the Draper Valley Indians. The Will Jackson Workshop site one mile south of Austinville revealed Indian relics including an ancient "rouge pot" holding grains of reddish purple "war paint." A large Indian fortress at Sugar Grove dating from 1450 has been found recently ten miles from Boone, North Carolina, where the waters of the New nearly touch the Watauga.[9]

The foregoing is a sampling of what anthropology has told of the New River people immediately before the coming of the white man. Tribal traditions reveal yet more.

Many peoples have wandered through the valley of the New. The Omaha and Kansas Indians, for example, have shells which they claim their ancestors brought with them from the "great water of the sunrise" after migrating through mountain passes to the east. According to Osage tradition, the western migrating tribes, after crossing the mountains, went from New River and Big Sandy to the Ohio and its mouth where the division of bands took place. On the other hand, Siouan tribes, the Catawbas, Saponi, Tutelo, Occoneechee and Monocans, had come from the west into Virginia and were living eastward of the Blue Ridge when white men first came to Virginia. One authority believes they entered Virginia by way of the Kanawha-New Valley.

The Catawbas have a tradition of flight from the Great Lakes pursued by Iroquois. Moving southward they entered into a league with the Cherokees bringing upon them the undying hatred of the Iroquois. The Cherokees were of the Iroquoian language group but had split from them centuries before. Another tradition of the Catawbas says they were driven from Canada about 1650, fled to the Kentucky River where they had a terrific battle with their pursuers and afterwards one group came through the mountains to Catawba Creek, Botetourt County, Virginia, where they settled only to move later to South Carolina. This tradition, not accepted by all historians, yet if true means the Catawbas must have arrived at Catawba Creek by way of New River. One of the first trails into the New River Valley follows Catawba Creek. Along this would be built the first white man's road to the New.[10]

In prehistoric times the Allegeni inhabited the Ohio Valley and the mountains that bear their name. The Delawares moving from the west were stopped by the Allegheni who built fortresses to stop their invasion. The Allegeni, ancestors of the modern Cherokees, were finally defeated by a Delaware-Iroquois alliance. According to this tradition, after defeat the Allegeni moved into Virginia living near Charlottesville, at the Peaks of Otter in Bedford County and finally in the New-Holston Valley. Here they made temporary settlements but left due to repeated invasions by northern Indians. They went on to Watauga and the Tennessee Rivers establishing their headquarters at Chota.

Anthropologists agree, calling the Cherokee the Pisgah culture, and saying they were driven from the Ohio Valley, possibly a remnant of the Adena-Hopewell culture.

Chota, their most ancient town, the Cherokees made into a sanctuary town, and so it would be to some whites from New River. The Cherokees had been established in the south two centuries before De Soto found them in 1540. His men came as far north as Xuala in the southwestern corner of North Carolina but miles from the New River.[11] There is no evidence that Spanish explorers came into the New River Valley.

In their progress south the Cherokees had traversed the New River Valley and would continue to travel it after the coming of the white man. One of the principal trade routes to them would follow the New and Holston into Tennessee.

Algonquian tribes inhabited the lower New-Kanawha Valley at the coming of the whites. The Delaware, Mohican and Shawnee as well as Kanawhas were Algonquian.

The Shawnee who the French called Chauvanoues were engaged in making salt on the Kanawha in the 1670's finding it took only 90 gallons of Kanawha water to make one bushel of salt as opposed to 840 gallons on the Licking River and others. The Shawnees built permanent structures which they had to leave behind when they moved which is in contrast to other New River Indians. It may have been their cabins which the Batts-Fallam party found near Narrows and it was certainly the Shawnees which were the fearsome salt-makers the Batts-Fallam guides quaked before.

Map-maker Dr. John Mitchell said that the Shawnees "who lived to the westward and north" of the Batts-Fallam discoveries were that same year, 1671, "engaged is a hot and bloody war with the Iroquois, in which they were so closely pressed that they were entirely extirpated or incorporated with the Iroquois the year following."[12]

These Shawnees, who were themselves under-dogs among their fellow Indians, would prove to be the most fearsome of all Indians to the New River settlers.

FOOTNOTES—Chapter V

1. Dr. John Mitchell, 1755, Notes on the Batts-Fallam Journal, Alvord-Bidgood, **Explorations,** pp. 197-198.

2. Cadwalleder Jones to Lord Baltimore, February 2, 1681, **VMHB,** v. 30, p. 327.

3. Joshua Fry, "Report on the Back Settlements," 1751, Delf Norona, ed., **VMHB** v. 56, p. 40.

4. Dr. John Mitchell, Map, Alvord-Bidgood, **Explorations,** pp. 197-198.

5. R.A. Streitmatter, "Blue Beads Cast Light on History," **Roanoke Times and World News,** April 29, 1975.

6. A.J. Morrison, "The Virginia Indian Trade to 1673," **WMQ** (2) I, p. 221.

7. **The News Messenger,** February 28, 1982, p. H-5.

8. Joseph Benthall, **Archaelogical Investigation of Shannon Site Montgomery County, Virginia** (Richmond: The Virginia State Library 1969) pp. 20-22, 43-44, 50-55, 93, 145-148.

9. John H. Reeves, "Draper Valley Indian Village Site," **Virginia Archaeological Bulletin,** September 1958; C.A. Michael, "Rock Materials Used in American Indian Artifacts from Central Southwestern Virginia,' **Virginia Archaeological Bulletins,** 1960; and Dr. Eric J. Olson, Appalachia Collection, Belk Library, Appalachia State University, letter to author, April 25, 1981.

10. Douglas Summers Brown, **The Catawba Indians The People of the River** (Columbia: The University of South Carolina Press, 1966) hereafter cited as Brown, **Catawba,** p. 29, and Charles M. Hudson, **The Catawba Nation** (Athens: University of Georgia Press, 1970) hereafter cited as Hudson, **Catawba,** p. 7, 14, 28-29.

11. John R. Swanton, **The Indians of the Southeastern United States** (Washington: Government Printing Office, 1946) p. 46 and Ruth Y. Wetmore, **First on the Land The North Carolina Indians** (Winston-Salem, N.C.: John F. Blair, 1975) p. 54.

12. Alexander S. Withers, **Chronicles of Border Welfare,** reprint of 1831 ed. (Parsons, W.Va.: McClain Printing Co., 1961) hereafter cited as Withers **Warfare,** p. 265 and Alvord-Bidgood, **Explorations,** pp. 197-198, 235 and Jerry E. Clark, **The Shawnees** (Lexington: The University Press of Kentucky, 1977) pp. 41-43.

Chapter VI

Curious Rising Hills and Brave Meadows

A fierce sea battle in the West Indies seems to have little connection with the ancient New River hidden deep in the folds of the
Alleghenies. Yet in 1620 on board the tiny English vessel **Margaret
and John** reeling in battle with two Spanish men-of-war was
ten-year-old Abraham Wood. Abraham was one of the few survivors
as the ship broke from the Spaniards and raced for Virginia. The
frightened child who stepped ashore at Jamestown could not know
that one day he would be the European discoverer of New River
which twentieth-century geologists would judge the second oldest
river in the world. Nor did he know that for nearly one hundred
years it would be called by his name, Wood's River.

Young Abraham by 1625 was apprenticed to Captain Samuel
Matthews of Matthews Manor recently excavated on Warwick River
who taught him soldiering. By 1644 he was soldier enough to be
given command of Fort Henry at present Petersburg and popular
enough to be chosen Burgess. He owned a house, a boat, some land
and had a captain's commission.

In 1642 the Virginia Assembly authorized Walter Austin and
Rice Hoe to explore unknown lands or new rivers southwest of
Appomattox River. If they made any discoveries they are unknown.
In 1649 a tract "A Perfect description of Virginia" written in
Virginia says, "The Indians acquainted our Governor that within five
days journey to the westward and by south there is a great high
mountain and at the foot thereof great rivers that run into a great
Sea. . .men come hither in ships, they wear apparell and have red
caps on their heads and ride on Beasts like our horses but have much
longer ears."[1] A great river behind a great mountain five days journey distant that flowed westward into Spanish territory — our first
description of New River — known in Virginia by 1649.

By this time the Great Trading Path to the Indian nations had penetrated 400 miles in a southwesterly direction from James River. In August of 1650 Abraham Wood steps upon stage as an explorer, when he and Edward Bland went along that Trading Path penetrating the Carolina region southwest of the Roanoke-Staunton River. Contacts with the Appomattox Indians and others gave information which Bland published in a 1651 pamphlet describing "New Brittaine" lying in latitude 35-37 abounding with "great rivers of long extent." He told of seeing "Indian pipes tipt with silver" and Indians wearing "copper plates about their necks." [2]

Silver and copper were both later mined along the New River in North Carolina (one of the world's best copper veins was in Ashe County) so most likely these materials came from there. Since the English were keen for gold and silver, it is certain Bland and Wood got some clue these items came from the mountains to the west, possibly along a river winding there. Since the New lay in the latitudinal bounds described by Bland it is possible they learned of the New at this time. Wood must have known something that whetted his appetite for in 1652 he petitioned "to discover the mountains." The Assembly granted permission "encouraging discoveries" to the southwest "granting all profits arising for 14 years." [3]

With permission from the Assembly to explore the west granted upon his request it would seem that Wood immediately did something in this regard. Daniel Coxe in a memorial presented to King William in 1699 related that Wood had discovered the western parts of Virginia "in several journeys from 1654 to 1664." In his 1722 book **Carolana**, Coxe repeats, "Parts of this country were discovered by the English. . .long before the French had the least knowledge. . .Colonel Wood in Virginia. . .from the year 1654 to 1664 discovered at several times several Branches of the great rivers Ohio and Mesechaceba." [4]

Historians for two centuries copied Coxes' claims that Wood came over the mountains in 1654 to western flowing waters. Recent historical scrutiny questions this though does not refute it. Twentieth-century scholars Alvord and Bidgood, foremost students of Wood's activities say only that Wood could have been on western waters prior to 1671 but there is no proof of it.

Virginia historian Lewis Preston Summers even gave Wood a gap to come through to New River. He says from the earliest traditions of the white man there has been a Wood's Gap lying between Smith or present Irvine River in Patrick County and Little River in Floyd through which Wood came to the New. This gap does not seem to be on twentieth-century maps. One questions if Summers could have confused Wood's Gap with Ward's Gap which is well-documented in court records and old journals.

Ward's Gap is an ancient gap in Carroll County through which ran one of the first roads from North Carolina into the New River Valley. Moravian missionaries from North Carolina traveled the road through Ward's Gap to Poplar Camp on New River in 1799.[5]

On the other hand a 1758 ranger company came through the mountains to Little River thence to the New in the same vicinity Summers claims is Wood's Gap. On the 1650 expedition with Bland Wood had been as far west as the junction of the Dan and Staunton Rivers. If in 1654 Wood again went to this point on the Dan and followed it westward to Smith he would be in mountains. Following Smith through the Blue Ridge would bring them near the Little River. Indian guides could tell them that a short climb would bring them to westward flowing waters of Little River which flowed into a "Great River" such as described in the 1649 tract "A Perfect Description of Virginia."

Clues that something was discovered at this time by Wood comes from the Assembly proceedings. They had rewarded him with a Major's promotion when he returned from his explorations with Bland in Carolina. In 1655 they rewarded him with a Colonel's promotion and again in 1657 with a nomination to the Council. Were these rewards for a new discovery — the discovery of New River?

In 1659 Francis Hammond asked permission to discover "places where no English ever have been." The Assembly agreed but reminded him in 1652 they had passed an act encouraging western discoveries (after Abraham Wood had petitioned for such) so Hammond must not stop others from "taking up lands and planting in those now **new discovered places** in Virginia."[6] This indicates that the Assembly felt some "new discoveries" had been made as a result of their 1652 directive to Abraham Wood and others.

Also in 1655 upon Wood's request Captain William Harris was promoted to Major and shortly the Assembly commissioned him "to discover the westward mountains to find commodities to benefit the country."[7] Had Harris already accompanied Wood into the mountains, thus his promotion and commission to explore further? In 1670 Harris led the German explorer John Lederer on his second trip of discovery following the James River into present Buckingham County. There Harris turned homeward but Lederer and a lone Indian continued south to a northern branch of the Yadkin.[8] This was as close to New River as Lederer came. Yet after this trip the Virginia government wrote London they were "very confident" that "there are rivers falling the other way into the sea as well as to the east."[9] This knowledge must have come from Wood's man Harris and Lederer.

Thus matters stood in the summer of 1670. Proof that the New River was already discovered seems tatalizing close yet we will never know absolutely unless more documentation is discovered in England or elsewhere.

In 1671 Wood, by now a major-general, one of four commanding the military districts of Virginia, gave a commission to Thomas Batts, Thomas Wood and Robert Fallam "for finding the ebbing and flowing of the waters on the other side of the Mountains in order to the discovery of the South Sea."

Batts was a grandson of Robert Batts, vicar master of University College, Oxford, and possibly brother to Nathaniel Batts first permanent settler in North Carolina and governor of Roanoke Island. Nathaniel by 1655 had a busy Indian trade from his house on Albemarle Sound. Thomas Wood may have been Abraham's son. Robert Fallam is a question mark. The journal he kept of their experiences shows him to be a literate, educated man.[10]

According to their journal they were accompanied by Perecute, "a great man of the Apomatack Indians" and Jack Weason, formerly Wood's servant. They also took along fourteen Englishmen and an equal number of Indians, according to Robert Beverley, historian of Virginia, writing twenty-eight years later.[11]

They set out from Appomattox Town on Appomattox River in Charles City County opposite present Petersburg at eight o'clock on the morning of Friday, September 1, 1671. For the next three days they traveled forty miles per day apparently along the Occoneechee Trading Path one branch which went into Carolina and the other over the mountains into the Roanoke Valley. On September 4 they arrived at the westernmost town of the Saponey, a Siouan village on the Otter River southwest of present Lynchburg. The cradle of this nation had been in the mountains of western Virginia on the Kanawha, Big Sandy and Monogahela. One scholar believes they entered Virginia by the Kanawha-New Valley.[12]

The Batts-Fallam party were kindly received, given supplies and a guide to take them to the Toteras, another Siouan tribe. Joined by seven Appomattox Indians sent by Major General Wood they went on to the Hanathaskies Town where they had to leave Thomas Wood ill with flux, the dangerous bloody bowel. Pressing on for three more days they arrived on September 9 at three o'clock at the Totera

Town in a rich swamp between "a branch and the main river of Roanoke circled about with mountains." They were in the vicinity of present Roanoke, Virginia.

Batts and Fallam do not describe these Siouan people but another traveler of the era says, "The women wear a hairy match-coat. . .the hair of their heads is made into a long roll like a horses tail and bound around with Roanoke. . .a sort of beads. The men have a matchcoat of hair, furs or feathers. Their hair is in a roll on each ear or the crown of the head. Betwixt their legs comes a piece of cloth tucked in by a belt both before and behind."[13]

Historian Beverley describes the terrain along the Roanoke where the explorers now found themselves. The mountains "seem'd to reach the clouds, and were so perpendicular and full of precipices that sometimes in a whole days march they could not travel three miles in a direct line. In other places they found large level plains and fine savannahs, three or four miles wide, in which were an infinite quantity of turkies, deer, elks, and buffalo, so gentle and undisturbed that they had no fear at the appearance of men" but "would allow them to come within hand's reach." The "grapes were so large they appeared more like plums than grapes."[14]

An Appomattox Indian and Perecute became ill so the Appomattox was left at Totera Town but Perecute pushed on with the expedition when it set out guided by a Totera on September 12, 1671. "We left the town west and by north," writes Fallam. "We travell'd that day sometimes southerly, sometimes westerly as the path went over several high mountains and steep vallies crossing several branches and the Roanoke River several times all exceedingly stony ground until Perecute being taken with his fit and very weary we took up our quarters by the side of Roanoke River almost at the head of it at the foot of the great mountain. Our course was west by north, having travell'd twenty five miles."

The morning of September 13 they set out early. It was this day that they would come to New River. They traveled three miles to the foot of a great mountain so steep they could hardly keep from sliding down as they climbed. "When we got up to the top of the mountain and set down very weary we saw very high mountains lying to the north and south as far as we could discern," says Fallam. "Our course up the mountain was west by north. A very small descent on the other side and as soon as over we found the vallies tending westerly. It was a pleasing tho' dreadful sight to see the mountains and hills as if piled one upon another."

"After we had travelled about three miles from the mountains, easily descending about twelve of the clock we came to two trees marked with a coal MA NI the other cut in with MA and several other scratchments," continues Fallam.

Thus we see that they were not the first Europeans in the New River Valley.

They marched on by a swift creek "emptying sometimes westerly sometimes northerly with curious meadows" on each side. "Going forward we found a rich ground but having curious rising hills and brave meadows with grass about man's height, many rivers running west-north-west and several runs from the southerly mountains which we saw as we march'd northerly into the great river," records Fallam.

After traveling about seven miles they came to a very steep descent where "are found a great run, which emptied itself as we supposed into the Great River northerly, our course being as the path went, west-southwest. We set forward west and had not gone far but we met again with the River, still broad running west and by north." [15]

This is the first surviving description by white men of their approach to New River. Historians have never been sure where Batts and Fallam first touched the river. Although some say they followed the route of the present railroad descending down the divide between Crab and Lick Creeks near Blacksburg, Virginia, the terrain Fallam describes is more like that in the Snowville area. Here the streams run "west-north-west" flowing from "the southerly mountains". The very steep descent to a "great run" describes Little River's approach through a deep gorge into New River. One local historian says "It seems most probable that the great run which empties itself into the Great River northerly" refers to Little River. [16] Dr. John Mitchell who in 1755 published his **Map of the British and French Dominions in North America**, the most accurate map of the time, says people "frequently pass the mountains now in going to and from Wood River about the same place that is described" in the Batts and Fallam Journal. Mitchell says he has placed the trail in his **Map of North America** "exactly as they are described in this Journal." When we examine Mitchell's map we see the approach is southwest of the mouth of Little River. [17]

FOOTNOTES—Chapter VI

1. Biographical Dictionary of Early Virginia 1607-1660; p. 3825-3826. Alvord-Bidgood, Explorations, pp. 34-35, 46; Louis Don Scisco, "Explorations of 1650 in Southern Virginia, "THQ, VII, p. 169; William and Mary Stanard, ed., "The Colonial Virginia Register A list of Governors, Councillors and other High Officials and also of Members of the House of Burgesses and the Revolutionary Conventions of the Colony of Virginia (Albany, N.Y.: Joel Munsell's Sons, 1901) p. 64; William W. Hening, ed. The Statutes at Large being a collection of all the Laws of Virginia from the first session of the Legislature in 1619 (Richmond: George Cochran Printer, 1823) hereafter cited as Hening Statutes, I, pp. 262, 328. For Matthews Manor see Ivor Noel Hume, Martin's Hundred (New York: Alfred A. Knopf, 1982, p. 25.

2. Lefler, Carolina History, pp. 12-13 and Brown, Catawba, p. 48.

3. Hening, Statues, I, pp. 376-377, 381, 548.

4. Alvord-Bidgood, Explorations, p. 202 and Daniel Coxe, A Description of the English Province In Carolana By the Spanianrds Called Florida and by the French Louisiana (Gainesville: The University Presses of Florida, 1976) p. 120.

5. Lewis P. Summers, History of Southwest Virginia 1746-1786 (Richmond: J.L. Hill Printing Company, 1903) hereafter cited as Summers, Southwest Virginia, p. 36 and Fries, Steiner Journey, pp. 330-333.

6. Stanard, Colonial Virginia Register, pp. 69, 72; "Extracts from the Proceedings of the House of Burgesses of Virginia, 1652-1661, VMHB, VIII, p. 391; Hening, Statutes, I, p. 548 and 19 VMHB, p.259.

7. Hening, Statutes, I, pp. 391-392 and HJ, 1619-1659, v. I, p. 101.

8. Alvord-Bidgood, Explorations, p. 68.

9. Thomas Ludwell to Lord Arlington, June 27, 1760, Alvord-Bidgood, Explorations, p.178.

10. Journal of Batts and Fallam, September 1671, Alvord-Bidgood, Explorations, pp. 183-184 and Hugh T. Lefler and William S. Powell, Colonial North Carolina A History (New York: Charles Scribner's Sons, 1973) hereafter cited as Lefler and Powell, Carolina, p. 32.

11. Robert Beverley, The History and Present State of Virginia, 1699 ed. Louis B. Wright (Chapel Hill: The University of North Carolina Press, 1947) hereafter cited as Beverley, Virginia, p. 73.

12. Hudson, Catawba, p. 7 and James Mooney, The Siouan tribes of the East, (Washington: Government Printing Office, 1894) p. 203.

13. Chapman J. Milling, Red Carolinians (Columbia, S.C.: The University of South Carolina Press, 1969) hereafter cited as Milling, Red Carolinians, p. 9.

14. Beverley, Virginia, p. 73.

15. Alvord-Bidgood, Explorations, pp. 184-189.

16. Conway Smith, Colonial Days in the Land That Became Pulaski County, (Pulaski:B.D. Smith & Bros. Printers, Inc. 1975) hereafter cited as Smith, Pulaski, p.7.

17. Alvord-Bidgood, Explorations, pp. 72, 197-198.

Chapter VII

Wood's River

The Batts and Fallam party now at New River continued forward and record, "We went over the great run emptying itself northerly into the Great River. After we marched about six miles northwest and by north we came to the River again where it was much broader than at the other two places. It ran here west and by south and as we supposed round up westerly. Here we took up our quarters, after we had waded over, for the night. Due west, the soil, the farther we went is the richer and full of bare meadows and fields."

These "bare meadows and fields" are described by Jamestown Reverend Clayton, who in 1686 sent their journal to the Royal Society in London, as being a "common expression for land that has been cultivated by the Indians and left fallow, generally overrun with what they call "broom grass". A hundred years later, in 1773, George Washington advertized his land on the New-Kanawha in the **Maryland Journal and Baltimore Advertizer** as having "meadows. . .in their present state, almost fit for the scythe." Openings in the forest in the 1670's on New River such as these "old fields" were man-made for the land in eastern North America was completely covered by forest except for the occasional "balds". These meadows or old fields were remnants of cornfields the Indians had abandoned. [1]

The Eastern Indians had extensively burned the forests of North America, having already burned in Kentucky an area about five thousand square miles. One authority says if the white man had not gotten into the Alleghenies when they did the prairie region would have extended to the base of the Alleghenies and in time all the great American Woods might have vanished. [2]

Batts and Fallam with their party set out again before sunrise on September 14. They traveled as the path went "sometimes westerly, sometimes southerly over good ground but stony, sometimes rising hills and then steep descents as we march'd in a clear place at the top of a hill we saw lying southwest a curious prospect of hills like waves raised by a gentle breeze of wind rising one upon another. Mr. Batts supposed he saw sailes; but I rather think them to be white cliffs," records Fallam.

On that day they had marched about twenty miles. "About three of the clock we took up our quarters to see if the Indians could kill us some Deer, being west and by north, very weary and hungry and Perecute continued very ill yet desired to go forward. We came this day over several brave runs and hope tomorrow to see the main River again."

On September 15 they set out describing themselves as having "a dog's life — hunger and ease."

"Our Indians having done their best could kill us no meat," Fallam wrote. "The Deer they said were in such herds and the ground so dry that one or other of them could spy them. About one of the clock we set forward and went about fifteen miles over some good, some indifferent ground, a west and by north course till we came to a great run which empties itself west and by north as we suppose into the great River which we hope is nigh at hand. As we march'd we met with some wild gooseberries and exceeding large haws with which we were forced to feed ourselves."

Since haws were the fruit of the hawthorn, a small round red berry, Fallam must have meant the red rasberry. English haws did not grow along New River.

On September 16 their Totera guide left them and their other Indians went ranging in search of deer or some other meat. "One came and told us they heard a Gun go off to the northwards. They brought us some exceeding good Grapes and killed two turkies which were very welcome and with which we feasted ourselves and about ten of the clock set forward and after we had travelled about ten miles one of our Indians killed us a deer and presently afterwards we had sight of a curious river like Apomatack River," continues Fallam. "Its course here was north and as we suppose runs west about a certain curious mountain (Angel's Rest?) we saw westward. Here we set up our quarters our course having been west. We understand the Mohetan Indians did here formerly live. It cannot be long since for we found corn stalks in the ground."

Although Beverley says the Indians were Mohetans, a Cherokee group, it is more likely they were Shawnees for it was after arrival at these cabins the guides became so fearful. Beverley continues in his 1699 narrative, "They discovered a river that descended backwards.

Down that stream they travell'd several days till they came to old fields and cabbins, where the Indians had lately been; but were supposed to have fled at the approach of Batt and his company. However, the Captain follow'd the old rule of leaving some Toys in the Cabbins, for them to find at their return, by which they might know they were Friends."

The old fields and cabins were obviously a site long inhabited by Indians. Such a site discovered in 1980 one mile west of Pearisburg on a point jutting into the river yielded Indian knives, arrowheads, and spear points of such nature that archaelogists believe the site may have been inhabited 8,000 years.

Beverley continues to say, "Near to these cabins were great marshes where the Indians which Captain Batt had with him, made a Halt, and would positively proceed no further. They said, that not far off from that Place, lived a Nation of Indians, that made Salt, and sold it to their neighbors. That this was a great and powerful people, which never suffer'd any Strangers to return that had once discovered their Towns. Capt. Batt used all the arguments he could to get them forward, but in vain. And so, to please those timorous Indians, the Hopes of this Discovery were frustrated and the detachment was forced to return.[3]

The New near Pearisburg, "The curious Mountain" of Batts and Fallam?
(Photo by Frank Shelton)

Thus was lost the opportunity to see conditions among the New River Indians or Shawnee "Salt-Makers". These salt works are believed located on the Kanawha above Charleston. If so they were not actually too distant from where Batts and Fallam terminated their exploration.

After finding the Indian fields Batts and Fallam claimed the territory for England. They marked four trees standing together on the New on September 17. "We first proclaimed the King in these words," Fallam records. "Long live Charles the Second, by the grace of God King of England, Scotland, France, Ireland and Virginia." They fired guns and marked the tree CR for Charles Rex. Next they marked WB for Governor William Berkeley. Third, they marked AW for Major-General Abraham Wood and lastly TB, presumably for Thomas Batts. Finally they marked RE.P. for Perecute. On another tree they marked TT, NP, VE and R. Perecute, the Appomattox chief, watching all this was so impressed he vowed "he would learn Englishman."

This simple ceremony of marking the trees so impressing to Perecute would have far reaching consequences. Batts and Fallam on this September day in 1671 on the New River claimed for England the westward flowing waters on the Mississippi watershed before La Sale or Marquette and Joliet claimed them for France. They were on a branch of the Mississippi two years before Marquette and Joliet touched the Mississippi. Although La Salle says he was on the Ohio in 1667 historians believe he was actually on the Wabash.[4] Their journal of their explorations on New River exists whereas the journals of Joliet and La Salle are lost. That of Joliet was lost when his canoe overturned and La Salle's journal was lost in Paris.

The implications of all this was far-reaching when France would try to seize the Mississippi Valley and all of North America eighty years later. Batts and Fallam would not live to know the continent-shaking consequences of what they did this day on New River. Nor did they know the vastness of the continent stretching beyond them. Truly seventeenth century men they were so intent on finding a passage to the Pacific Ocean that anything white shining in the distance must be sails on the "South Sea!"

After marking the trees they marched back to the riverside through impassable prickly thistles. They were now on a falls "like the James River at Colonel Stagg's" meaning Thomas Stegg uncle of William Byrd I near present Richmond. Probably these falls on New River beyond which they dared not proceed were Peters Falls where New River cuts through Peters Mountain near Pearisburg, Virginia.

Mr. Fallam now records, "We imagined by the water marks it flows here about three feet. It was ebbing water when we were here. We set up a stick by the water side but found it ebb very slowly."

When reading this we must remember their original intent, to find a passage to the South Sea. Surely therefore the New must be "ebbing water" as the tide went out!

Fallam continues, "Our guides kept such a hollowing that we durst not stay any longer," but before they turned homeward they climbed to a hill top and viewing the hills they imagined they saw "a glimmering light as from water. We supposed there to be a great Bay." They still believed they were seeing the Pacific or some mysterious water. We know they only saw the hills of West Virginia.

Returning to Toteras Town they learned that "Mr. Byrd and his great company" had made discoveries nearby. Nineteen-year-old William Byrd I whose uncle Thomas Stegg had established a Cherokee trade in the 1650's was exploring here in the present Roanoke area. Whether Byrd and his traders came into the New River valley we do not know. We do know that in 1673 when the French explorer Marquette, traveling down the Mississippi, reached the mouth of the Ohio he wrote a letter about his explorations and gave it to Indians who said they traded with Europeans. Through some trading network the letter reached Byrd.[5]

Batts and Fallam left Toteras Town and returned to the Hanahaskies village where they found Thomas Wood dead and buried. Continuing home they arrived October 1 at Fort Henry where Fallam finishing his journal wrote, "God's Holy name be praised for our preservation."

Two copies of Fallam's journal recording the trek to New River are in London. One, sent by Reverend Clayton, is in the British Museum. Ironically Clayton may be responsible for some of the early disinterest in the New River.

Twentieth-century historians draw these conclusions about the discovery of New River. "Wood may well have gone in person or sent men who passed the Blue Ridge before Batts and Fallam. The fact that he commissioned the latter simply to find out about the tidal waters beyond the mountains would seem to indicate that the passes were already known. The men who left their initials east of the Blue Ridge and again beyond the Alleghenies were probably not his; but whosoever they were, their markings show that by 1671 at least three parties of white men had been far beyond the Blue Ridge along the New River trail, and two of them beyond the Allegheny divide. The path which Fallam followed is seen from his references to it to have been a plain Indian trail, doubtless well-known to the guides. From the behavior of the Indians in firing salutes. . .it appears certain that in the villages along the route, as far as that of the Toteras, white men were welcome and familiar guests. So far had Virginians progressed on the way to Kentucky a century before Daniel Boone and forty-five years before Spotswood's pleasant summer picnicking excursion into the Shenandoah Valley."[6]

FOOTNOTES—Chapter VII

1. Alvord-Bidgood, **Explorations,** p. 189.

2. Hugh Maxwell, "The Use and Abuse of Forests by the Virginia Indians," 19 W (1) p. 100.

3. Beverley, **Virginia,** p. 73 and Doug Waters, "Pearisburg Plant site rich in Indian Artifacts," **Roanoke Times & World News,** May 30, 1982.

4. Francis Parkman, **La Salle and the Discovery of the Great West** reprint of 1897 edition (Williamstown, Massachusetts: Corner House Publisher, 1968) pp. 27-34 and Reuben G. Thwaites, **France in America, 1947-1763** (New York: Harper & Brothers, 1905) pp. 58-59.

5. Brown, **Catawba,** p. 54.

6. Alvord-Bidgood, **Explorations,** pp. 78, 184-193.

Chapter VIII

Pallatia

Governor Berkeley was so excited over the Batts and Fallam discoveries that he wrote London, January 30, 1672, that he hoped to send out another party in February. The records are silent as to whether he did.[1] Major-General Wood did send out another party in 1673 under James Needham and Gabriel Arthur which went to the Yadkin headwaters, crested the Blue Ridge descended across five shallow streams flowing northwest probably New headwaters and on to Tennessee Cherokee villages who they called Tomahitans. Needham left Arthur in a Tomahitan town, probably Chota, to return to Virginia and was killed. Arthur, meanwhile, was going on the warpath with the Tomahitan king into both Spanish and English territory. One excursion took them into the mountains where they came to the New-Kanawha Valley.

As far as we know, Gabriel Arthur, surely an indentured servant who Major-General Wood called "my man Gabriel", was the first Englishman to see the Kanawha Valley.

Wood, writing to England of Arthur's New River trip, relates, "Now ye king of the Tomahitans must goe to give ye monetons a visit. Gabriel must go with him. They set forth with sixty men and traveled ten days due north and then arrived at ye monyton town situated upon a great river at which place ye tide ebbs and flowes. Gabriel swom in ye river several times, being fresh water. This is a great towne and a great number of Indians belong unto it, and in ye same river Mr. Batt and Fallam were upon the head of it as you read in one of my first journals. This river runs north west and out of westerly side of it goeth another very great river."[2]

It is impossible to know exactly where Gabriel Arthur was in the New-Kanawha Valley except there was a very large Indian settlement near.

"About a days journey downstream are an inumarable company of Indians as the monytons, which is twenty days journey from one end to ye other of ye inhabitance, and all these are at warr with the Tomahitans. When they had taken their leave of ye monytons," continues Wood in his Elizabethan way, "they marched three days out of their way to give a clap to some of that nation, where they fell on with great curage and were as curagiously repulsed."

Apparently these Indians to whom they gave "a clap" were the Shawnee and Kanawha salt-makers so feared by the Totera guides with Batts. Gabriel was wounded in this "clap" and taken captive to their towns. Thus we have a first glimpse by white men of the Ohio Indians who would so terrorize New settlers.

"They took Gabriel and scowered his skin with water and ashes," writes Wood, "When they perceived his skin to be white they made very much of him and admired his knife, gun and hattchet which they took (but later returned). He made signes to them the gun was ye Tomahittans which he had a desire to take with him but ye knife and hatchet he gave to the king. They not knowing the use of guns, the king received it with great showes of thankfulness for they had not any manner of iron instrument that he saw amongst them while he was there."

Although Gabriel saw no iron instrument among these Indians we have the mysterious 1600's iron hatchet found in the tree on the Kanawha mentioned earlier.

Gabriel saw these Indians bring in a fat beaver and he made signs "that those skins were good amongst the white people toward the rising sun." Asking "how many such skins they would take for such a knife," Gabriel told them "four and eight for such a hatchett and made signs that if they would let him return, he would bring many things among them. They seemed to rejoice at it and carried him to a path that carried to ye Tomahittans — gave him Rokahamony for his journey and so departed."

Gabriel arrived back in the Tomahitan camp by May 10, 1674 in time to accompany a party laden with trade goods heading to Fort Henry. In an Occoneechee village he was separated from them and wandered home alone arriving at Fort Henry on June 18. "Praise be to God for it," said Wood.

Though Arthur promised to return to the Kanawha Indians we do not know if he did or was allowed to do so. According to historian Beverley, "Upon Captain Batt's report to Sir William Berkeley he resolved to journey himself so there might be no hindrance of sufficient authority as had been in the aforesaid expedition. His plans came to nothing because of the confusion soon after of Bacon's Rebellion. Since that there never has been any such discovery attempted from Virginia."[3]

Repressive measures after Bacon's Rebellion in 1676 were not the only reason no more explorations were made on New River. Exploration into the interior was generally discouraged. After John Lederer's explorations of 1671-72 Sir William Talbot of Maryland said there was such an uproar over Lederer's explorations that he fled to Maryland because he "was not safe in Virginia from the outrage of the people" and "instead of welcome and applause met nothing but affronts and reproaches." Talbot said that even with Governor Berkeley's blessing, "To go into those parts of the American continent where Englishmen never had been. . .was in Virginia looked upon as so great an insolence."[4]

This outrage against western explorations was due to fear that the Indians aroused by meddling explorers would in their anger fall upon the white settlements.

As to why he made no more explorations Major-General Abraham Wood explains, "Self-ended traders" had "strove what they could to block up ye designe from the beginning."

"If I could have ye countenance of some person of honor in England," Wood claimed, "to curb and bridle ye obstructers here for here is no encouragment at all to be had for him that is your humble servant Abraham Wood."[5]

The Byrd family, competitors of Wood, were beginning to have tremendous influence in Virginia. Reverend Clayton who originally sent the Batts-Fallam journal to the Royal Society may have discouraged New River exploration by voicing around the colony what William Byrd told him. "I know Col. Byrd that is mentioned to have been about that time as far as the Toteras," writes Clayton. "He is one of the intelligentest Gentlemen in all Virignia and knows more about Indian affairs than any man in the country. I discoursed with him about the river on the other side of the mountains said to ebb and flow which he assured me was a mistake." Clayton claimed Byrd said the river merely drained into a lake "at the back of Virginia where Fallam and the rest supposed there might be a bay" where the French had settled and were "absolute masters of the Beaver trade."[6]

Possibly Wood meant Byrd when he talked of "self-ended traders". Byrd seemed to belittle the New River discovery when he said it merely drained into a lake inhabited by the French. Could Byrd's talk have been a ploy to monopolize the beaver trade and keep competitors out of the New River Valley? Gabriel Arthur had come back telling of beaver (but no French) and surely this kindled interest with Wood, Byrd and other traders. Pound per pound beaver skin was one of the most valuable exports of Virginia. Is it likely that the New-Kanawha Valley where there was an abundance of beaver would soon be forgotten?

Certainly the French were interested in the valley. In 1676 Richard Wharton a Boston merchant wrote, "The French are reported to be very diligent in discovery of the land behind Virginia. Some persons have been three years upon discovery (and) are returned to Canada."[7]

In 1692 a Dutch trader Arnold Viele from Albany led a party of traders down the Ohio to the mouth of a river where lived many Shawnee and traded with them. They returned home in 1694.[8]

The French anxiously watched the Ohio and its tributaries for English traders. In 1694 the same year Viele returned to Albany Henri de Tonty chief commandant in the Illinois country sent word to Canada that "Carolinians are established on a branch of Ohio."[9]

This shadowy reference may refer to the Tennessee, or Cumberland but could mean the New-Kanawha. Certainly some English trading goods were getting into the New-Kanawha Valley and to the Ohio for in 1700 the French commandant at Detroit told his Indians to go to the Beautiful River (Ohio) and seize the English trading goods.[10] Certainly in the interval between 1674 and 1730 it is likely hunters and traders came into the New River Valley and we have some inkling who they were.

When Virginia established a fort on the Appomattox commanded by Abraham Wood they also placed one on the Rappahannock at the site of present Fredericksburg to protect Rappahannock and Essex Counties. In command was Colonel Cadwallader Jones, son of a London merchant, who in February 1681 wrote Lord Baltimore, "I have an inland trade about four hundred miles from here, south southwest."

There is a tradition that Jones was a brother of Peter Jones, Abraham Wood's son-in-law, who had a trading post at Petersburg, which would explain how he became interested in the Indian trade to the west. Whether from this connection or his own explorations Jones knew much about the mountains toward New River. He called the Blue Ridge "Cawcaseans" and said he had explored beyond them on Shenandoah and knew well the mountains where headed the James as well as the Roanoke which he called Occoneechee River. By 1698 he claimed "those mountains is now to me well known."[11]

The Roanoke and New head within a stone's throw of each other. In Blacksburg, Virginia on Cohee Drive the water on one side drains toward Strouble's and Tom's Creek into New River and on the other side into Roanoke River. It is worth noting that Tom's Creek was first known as Jones Creek.[12]

Because Virginia stiffled western Indian trade Jones got in debt so left Virginia to become governor of the Bahamas. There, accused of trafficking with pirates, he was dismissed. By 1698 he was back in Virginia still trying to arouse interest in western Indian trade. He made a map of western Virginia and the Mississippi Valley to accompany his **Essay, Louissiana and Virginia Improved** which he presented to Governor Nicholson with the express purpose of establishing trade with the Indians on the Great Lakes and the Mississippi. His map shows the western Indian nations and rivers that drained the Appalachian region with the headwaters of the Ohio arising in those mountains. He shows one branch of the Ohio bisecting the Appalachians placed where New River should be on a map but does not name it, the land drained by the Ohio lying south in the New River region Jones calls Pallatia.[13]

Governor Nicholson supported Jones' scheme, presented it to Council, Assembly and Board of Trade in London where they cautiously urged that adventures westward not "interfere with or discourage the planting of tobacco which is the main thing to be pursued in that colony."[14]

Pallatia, taking its name from the mountains which Jones called "Appelatinian", has a strange sound today but may have been well known to hunters and traders threading their way from the Appomattox and Rappahannock River forts into the southwestern mountains.

Whether Jones had gotten into Pallatia and the valley of the New we do not know. After 1698 he seems more concerned with establishing trade through the Potomac Valley. We do know that Rappahannock River men were engaged in trade in southwestern Virginia. Hunter and fur trader Abraham Little living in Essex County in 1704 hunted deep into the mountains. He had a "Meat House" on Leatherwood Creek in Henry County, an early landmark. One historian believes Little came into the New River Valley hunting and Little River is named for him.[15]

Though evidence is slim yet there are indications that the name of Cadwallader Jones should be added to those who made some contribution to knowledge of western Virginia in the region of the New River Valley.

FOOTNOTES—Chapter VIII

1. Alvord-Bidgood, **Explorations,** p. 77

2. Ibid. pp. 210-226 Abraham Wood to John Richards August 22, 1674.

3. Beverley, **Virginia,** p. 74.

4. Sir William Talbot, Foreword to the Discoveries of John Lederer (1672), Alvord-Bidgood, **Explorations,** p. 136.

5. Wood to Richards, August 22, 1674, ibid, p. 210.

6. Reverend John Clayton to the Royal Society, October 24, 1688, Alvord-Bidgood, **Explorations,** p. 194.

7. **Mississippi Valley Historical Review,** 1934, v. XXI, p. 256.

8. Hanna, **Wilderness Trail,** I, p. 143.

9. Archibald Henderson, **Conquest of the Old Southwest** (New York: The Century Company, 1920) hereafter cited as Henderson, **Old Southwest,** p. 45.

10. Harriet S. Arnow, **Seedtime on the Cumberland** (New York: The MacMillan Company, 1960) hereafter cited as Arnow, **Seedtime,** p. 83.

11. John Holt Rice, "Western Explorations in Virginia Between Lederer and Spotswood," **VMHB,** v. 30, pp. 325-327, 338-340.

12. CS, I, pp. 307-308.

13. **VMHB,** v. 30.

14. Verner W. Crane, **The Southern Frontier, 1670-1732** (Durham: Duke University Press, 1928) p. 62, quoting VMHB, XXII, p. 40.

15. Maud C. Clement, **The History of Pittsylvania County, Virginia** (Lynchburg, Virginia: J.P. Bell Company Inc., 1929) hereafter cited as Clement, **Pittsylvania,** p. 44 and Brown, **Catawba,** p. 52.

Chapter IX

A Trip Through Pallatia

Whether or not Cadwallader Jones's traders frequented the New River Valley fierce Iroquois traveled it every season. For decades they had used it as a corridor to pass to their southern battlegrounds among the Catawbas and Cherokees.

One major Indian trail was the Seneca Trail which came from Seneca Country in New York, through western Pennsylvania, thence to Parsons, West Virginia, to Elkins, to Lewisburg, following generally the route of present U.S. 219 to Union, south along Rich Creek to Peterstown and across New River at Rich Creek and Glen Lyn. Here was a great Indian rendezvous point. In the area around Indian Creek, under Bluestone Dam Lake, and in the surrounding area have been found thousands of Indian relics, hieroglyphics and burials. The size of the encampment is witness that the Seneca Trail was heavily traveled.

One of the earliest historians of western Virginia, Alexander S. Withers, relates that on the Ohio there were two rendezvous points for the Ohio Indians such as the Shawnees and Miamis. One was at the mouth of the Great Kanawha and another at the mouth of Great Sandy. From the mouth of the Great Kanawha they would ascend the Kanawha and Greenbrier rivers to the New. Two major Indian trails transverse the Gorge area, the Buffalo or Kanawha Trail following present U.S. 60 and the path leading up Paint Creek. From the Great Sandy rendezvous point they would ascend the Great Sandy and by way of the Bluestone come over on to New River. From either point they would end up on the New at the big camping ground at Indian Creek and Bluestone.[1]

Possibly this is the camp site William Preston mentions when Ohio Indians raided Fort Vause in 1756. He says one of the white captives was taken prisoner to "a camp they had in the Gap of a mountain beyond New River."[2] This area is a rich ground in which amateur and professional anthropologists might search for early New River Indian remains.

Also approaching New River Valley was the Great Iroquois War Trail down the Valley of Virginia which crossed the Blue Ridge near Roanoke and continued south into the Carolina Piedmont. A branch of this trail came up Catawba Valley where the Catawba Creek Road or Indian Road would come into the New River Valley.

A third trail for traders and Indians coming into the New River Valley approaches from the east over the Blue Ridge to Little River. This may be the trail followed by Batts and is later the Warwick Road.

A fourth trail was the one beginning at Totera Town (Roanoke) following the course of New River and connecting with the Occonee trail near present Wilkesboro, North Carolina.

It was a certain fact that anyone living in the New River Valley in the 1700's was directly in the path of northern Indians coming south to war. A friend told William Preston at Smithfield on the New in 1774, "You lay too much in the way of Indians. New River has been the course they came formerly to war."[3]

Only about 1730 do we begin to pick up clues in historical documents of their activities in that valley. A Mr. Wates meeting in council May 10, 1731, with a Tuscaroroa chief in North Carolina reported, "Last fall some Indians came to the head of New River and killed Captain Jack and wounded one more of their people. A party of Senecas coming to their town to go against the Catawbas they went out with them."[4] Although there is a New River in eastern Carolina the **North Carolina Colonial Records** editors have classified this incident as happening on New River of western Carolina.

By the 1730's the Shawnees, the old "salt-makers" of the Kanawha, were well incorporated into the Iroquois League and going with them against the Catawbas and Cherokees. In 1732 they had a battle with the Catawbas on New River. A Catawba warrior killed a Shawnee chief in this battle, a great victory for the southern Indians. The Catawba was given the name New River. He became Chief New River and it was said, "New River had no other name, he would have felt insulted" to change his name. "He gloried in that of New River." He married Catawba princess, Sally, daughter of Chief Hagler and began the family of New River which became numerous among the Catawbas. Chief New River's friend Thomas Spratt was named Kanawha.[5]

By the 1730's little was still known in England about the New and the Mississippi watershed. The French had busily explored the

Mississippi but did not know much about New River. Guillaume De l'Isle's 1718 **Map of Louisiana** shows the Ohio but not the Kanawha-New. However the French were trading there calling it the Sault. In 1720 Herman Moll's **New Map of the North Part of America claimed by France** shows the Kanawha labeled as Sault River. In 1729 Moll's **Map of Carolina** shows the New rising in North Carolina and labels it Sault. Neither John Barnwell's 1722 map of southeastern North America nor Henry Popple's 1733 **Map of Virginia** ordered by the Lords of Trade show the Sault or New.[6] If the state of cartography is any measure of knowledge less and less was being known about Pallatia and the Sault or New River.

Consideration should be made of London's policy not to provoke the French in the Mississippi Valley and bring upon the Virginia frontier an Indian war. Perhaps Henry Popple deliberately left the New off his 1733 map. Whatever London's reasons the humble people hungrily seeking land knew little of them as they began following the trails to the New.

A tiny cabin at Forest Hill near Hinton, West Virginia, is said to have been discovered years ago with the date 1738 carved over the door. This is years before whites are said to have penetrated the river valley that far west but the story is given credence by a stone at the mouth of East River on the New inscribed, "Mary Porter was killed by the Indians, November 28, 1742," revealing that there were white settlers that far west at that early date.[7]

Settlers between East River and Hinton, at the mouth of Greenbrier, though far to the interior, might have arrived there by the way of the Greenbrier, coming down from settlements in the Shenandoah area. Far-fetched but possible.

About 1740 a Mr. Vaughan of Amelia County who died in 1801 was employed to go as packman with a party of Indian traders to the Cherokee nation. The last cabin he saw was on Otter River in Bedford County. The route he traveled was an old trading path following the same route the stage road later followed from Buchanan to Ingles Ferry (Radford) where they crossed the New. From there they went on to the Holston and Tennessee.[8]

In the late 1730's John Howard living on the Shenandoah petitioned the Virginia Council to make discoveries on the "Lakes and Rivers of the Mississippi." On October 17, 1737, the Council gave Howard the permission. Arming him with 40 pounds of powder and bullets and four kettles they told him not to fight Indians or attack French forts.[9] As if a few men with four kettles would attack French forts!

Trying to find people to go on this wild goose chase delayed Howard until March 1742. At that time he came to John Peter Salling on the upper James to ask him to accompany the party. Salling, a German who had bought land in Lancaster County, Pennsylvania, in 1735, by 1740 had moved to the first fork of the James west of the Blue Ridge and was one of the westernmost settlers in Virginia. According to his descendants, in 1736 Salling had been captured near Salem, Virginia, by the Cherokees and carried by them along the New to the Ohio. Withers in his **Border Warfare** makes the same claim.[10]

On March 16, 1742 Salling, Howard, his son Josias Howard, John Pottett and Charles Cinekler (St. Clair) set out on their exploration of the Mississippi Valley. They went to Mondongachete or Wood's River as Salling called the New. They killed five buffalo and with their hides made "bullboats" to carry the party down New River. They found the river very rocky having many falls "one of which we computed to be thirty feet high". Surrounded by high mountains and rough precipices they had to leave the river near present Richmond or Sandstone Falls, West Virginia. Going southwest by land they came to Coal River which they followed and named for the

Sandstone Falls where Salling and Howard left the New to go overland to Coal River.
(Photo by West Virginia Governor's Office of E.C.D.)

exposed coal. They rejoined the river where the Coal joins in level country below present Charleston which they found very fertile and well-watered.

Soon they came to the Ohio and went down it to the Mississippi. Floating along the "Father of Waters" they were captured by the French near Natchez and interrogated by none other than Le Moyne de Bienville, the foremost Frenchman in the Mississippi Valley. They were sentenced to the New Mexico mines, a French Devil's Island, but ended up in prison in New Orleans. Du Pratz's **History of Louisiana** (London: 1774) tells of them in prison in 1742 at New Orleans, where Salling stayed at least two years. Aided by a fellow prisoner he escaped and after many adventures got to Charleston, South Carolina, and finally overland home to Virginia in May 1745. Howard and the others were sent to France, captured enroute by the English and taken to London. [11]

Salling's eye-witness account of the far reaches of Wood's River was of great interest to land speculators and map-makers. The land speculator most interested in Salling's experiences was James Patton, who had petitioned for a land grant on Wood's River in October 1743, while Salling was in New Orleans in prison. In April just before Salling returned to Virginia Patton was granted 100,000 acres on Wood's River. Now comes to center stage the man who would do the most in the next decade to develop the New River Valley.

FOOTNOTES—Chapter IX

1. New River Travel Council, Beckley, West Virginia, **Pamphlet**, Withers **Warfare** p. 61 and Rice, **Gorge**, p. 2.

2. Captain William Preston to Governor Dinwiddie ? June 24, 1756, **WH**, 1 QQ pp. 134-135.

3. Johnson J. Hayes, **The Land of Wilkes** (Wilkesboro: Wilkes County Historical Society, 1962) hereafter cited as Hayes, **Wilkes**, p. 9; Reverend John Brown to William Preston, 1774, **WH**, 3 QQ p. 29.

4. Mr. Wates Journal, May 10, 1731, **NCCR**, XI, p. 11.

5. Joseph White to Lyman C. Draper, December 13, 1870, **WH**, 15 VV pp. 90-100 cited in Brown, **Catawba**, p. 276.

6. The Moll and Popple maps may be seen at the Library of Congress, Map Division, Washington, D.C. De l'Isle's map is in Hanna, **Wilderness Trail** v. I, p. 122. Barnwell's map is in William P. Cumming, **The Southwest in Early Maps** (Chapel Hill, North Carolina: The University of North Carolina Press, 1958, 1962) hereafter cited as Cumming, **Southeast Maps.**

7. Related to the author by a descendant of the man who found the date 1738 and Johnston, **Middle New**, p. 9.

8. John Haywood, **The Civil and Political History of the State of Tennessee from its earliest settlement up to 1796** 1891 reprint (Nashville: Methodist Episcopal Church, 1915) p. 40 quoting Ramsay, **Tennessee** (1853) which first gives this account.

9. Fairfax Harrison, "Virginians on the Ohio and the Mississippi in 1742", **VMHB**, v. 30, pp. 205-206 hereafter cited as Harrison,

10. **CS**, II, p. 364; W (2) v. 5, p. 264; Withers, **Warfare**, p. 49; Salling's descendants told Lyman Draper the story of his 1726 capture.

11. Lewis, **West Virginia**, p. 32 and Harrison, **Virginians**, pp. 211, 219-222.

Chapter X

Patton's "Great Grant"

James Patton, a sea-captain bringing with him many Northern Irish settlers, had settled in 1738 at the "Irish Settlement" on the Shenandoah, later known as Augusta Court House at Staunton. This settlement though west of the Blue Ridge was in Orange County with its county seat east of the mountains. Patton immediately became involved in land speculation and got control of the 100,000-acre Roanoke River grant in 1742. In 1743 he asked Virginia's Council for a Wood's River grant.

Whether Patton himself had come up the old Indian trail along Catawba Creek and climbed the thousand feet above the Roanoke Valley to the New River Valley by 1743 is uncertain. According to his accounts, in May 1743 he sent John Buchanan and Stephen Holston with a party of chain carriers to the New River to "view 100,000 acres on the Mississippi." Buchanan purchased 30 yards of canvas for tents, twenty gallons of whiskey, Indian corn, peas, beans and flour — "to be carried to the Wood's" by four baggage horses belonging to Patton and Buchanan. Chain carriers and hunters were Jacob Goldman's sons, Mordicia Early, John Bowman, Anthony Plates, Thomas Delaney, Peter Rentfro, William Foreman and George Smith.

Later Patton claimed, "I was the first British subject that petitioned for land on Mississippi waters which I discovered at vast expense." He was truthful when he said he was the first British subject to petition for land in Virginia on Mississippi waters. He was not truthful when he said he discovered them.

He first asked the Council for 200,000 acres proposing to place one family per thousand acres. Not knowing how London would feel about granting land in the Mississippi drainage also claimed by France, the Council refused. Since the distance was so great from the Atlantic Ocean they "could not conceive of any benefit to the King's revenues or the strength of this colony by a handful of poor people that might venture to settle there."

"I then set forth the practicableness of my scheme," Patton said, "shewing the great distance it was from the French, what a useful barrier might be there in time between the French, French Indians and Virginia."

"It would increase His Majestie's revenues," he argued, "by 'othertakers' who would follow my example should I succeed."

Thus James Patton shows himself to be the first New River land promoter. Finally he asked the Virginia Council to remember that he was the first subject to petition for land in this region. "I feared the noise of my petition would spread and other petitioners might come in before me and reap the benefits of my industry."

The Council agreed to this and in June 1744 sent Patton off to the Treaty of Lancaster to help in purchasing land between the Alleghenies and Ohio from the Iroquois. By April 1745 France and England had gone to war. Policy regarding the frontier had changed.

"In April 1745 I had notice to attend the Council," Patton says. "They gave me and others a grant for 100,000 acres on the river known by the name of Woods." At the same time 100,000 acres was granted to John Robinson on the Greenbrier. Patton was told by a "friend in the government" that as soon as he complied with his promise to settle families he would be given another 100,000 acres.[1]

Council President William Nelson said years later that when Patton got his New River grant the policy was to make "large grants to persons who were likeliest to procure people to inhabit and cultivate the lands."

"It was thought good policy," said Nelson, "to settle those lands as fast as possible, and that granting them to men of the first consequence who were likeliest and best able to procure large bodies of people to settle on them was the probable means of effecting the end."[2]

James Patton certainly fulfilled the requirements. By this time Augusta County was organized west of the Blue Ridge, including all territory to the Ohio. Patton was appointed County Lieutenant, an office similar to the Lord Lieutenant in England given to the first man of the county. He commanded the county militia, regulated all military affairs and courts martial, was President of Augusta Court, directing the judiciary of the county. A man of "first consequence." He immediately organized a company of twenty men into the Wood's River Company and called his grant "The Great Grant." From the beginning management was in the hands of Patton. "It was agreed that the division of the lands should be left wholly to Colo. Patton. Upon the dissatisfaction of any of the parties it should be left to arbitration."[3]

The partners in the Wood's River Company were a composite of Orange, Augusta, and Frederick County politicians and landowners, Fredericksburg merchants and Tidewater land speculators.[4]

James Patton's Land Entry Book for his "Great Grant" on New River when it was still called Woods River
(Photo Courtesy of the Filson Club)

Receipt for land in Patton's "Great Grant"
(Photo from Perkins Library Duke University)

John Buchanan, later married to Patton's daughter Peggy, was chief surveyor. Peter Rentfro of Rentfro's Mill on Blackwater in present Franklin County, was to show people over the land. Patton provided Buchanan with a survey entry book which had **Wood's River Land Entry Book** on the cover but inside the surveys were registered as being on **New River**. Patton naturally told prospective buyers the important fact mentioned later by Joshua Fry that "anywhere on the New River there are no Indians seated."

In October 1745 Buchanan started for the New to notify people already there that they would have to buy their land from him to get title. He stopped at John Peter Salling's cabin on the upper James and listened as Salling told what he had seen on the New — salt works, clover as high as the calf on a man's leg, coal lying on the ground, rich soil, huge trees and bountiful game. They decided to record Salling's experiences. Buchanan in his own journal of his trek to New River tells of recording Salling's story in English.[5]

Salling's journal would be read by many important people, including map-maker Dr. John Mitchell who made the 1755 **Map of the British and French Dominions in North America** and says he referred to Salling's journal in making his map.[6] Mitchell's is the most accurate map of the time.

Salling does not mention seeing a single inhabitant in the New River Valley in 1742 yet Harman family tradition says they were on the New by 1738. It appears that Heinrich Adam, Jacob, and Valentine Herrman, three brothers whose grandfather had fled Moravia in present Czechoslovakia because of his religion, early came to the New River. Adam married his Louisa Katrina in 1723 probably near Mannheim, Germany. Son Adam was born in Germany in 1724, son Henry on the Isle of Man in 1726, as the family were beginning their migration to America. They bought land in Philadelphia County, Pennsylvania in 1734 and family tradition says when Henry was eleven years old they came to New River.[7]

Other Moravians would come to the New. The Moravians had been followers of John Huss, a Bohemian religious reformer burned at the stake in 1415. Ironically his ashes were thrown into the Rhine River which thousands of persecuted Protestants would follow to religious freedom in America. Many persecuted Rhinelanders sought sanctuary on the New. John Buchanan found some of these already there when he arrived.

After translating Salling's journal Buchanan picked up Andrew Gahagen and John Vance at Gahagen's Island on the upper James and stopped to see George Robinson, New River company partner from Mill Creek Hundred in New Castle County, Delaware. Robinson would bring a large collection of relatives from Delaware to the New River including the Robinsons and McDonalds. Robinson Tract on the New would be named for this family.

Buchanan and companions followed the Catawba Creek path toward New River often "in great danger of trees falling very near us." They climbed a rib on the Alleghenies a thousand feet above the valley they had left. They were now on the watershed of the New River and arrived that night at immigrant Israel Lorton's place at the mouth of Tom's or Jones Creek where on October 16 Buchanan began making the first entries in the **Woods River Land Entry Book.** He wrote "Entrys made with Colo. John Buchanan augent for the New River company". Why did he write New River on the inside when Woods River was written on the outside?

Buchanan's entries at Horseshoe Meadow, Beaver Dam, Thorn Spring, Eagle Bottom and Buffalo Wallowing Hole, are aptly descriptive of the New at the time.

Buchanan left Lorton and rode to Charles Hart's cabin on land James Patton later claimed in his Springfield estate on Back Creek. Buchanan offered Hart land for three pounds per hundred "he paying the surveying charges." Hart said he had bought of Captain Robinson "clear of charges." Buchanan said Robinson did not have authority to sell the land, that he had that power. Hart then said he wanted 500 acres on the side of a creek to turn as the creek turned. Buchanan said the survey would be "laid off as the land would bear and that if in running it the manner did not hurt or prevent the sale of other land I would agree." All this sent Hart into a passion so Buchanan rode on to William Mack's place at present Max Meadows. Mack was probably from the noted Mack milling family in Schriesheim, Germany, whose father Yost Mack had a mill and whose cousin Alexander Mack founded the German River Baptist (Dunkard) faith.

Buchanan found Mack dead in his cabin but with him several "Long Beards" or Siebentangers from Ephrata Cloister, Lancaster County, Pennsylvania. Newly arrived they would build a settlement called Mahanaim. Buchanan questioned them about their life as celibate, vegetarian pacifists. Buchanan asked why a man should deprive himself of so "great a blessing as the enjoyment of a good wife." Buchanan already had a lingering eye for Peggy Patton. The celibate answered in the words of Paul, "He who marries does well, but he that did not did better."

Their conversation was interrupted by a "new arrival" probably Adam Harman who on this day took a place called Tom's place and a place on Thorn Spring. The next day Buchanan with Adam and Jacob Harman appraised Mack's estate agreeing with the "Long Beards" to gather the crops and committing the rest to Phineas Griffith. Returning to Hart's Buchanan argued again. Hart said unless he got his "land in such and such a manner he would burn all and so off." Buchanan told Hart such talk would make him "take particular notice of him above all the men" in the settlement. "Neither would I give him any land but upon his good behavior." Buchanan then went "to the woods with Jeremiah" probably Jeremiah Pate who became Adam Harman's son-in-law and found land on "Sink's Creek." Then Buchanan rode to Jacob Harman's place on the west side of the New at present Neck Creek at the Big Spring north of Morgan's Glade in modern times known as Spring Dale Farm off U.S. route 11 at Dublin. The ruins of an old log house still lie there. Here Moravian missionaries would receive a joyous reception several years later. Buchanan later met with John Stroud and Samuel Stalnaker, Stroud contracting for Eagle Bottom near Little River and Stalnaker for the Buffalo Wallowing Hole. Buchanan was told that Frederick Starn who had settled "last spring by ye river" intended to take 400 acres. This entry for Starn is historically significant for the New since it is an early recorded date of actual settlement. Adam Harman was established there by March 1745 because the "Indian Road" ended at his ford on New River according to an Orange County road order. These are the first documentary evidences of white men settled on New River.[8]

After meeting these New River people John Buchanan rode home to Augusta Court House to wait for the spring when he would return and begin surveying.

FOOTNOTES—Chapter X

1. John Buchanan, Account with James Patton, May 1, 1743, **LCPP**, Reel II, folder 13; **WH**, 1 QQ p. 75-76, James Patton to Governor of Virginia, January 1753; **VEJ**, V, p. 134 and Patricia Givens Johnson, **James Patton and the Appalachian Colonists** (Verona, Virginia: McClure Press, 1973) hereafter cited as Johnson, **James Patton**, p. 67.

2. **VEJ**, VI, pp. 688-689 and William Nelson to Lord Hillsborough, October 18, 1770, P.R.O.: C.O. 5:1348/ p. 326.

3. John Wood to William Thompson, January 18, 1774, **WH**, 3 QQ p. 3.

4. For more about Wood's River Company see Johnson, **Patton**, pp. 67-70.

5. John Buchanan, **Journal**, October 1745, **WH**, 1 QQ pp. 38-52 hereafter cited as Buchanan, **Journal**.

6. Alvord-Bidgood, **Explorations**, p. 204.

7. Harman family tradition told the author by family members; John Newton Harman, **Harman Genealogy (Southern Branch) with Biographical Sketches 1700-1924** (Richmond, Virginia: W.C. Hill Printing Company, 1925) pp. 49-50; and William Elsey Connelley, **The Founding of Harman's Station with an account of the Indian Captivity of Mrs. Jennie Wiley** (New York: William E. Connelley The Torch Press, 1918) hereafter cited as Connelley, Harman's Station, p. 26, 52, 89.

8. Wust, **Saints,** pp. 18, 108; Smith, **Pulaski,** p. 12; **LCPP,** Reel II, folder **Wood's River Land Entry Book,** October 1745; hereafter cited as **Wood's River Land Entry Book:** F.B. Kegley, **Virginia Frontier,** 3rd ed. (Roanoke: The Stone Press, 1938) hereafter cited as Kegley, **Virginia Frontier,** p. 122; David Mays, **The Letters and Papers of Edmund Pendleton 1734-1803** (Charlottesville: The University Press of Virginia, 1967) hereafter cited as Mays, Pendleton Papers, v. I, p. 9 and Buchanan Journal.

The "Great Grant" lands on the New near "Buchanan's Bottoms"

(Photo by Walter L. Johnson)

Chapter XI

Hunters and Mahanaim

The first settlers, the Harmans, Stalnakers, Starns, Strouds, Harts and others found by John Buchanan, were hunters and traders. The Stalnakers would establish an Indian trading post on the Holston and the Strouds were fur traders some years at Fort Pitt. The fur trade was one of the most lucrative in Virginia. The presence of the "Beaver Dam on Tom's Creek" and "Buffalo Wallowing Hole" shows why these hunters were here. Beaver skins were the third largest export in Virginia before 1750, the first being tobacco and the second beef and pork. New River travelers from the time of Batts and Fallam to J.F.D. Smyth remark on the abundance of wild turkeys. In 1671 the Batts party mention an "infinite quantity" of turkeys, elk, buffalo and deer in "great herds." In 1781 Smyth said turkeys in the New River Valley "were so very numerous that we could have easily subsisted a company of men upon them."[1]

The second group of settlers on New River were a body of religious mystics from Lancaster County, Pennsylvania. The Treaty of Lancaster in 1744 had given Virginia claim to the Valley of Virginia allowing the Iroquois freedom to travel unmolested through the valley. The Iroquois agreed to sell to the English the territory lying between the Alleghenies and the Ohio for four hundred pounds.[2] James Patton had been present at the Treaty and probably with the Treaty Commissioners when they visited the Ephrata Cloisters in Lancaster County a communal society of German mystics led by Conrad Beissel. They were formerly associated with the German River Baptists founded by Alexander Mack possibly cousin of William Mack who had settled on New River. This apostate group of River Baptists called themselves Sabbatarians though they are commonly called Dunkards. The Eckerlin brothers, Samuel, Israel and Gabriel from Alsace had joined the society and turned Ephrata into such a model of communal self-sufficiency that the Lancaster Treaty Commissioners were amazed.

The Eckerlins probably learned of the New River which the Treaty of Lancaster made available for settlement when the Commissioners visited Ephrata.[3]

Ephrata Cloisters, Lancaster, Pennsylvania from here Sabbatarians came to Dunkard's Bottom on New River 1745
(Photo by Walter L. Johnson)

Dunkard's Bottom (Mahanaim) before submerged under Claytor Lake
(Photo by John Ingles Barton)

Though from outward appearances Ephrata appeared the ideal community all was not well. A power struggle was going on between the Eckerlins and the Superintendent, Conrad Beissel. It was bitterly waged, Beissel burning the Eckerlin's writings in a huge bonfire and not allowing them to eat with the other brothers. Humiliation followed humiliation. Finally the Eckerlins and Alexander Mack Jr. sought refuge on New River.

Their flight on September 4, 1745 created such a stir Beissel was forced to explain in his newspaper **Chronicon Ephratense**, "They fled about 400 English miles, towards the setting sun. . .until beyond all Christian governments, they reached a stream which runs toward the Mississippi — New River by name. Here they settled in the midst of nothing but ragamuffins, the dregs of human society, who spent their time murdering wild beasts."[4]

"The scandal of this schism spread through the whole country," the **Chronicon** reported. Philadelphia merchants heard of it as well as a man far away in Frankfort, Germany, who wrote, "The flight of the Eckerlins into the wilderness is a great marvel, let me know the result of it."

So much commotion was caused that "friends of the separation in Germantown were all ready to follow them, but were prevented by the subsequent Indian war."[5]

And here they were when John Buchanan arrived in mid-October at William Mack's cabin. They named their settlement Mahanaim, meaning "two-camps", showing their dependence upon their friends in Pennsylvania. During the winter they returned there to get supplies and recruits. Jacob Hohnly and Gabriel Eckerlin accompanied them back to New River. Wild rumors flew in Lancaster County. Everybody was heading to New River!

Revealing how truth was being distorted, a local newspaper published, "Not 70 but 5 brothers went from the Cloister. . .to New River. . .to lead a solitary life there each in his hut according to his needs."[6]

Other religious groups heard about Mahanaim on New River. A Lutheran minister wrote, "They have one society in New Virginia upon New River. There they dwell in separate houses, but in one neighborhood, and so by themselves that they neither help nor desire help from other people. The land they cultivate has an excellent soil. The brethren often receive messages in these nests from traveling brethren, who always journey on foot, two and two together, never nore and never less. Sometimes, also the sisters are thus seen upon the roads."[7]

Mahanaim flourished under the leadership of the Eckerlins. Samuel became a herb doctor learning so much about herbs on New River that he opened an apothecary after he left New River and settled at Sandy Hook in Shenandoah country where people came from miles to be treated by him.[8]

Gabriel became a hunter like the neighboring folk and Israel spent all his time writing vindicative letters to Conrad Beissel at Ephrata. A mill was built probably by Alexander Mack Jr. whose family were Schriesheim millers.

While the Dunkards were establishing their hermitage at Mahanaim the New River hunters were busily setting their traps, stalking game and quarreling over their catch. James Connolly accused Humberston Lyon living on Reed Creek of stealing 43 red deer skins from James Scaggs' house. Traders Samuel Stalnaker and Erwin Patterson along with Frederick and Mary Starn, Jacob Miller and George Gabriel were all involved in the case at Augusta Court in February 1746/7.[9]

Meanwhile many from Germantown and Ephrata were coming to New River. "A pilgrimage was undertaken to those regions," commented the **Chronicon,** "for whoever became troubled about his salvation took refuge with them, and they undertook how to cure him. Others hoped to find out some of the sins and infamies which were carried on in the Settlement."[10]

John and Henry Miller, George Hoopaugh, Peter Shafer, John Negley, the Graffs, Webers, Grebils, Freys, Landes, Huffacres from the Germantown area came to Mahanaim.[11]

"A famous doctor was most likely induced to undertake his long journey to them," reported the **Chronicon.** This is thought to be Christopher Witt, Germantown botanist, who came to Virginia at this time. Knowing the botanical paradise the New River later proved to be, it is possible Witt did visit the New. Others have suggested this mysterious doctor was Dr. George Benneville, founder of the Universalist faith.

Even the very young came to the New. "A young brother, Henry Zinn by name, also longed at last for such a life of license, and begged the Brethren to accompany him thither," reported the **Chronicon.** Henry could not foresee his terrible fate on the New.

Conrad Beissel did everything he could to discredit and discourage people from going to New River. He torn out of the ground an entire orchard the Eckerlins had planted and of them at New River he said, "Though they tried to establish divine service they could not establish anything with people who had stepped beyond God."

Finally Beissel daringly told everyone at Ephrata that if anyone wanted to leave they could. "Some left in the day time, others secretly at night; some asked for their wages, others demanded again what they had contributed."

We even learn there were some liberated women in Pennsylvania that set out for New River. "Some in the Sister's House took their leave and followed this licentious life, which gave risk to marriages and other forbidden deeds. This disorderly crowd of people turned towards New River. Several from the Men's Cloister also followed them, for there they found an altar erected for flesh and blood and the number of disorderly persons increased so fast among these Solitary that they sent a request to the Cloister not to send any more people to them." [12]

Meanwhile other settlements on the New were developing. During the spring and summer of 1746 John Buchanan was busy surveying and James Patton was advertising his New River land. By the fall a number of families had arrived and centered in two distinct settlements, one at Reed Creek and the other at Draper's Meadows.

Patton called the Reed Creek settlement the "Valley of Contention and Strife". Patton tracts there were called "Anchor and Hope", "Pride and Self-Conceit" and "Biggotrey". Why these tracts had these names may be seen from future events.

Humberston Lyon, and James Scaggs, who went to court over stolen deerskins, had been living on Reed Creek. They had their problems but it appears the Calhoun family are the ones who turned Reed Creek into the "Valley of Contention and Strife." At least in Colonel James Patton's opinion they did.

The Calhouns — Zachariah, James, George, Ezekiel, William and Patrick — had come to Augusta County and bought from the Wood's River Company in the fall of 1746. Their land was immediately opposite "Col Jameses place" on Reed Creek. Joining them on Reed Creek were John Noble whose wife was Mary Calhoun and their children, James, Patrick, Ezekiel, Alexander and Jean Noble. Even as the Calhouns were agreeing to buy land they were spreading rumors against Patton who called them to court claiming that "James, Ezekiel, William and Patrick Calhoon were divulgers of false news to the great detriment of the inhabitants of this colony." [13]

These Calhouns, ancestors of Mark Twain, and uncles and grandsire of John C. Calhoun who led the South into secession, were related to Patton's rival in land speculation, John Lewis, whose mother was Mary Calhoun. The news they were spreading involved the New River grant. George Robinson, New River Company partner, was called to testify against them.

Two years later James Calhoun petitioned against Patton to the Virginia Executive Council which called for arbitration. Again in 1750, the year Patton made his will, James Calhoun started rumors that Patton had made over his estate to his children to defraud his creditors and could give no good title to New River lands. Patton instituted proceedings against Calhoun for slander. In an ensuing trial John Smith a juror jumped from the Augusta Court House window when the sheriff called for the jury to take their places. At the next court none of the jurors appeared. Samuel Stalnaker, living on Patton's land on the New and Holston, was Patton's principal witness. The next bout was brought by Patton against William Calhoun for refusing to execute a warrant directed to him by Patton in the name of the King. This case was still in court when the Calhouns fled from New River.[14] No wonder Patton called Reed Creek the "Valley of Contention and Strife."

In order to balance things in the Reed Creek area, relatives of Patton arrived. These were the Crocketts, Sayers and Buchanans. Samuel Crockett's wife was Esther Thompson, daughter of Reverend John Thompson, Presbyterian graduate (M.A. 1710/11) of the University of Glasgow and his first wife, reputed sister of James Patton's wife, Mary Osborne.

Esther was born about 1710 and her father came in 1715 as pastor to Lewes, Sussex County, Delaware, to the Scotch-Irish settlement. John Goodwin Herndon says in **Some of the Descendants of the Reverend John Thompson** that he visited the back parts of Virginia often between 1733 and 1744 and was minister at the Augusta "Irish Settlement" in 1739. Later he moved to Spring Creek, Prince Edward County, Virginia and then to Mecklenberg County, North Carolina.

Meanwhile Esther married Samuel Crockett living in Baltimore County, Maryland and their children's births are there recorded in the Register of St. John's and St. George's Parish, where they lived from 1738 to 1748. In 1748 Samuel and his brother Joseph Crockett sold their land in Maryland. Soon they were on New River where their cabin was near a bold spring that still flows in the yard of the Williamson McGavock mansion place. The cabin was later moved to a site beside the highway and still later when I-81 was built.[15]

The Sayers came to New River as early as 1746. John Buchanan's mother was Jane Sayers Buchanan. The Sayers and Buchanans had lived in Northumberland County, Pennsylvania. When John

Buchanan became Patton's chief surveyor he located good tracts for his Sayers cousins, Alexander and William. On Tate's Run, on March 6, 1746 over five hundred acres was surveyed for Alexander Sayers. William Sayers settled next door to Samuel Crockett. John Buchanan took deceased William Mack's place which later became his 1,200 acre estate "Anchor and Hope." So it was that James Patton settled his kin among the contentious Calhouns.

Mention should be made of the Montgomerys now come to the New and connected to both the Calhouns and Crocketts. John Montgomery and sister Elizabeth born in Donegal, Ireland, married Crocketts, she to John and he in 1753 to Samuel and Esther's Anne Agnes. Their Calhoun connection was through James Calhoun married to Catherine Montgomery whose sons caused Patton so much trouble. After the Calhouns fled John handled their New River affairs.[16]

In November 1746 Augusta Court ordered a road from Reed Creek to Eagle Bottom, John Stroud's place near the mouth of Little River. From Eagle Bottom it went to the top of the ridge that parts the waters of New River from those of the South Fork of Roanoke. It is difficult to decide exactly where this road was since the South Fork of the Roanoke sometimes meant the Blackwater River in present Franklin County. The workers were the Calhouns, Bryan White, William Handlow, Peter Rentfro and sons, George the Tinker, Jacob Goldman and sons, John Black, Simon Hart, Michael Claine, John Stroud, Samuel Stalnaker, and the Dunkards with overseers Charles Hart and James Calhoun.[17]

The other settlement established on New River in 1746 was Draper's Meadows, present Blacksburg, Virginia. George Draper brought his wife Eleanor Hardin Draper and their children Mary and John to five hundred acres on Tom's and Strouble's Creek on the "west side of the ridge that parts the waters of the Roanoke from those of the New." This land was bought from Adam Harman acting as Patton's agent and Harman set no price "but refered them to make their bargain or price with Col. Patton."[18]

The Drapers had come from County Donegal, Ireland, in 1729, to Pennsylvania. Donegal was James Patton's home county in Ireland and he may have known them there or even brought them to America on one of his many voyages across the Atlantic. From Pennsylvania they came to Patton's settlement at Cherry Tree Bottom on the James and from there they came to the "Glades" on Strouble's Creek. John Draper had been there only a few years when in 1749 he went hunting and never returned, presumed killed by Indians.

In November 1746 a road was ordered from Adam Harman's place to the river and to the north branch of Roanoke River. Adam was to oversee workers George Draper, Israel Lorton and son, Thomas Looney, John Lane, John Davis, Frederick Stering (Starn) and sons, George Harman, Jacob Harman and sons, Valentine Harman, Adren Moser, Jacob Castle, Humberston Lyon and James Scaggs.

John Buchanan had left Adam Harman and Israel Lorton as agents for the Wood's River Company. In July 1748 Lorton sold to Michael Price and Philip Harless 400 acres at the mouth of Jones' or Tom's Creek and 400 acres to Augustine, Henry and Daniel Price at the Horseshoe Bottom. These men, including Lorton with Caspar Barger, Adam Wall and Stephen Lang, were all German immigrants who had arrived September 5, 1738 in Pennsylvania on the Winter Galley out of Rotterdam.[19] All came to New River.

The eldest Price brother was John Michael, aged nineteen, in 1738. With him were Augustine, aged sixteen and brother-in-law Philip Harless married to Anna Margaretha Price the elder sister of Michael. Not on the ship's passenger list because they were under age were Daniel, fourteen and Henry, twelve. Nor was the name of Anna Margaretha. Although there were 113 women and children on board their names are not listed. This Price family were the children of David Preisch (Breisch) and Agnes Hoffman of Offenbach, Landau, Rheinland Pfalz, Germany. Their father David had recently died in 1735.

After immigration the Prices and Harlesses remained for a time in Lancaster County, Pennsylvania, for the first child of Philip and Anna Harless was christened in a Moravian church in Lancaster town though the Harlesses had been Lutherans at Muhlhofen, Rheinland Phalz. The Prices for several generations were registered in the Catholic Church baptisms at Offenbach. However their true religious aspirations seem apparent when they came to America and were free to choose their religion. In the New River Valley one of the first acts was to establish a Lutheran church on land that James Patton promised. St. Peter's or St. Michael's Church at Price's Fork, Montgomery County, Virginia, dating from 1750, is built on this site and is said to be the oldest Lutheran church west of the Alleghenies.[20] Samuel Burgell or Brugell from the Haw River settlements in Orange County, North Carolina, is said to be the earliest minister.

The fact that these people were Lutheran explains why they came to New River. The Lutherans were later coming to Pennsylvania than other Germans and found the best land taken.

"Our German Evangelical settlers in Pennsylvania are the most

SITE OF ST. PETER'S
EVANGELICAL LUTHERAN
CHURCH
1750 — 1885
ST. PETER'S WAS THE FIRST CHURCH WEST
OF THE ALLEGHANIES AND THE THIRD
LUTHERAN CHURCH IN VIRGINIA. ITS ORIGINAL
MEMBERS WERE PIONEERS WHO, HAVING
SUFFERED RELIGIOUS PERSECUTIONS, HAD
COME FROM THE PALATINATE IN GERMANY
TO PHILADELPHIA, PENNSYLVANIA,
SEPTEMBER 5, 1738, THENCE TO AND
AROUND THE HORSE SHOE BOTTOMS ON
NEW RIVER. THIS MONUMENT ERECTED
IN 1946 IS IN MEMORY OF THESE STURDY,
GOD-FEARING PIONEERS:
RICHARD HAEVEN   SAMUEL PEPPER
PHILIP HARLESS   AUGUSTINE PRICE
ADAM HARMAN   DANIEL PRICE
JACOB HARMAN   HENRY PRICE
VALENTINE HARMAN   MICHAEL PRICE
JACOB HARNBERGER   JACOB SHELL
ISRAEL LAURTON   ADAM WALL
COMMITTEE
ULYSSES S. A. HEAVENER, D. D.
MRS. LOUISE PRICE MOFFATT

The first church founded on New River
(Photo by Frank Shelton)

recent immigrants," writes minister Henry M. Muhlenberg, father of Revolutionary General Muhlenberg. "Most of them had to be slaves for several years to repay their passage and then make shift with the poorer lands."

"Finally, even poor land was no longer to be had, hence they are moving farther," writes Muhlenberg in the summer of 1747, when the Prices and Harlesses were planning to move to New River.[21]

The next summer of 1748 when the Prices bought land from Patton he is said to have made a long trek down the New and deep into the Holston Valley to present Tennessee where he discovered and named Cumberland Gap and Mountains, credit for which is usually given Dr. Thomas Walker. That Patton was on a surveying trip at this time is substantiated by the fact that his grant was up for renewal so he had to make surveys in order to renew and by his absence from Augusta Court of which he was President the entire month of April 1748. The land records show surveying parties on branches of the New and Holston in spring 1748 but no land was entered as far south as Cumberland Gap. George Robinson, Charles Sinclair, James Patton, John Shelton, Charles Campbell, James Davis,

Dr. Thomas Walker, New River Colonizer
(Photo Courtesy of Virginia State Library)

James McCall, Robert Evans, William Calhoun, James Wood and John Miller had land surveyed at this time.

Dr. Thomas Walker, John Buchanan, chain carriers, cooks and packhorsemen among whom were James Burke and John Finley, were reported in the group. Dr. Walker, the Albemarle doctor who loved exploring, says he was on the New in 1748 where he met Samuel Stalnaker at Reed Creek on his way to the Holston. James Patton was claiming a large tract at present Chilhowie called "Indian Fields", settling Stalnaker there giving him "liberty to crop only". Stalnaker would raise corn to sell to the Cherokees and establish a trading post. Dr. Walker would have great influence upon New River settlement. Both a physical and character description of him is given by John Redd of Henry County who knew him. He was "slightly built, round-shouldered, black-haired, highly educated" and of the "very highest order of intellect. No man bore a more irreproachable character than he."[22]

Meanwhile at Mahanaim existence on New River was not idyllic. In 1747 Alexander Mack Jr. had a bad dream where he saw Indians burning cabins and killing. A few days later they did come to Mahanaim and "laid waste the corn" Fearfully Mack hurried away to Pennsylvania saying he had no "intention to return to New River unless Divine Providence directed him to do it." Henry Miller who once praised Mahanaim also became unhappy saying "he despises the life of the brethren at New River."

After the Mahanaim corn was destroyed Adam Harman's fur cache was wrecked about the same time he lost his wife who died in childbirth March 18, 1749. At the same time Adam was embroiled in a lawsuit with Jacob Castle. Augusta Court ordered the goods of Jacob Castle seized because he planned to go to the French dominions on the Mississippi. Such commerce was traitorous when relations with France were so precarious. In April Adam and Valentine Harman were imprisoned in Augusta jail for the violent robber of Castle's goods done apparently when they tried to stop Castle. Castle was arrested, tried, acquitted and later went to Castle's Woods.[23] It is significant that these troubles happened in 1749 the year the French came down the Ohio planting leaden plates claiming all for France.

The next summer the Harmans obtained 7,000 acres on the New near the mouth of Bluestone in the names of Adam and Valentine and Valentine Sevier. Was this a reward for their vigilance for watching for trouble with France?

Regardless of what the French were doing on the Ohio, New River people were having their problems locally. In August 1749 terrific rains hit southwest Virginia. Samuel Eckerlin writing from Mahanaim to Alexander Mack Jr. in Pennsylvania describes the floods, "I want to report to you about the great inundations which occurred on the 25th of August, a little past midnight, on the Roanoke. Our river as well as Little River were also very high but nobody here suffered mentionable damage. On the Roanoke. . . which was a mile wide. . .and other places there was much damage." He describes terrible devastation where hills were leveled and entire families swept away. [24]

FOOTNOTES—Chapter XI

1. J.F.D. Smith, A Tour in the United States of America (London: 1784) reprint (New York: The New York Times and Arno Press, 1968) hereafter cited as Smyth, Tour, p. 311, and John W. Jordon, ed. "Journal of James Kenny 1761-1763" PMHB, v. 37 p. 152-201.

2. Johnson, James Patton, pp. 54-56.

3. Ibid. p. 91 and Wust, Saint, p. 1-12.

4. Sachse, German Sectarians, II, pp. 213-216, 334-335; Wust, Saint, p. 18.

5. Joseph Hark, ed. and translator, Lamech and Agrippa, Chronicon Ephratense. A History of the Community of Seventh Day Baptists at Ephrata, Lancaster County, Penn'a (Lancaster, Pennsylvania: S.H. Zahm & Co., 1889) hereafter cited as Hark, Chronicon Ephratense, p. 188 and Wust, Saints p. 16.

6. Wust, Saints, pp. 18-19 quoting Der Hoch-Deutsche Pennsylvanische Bericht no. 70, May 16, 1746.

7. Reichmann, Ephrata, p. 75.

8. Wust, Saints, p.45.

9. CS, I, p. 431.

10. Hark, Chronicon Ephratense, p. 188.

11. Der Hoch-Deutsch Pennsylvanische Berichte and Conrad Beissel, Letter Book, pp. 79-80.

12. Wust, Saints, pp. 21-23 and Hark, Chronicon Ephratense, pp. 188-189.

13. LCPP, II, folder 25; Wood's River Land Entry Book and CS, I, p. 23.

14. Johnson, James Patton, p 106; Agnes Riley, "John Montgomery 1717-1802" The Historical Society of Washington County, Virginia Publication Series II, no. 5, p. 9.

15. Information given the author by the Crockett family; Goodridge Wilson, "Southwest Corner" Roanoke Times and World News, June 9, 1975.

16. John Montgomery, ibid., pp. 5-7.

17. Mays, Pendleton Papers, I, p. 9; J.R. Hildebrand, Historical Map of Montgomery County Virginia 1970; CS, I, p. 23.

18. Wood's River Land Entry Book; Kegley, Virginia Frontier, p. 123; Hale, Trans- Allegheny Pioneers, pp. 9-10; CS, I, p. 23; and Johnson, James Patton, p. 94.

19. CS, I, pp. 23, 38, 307-308.

20. Information supplied by Christine Neuenschwander, Salt Lake City, Utah, from Catholic Church Register, 1685-1822, G.S. 367, 643.

21. William E. Eisenberg, The Lutheran Church in Virginia, 1717-1962 (Lynchburg, Virginia: J.P. Bell Company Inc., 1967) hereafter cited as Eisenberg, Virginia Lutherans, pp. 33-34 quoting Muhlenberg, Journal.

22. VEJ, v. 6, p. 692; Johnson, **James Patton,** pp. 71-72 and John Redd, "Reminiscences of Western Virginia," hereafter cited as Redd, **Reminiscenses,** VMHB, v. 7, p. 243; William Cabell Rives Papers, Library of Congress, Manuscript Division, Dr. Thomas Walker, Journal of an **Expedition in 1750,** hereafter cited as Walker, **Journal,** Entry March 31, 1750.

23. CS, I, pp. 38, 102, 432-433; CS, II, p. 413; Sachse, **German Sectarians,** p. 338. and Wust, **Saint** p. 23, pp. 337-339; Harman Family member to author; Palmer, **Calendar,** I, p. 243, Deposition of Henry Lenard, April 1749

24. Johnson, **James Patton,** p. 63. for Wust, **Flood.**

Claytor Lake and Dam today on the site of Mahanaim or Dunkard's Bottom. Ingles Ferry was around the bend of the New toward the center of the picture.

(Photo courtesy Radford Chamber of Commerce)

Chapter XII

The Warwick Road

In 1749 North Carolina and Virginia decided to extend the boundary line between them. Surveyor for the Granville District, William Churton of Edenton and Corbin Town (Hillsborough) and Daniel Weldon were chosen surveyors for North Carolina. Joshua Fry, former mathematics instructor at William and Mary, and Peter Jefferson, father of Thomas, headed Virginia's survey party. Surveyor Peter Fontaine Jr. accompanied them. His father, Reverend Peter, had gone as chaplain with William Byrd II on the 1732 dividing line survey. Young Peter would be appointed surveyor for Halifax County in 1752 and that year made a map showing the Virginia boundary crossing the New. These were the men first officially hired by the colonies to cross New River surveying. In running the line from Peters Creek (Stokes County) to Steep Rock Creek (Laurel Fork of Holston) they crossed the New River sometime in 1749 and made a chart, **A Plan of the line between Virginia and North Carolina from Peter's Creek to Steep Rock Creek** which Governor Gabriel Johnston of North Carolina sent to London, February 15, 1750. Johnston says the surveyors "crossed a large branch of the Mississippi which runs between the ledges of the mountains and nobody ever dreamt of before." He was speaking of New River. [1]

In 1750 the part of New River on the Virginia side of the boundary line was in Augusta County which stretched to the Ohio River. The North Carolina part of New River was in Anson County.

At the same time the surveyors were running the line across New River in North Carolina the New River people of Virginia petitioned Augusta Court to have a road built linking the New settlements with eastern Virginia.

"We labor under great inconveniences for want of a road being open from our settlement towards the landing," they noted.

The "landing" meant Warwick Wharf on the James River below Richmond which was at that time the tobacco inspection station where ships bound for England loaded. There was already a road from Warwick into Lunenberg County which reached into the area now Franklin County. The New River people wanted to link up with it.

"We have a sufficient number of inhabitants to open one," they claimed. The route they wanted was from Zachariah Calhoun's on Reed Creek "thence the nearest and best way to Woods River, at the upper end of a small island below the mouth of Little River, and thence towards the forks of Meadow Creek, and thence to the top of the dividing ridge between Woods River and the South Fork of Roanoke."[2]

According to Maude Clement foremost historian of the area now known as Franklin County, eastward from the New River Valley, South Fork of Roanoke sometimes means Blackwater River in Franklin County rather than today's South Fork of Roanoke. If true this road from Reed Creek on the New went eastward over the Blue Ridge in the vicinity of present Check and Callaway toward Rocky Mount.

At the same time in 1749 that the Reed Creek people asked Augusta court for the road Lunenberg Court was petitioned by a large settlement at the foot of Blue Ridge for a road for them to Lunenberg Court House. This settlement on Blackwater and Pigg Rivers also needed access to New River Valley. This area later was Halifax County and even later Pittsylvania and Franklin. A petition was sent asking that the road extend to the top of the Blue Ridge.

Augusta Court ordered the "Warwick Road," appointing John McFarland and Joseph Crockett surveyors and workers William Crisp, William Pelham, Henry Patton, Mordecai Early, Jacob Goldman, John Goldman, John Downing, Charles Sinclair, Nathaniel Wiltshire, William Sayers, William Hamilton, Humberston Lyon, Frederick Carlock, Robert Norris, James Miller, James Cane, Samuel Montgomery, Steven Lyon, John Conley, Andrew Linam, James Wilbey, Sam Stanlick, James Maies, Robert McFarland, James Harris, John Vance, John Stride, (Stroud?) Robert Miller, Alexander Sayers, John Miller, Jacob Castle, Robert Alcorn, John Forman, William Miller.[3]

Work progressed slowly. In 1752 the people from the forks of the Roanoke to James Neiley's (Salem) complained, "We have to travel 25 to 30 miles to work on ye road from Reed Creek to Warwick" and asked that the road be laid off in precincts.[4]

By 1753 the road was coming along. In present Franklin County near Magotty Creek the Warwick Road was crossed by Moravian missionaries who said, "Warrick Road runs mostly westward and is a pretty good road." A little further they came to Rentfro's mill on Blackwater River established by James, Peter and Joseph, near present Callaway.[5] In 1754 Benjamin Pyborn got land "above James Rentfro's under the mountain on the road to the Little River."[6] "Rentfro's Path" along the Blackwater frequently mentioned by Pittsylvania surveyors is believed to be the Warwick Road which crossed the Blue Ridge to Little River. Definitely by summer 1754 there was a road or path traveling in this direction to New River. Colonel James Patton wrote Governor Dinwiddie to send ammunition to New River "by way of Warwick to Reed Creek." When Fort Chiswell was built on Reed Creek this became known as the "Chiswell Road". In 1769 a chapel was built at the future site of Rocky Mount near the crossroads of "the Carolina and Chiswell roads."[7]

A student of Franklin County says, "The oldest road appears to be the Warwick, crossing the ridge south of Boones Mill, going westward to Callaway and up the mountain via either Nearway Ridge or Pine Spur on the Blue Ridge Parkway. Most likely the oldest road crossed just south of this point where an old trail meanders from a neglected road at the bottom of the mountain up Nearway Ridge to the top of Blue Ridge. I suppose this early name is an indication of that route. Another route nearby and also possibly used was the Pine Spur route. Both are likely a continium of the Warwick Road which came across the mountain, extended down 122 to Bedford then eastward to Warwick."[8]

The best known record of people traveling this old Warwick road from New River eastward across the Blue Ridge is that of Captain Robert Wade's Ranger company out of Fort Mayo (Martinsville) ranging on the New in 1758. Returning to Fort Mayo they ate dinner on Blackwater (probably the Pine Spur route). Then they left the Warwick and went south to spend the night at Robert Jones' plantation on Pigg River before going home to Fort Mayo near Bull or Wart Mountain.

This route appears to be little more than a path though called a road. The conditions of traveling on it can be more clearly seen by an Englishman's description about 1781. J.F.D. Smyth set out from Wart Mountain heading west to New River by a gap "only used by hunters which is about twenty miles southwest of that which the Great Trading Path goes over. By this way we proposed to fall on the headwaters of Little River, which runs into the New just above the crossing place."

Smyth did succeed in reaching New River by this route after a journey of forty miles and "crossing a number of large streams" and the "Blue Ridge at a most disagreeable and dangerous gap."[9]

Map of the State of Virginia (Facsimile) by Herman Böy 1825-1859
(Photo courtesy of Carol Newman Library, Virginia Polytechnic and State University)

Certainly traveling into the New valley from the east by approaching Little River was a well established route from the time of Batts and Fallam to July 7, 1819 when Lutheran minister Paul Henkel left Roanoke and "drove to Montgomery County up Bent Mountain to the German congregation on Little River."[10]

This route was open enough by 1755 to be placed on Dr. John Mitchell's **Map of the British and French Dominions in North America** the most accurate eighteenth century map of the New River. Mitchell has the road crossing the New near Little River. Mitchell living at Urbanna on the Rappahannock may have talked with hunter Abraham Little or map-maker William Mayo who made the first map of the Rappahannock Valley (showing Blue Ridge passes) and had surveyed in southern Virginia. Mitchell comments about his map in relation to the Batts and Fallam journal, "You will see these roads laid down in our Map of North America exactly as they are described in (Batts and Fallam) journal, they being the two roads that lead from the falls of Appomattox River southward to Carolina and westward to our settlements on Wood River in Virginia."

Mitchell says in 1755 the road ran westward, crossed several branches of Roanoke River. "From these branches of Roanoke River they passed over the mountains, and came to a large River west of the mountains, running north and south which plainly appears from this account of it to have been what we call Wood River in Virginia, which is well known and well settled by our people there, both above and below the place where these people discovered it; and **they frequently pass the mountains now in going to and from Wood River, about the same place that is described in the Journal**(of Batts and Fallam)."[11]

This statement by Mitchell is extrenely important. Mitchell, noted for his expertise, having been commissioned by the British government before the French and Indian War to make his map, wrote this about eighty years after the Batts-Fallam expedition and discoveries. There were people alive who would have knowledge of the place they first touched New River. Mitchell had read the journals of Salling, Gist and Walker, his contemporaries. Therefore the place on his map where he shows the road crossing the New is approximately the place Batts and Fallam first touched upon the New. Mitchell's map shows this as a place near the mouth of Little River, the same place that the New River folk asked to place the road in 1749. It is also a different place than historians have assigned as the place Batts and Fallam first came upon the river.

The road building activity on New River would attract settlers and many visitors in the next years. One group who seemed to have an intense interest in New River and its people were the Moravians.

The Harmans were of Moravian ancestry and the Moravians in Pennsylvania knew of them. There were other New families who had attended Moravian churches in Pennsylvania before coming to New River. Philip and Margaretha Price Harless had two children baptized in the Moravian church, Lancaster County. Philip, born in 1743 and David born in 1745 were christened in 1744 and 1745 by the famed Moravian minister Laurentius Thorstonsen Nyberg, a Swedish pastor, passing for a Lutheran but secretly a Moravian. Nyberg was a renowned preacher and was successful in defeating a unification between the Swedish and German Lutherans.[12]

Although the Harless family were Lutherans in Germany the Lutheran church had a scarcity of ministers in America and the shepherdless flocks were fruitful ground for Moravian preaching. When the Harless and Prices were planning to move to New River, Lutheran minister Henry Muhlenberg wrote that the Moravians identified themselves with the religion of their intended converts. "When in Catholic lands they believe as the Pope. . .in Switzerland they live in accord with the Synod of Bern. . .in Sweden. . .with the Augsburg Confession."[13]

The Moravians were always looking for a field for missionary endeavour. In March 1748 Moravian Brother Gottschalk mentioned the "few German families on New River". In November 1749 Moravians Leonhard Schnell and John Brandmueller headed for New River which they said they had intended to visit for the past four years. As they neared the New they report, "We came to a house where we had to lie on bear skins around the fire like the rest. The manner of living is rather poor. The clothes of the people consist of deer skins. Their food of Johnny cakes, deer and bear meat. A kind of white people are found here who live like savages. Hunting is their chief occupation. We heard an awful howling of wolves in the morning quite near."

By now they were on the "Catawba Crick Road" climbing toward New River. "On Sunday November 19 we were glad in anticipation of seeing the New River," they wrote, "and asked the Lamb for a favorable reception."

"Towards noon we arrived safely at the New River. We were taken across the river to Jacob Herrman, who together with his wife, received us with great joy and love. We had hoped to preach today, but as it was late the sermon was appointed for tomorrow. There we enjoyed a spiritual and physical rest. I firmly believed that my visit to this district which I had longed for four years would not be in vain," wrote the Moravian.

"On November 20 I preached the words of the Saviour, "I am a King" (John 18:3). It seemed as if I had hungry souls before me. On November 21st we stayed quietly at Jacob Herrman's house and spoke with him much about the Saviour and the congregation at Bethlehem, Pennsylvania."

Jacob Herrman told them that "his grandfather was by birth a Moravian who had been driven from his country because of his religion."

November 22 dawned very cold so no people came to the sermon. The next day, "Mr. Herrman went with us to visit Jacob Goldman whose wife is sister of my father-in-law. We were kindly received." It was a fifteen mile trip to Goldman's place. They may have found Jacob the elder Goldman ill for he died a short time after this.

Returning to Harman's they preached a sermon on the Ten Virgins and the "audience received the Word with good attention." "We were only a few miles from the Seventh Day Baptists who live here on New River. But we had enough of the description the people gave of them," reported the missionaries as they returned home. [14]

The Moravian's description of New River people as "hungry souls" who "received the Word with good attention" is in sharp contrast to Sabbatarian Conrad Beissel who called them "nothing but ragamuffins."

FOOTNOTES—Chapter XII

1. Cumming, Southeast Maps, pp. 216, 221; NCCR, v. IV, xiii; and Edward P. Alexander, The Jouranl of John Fontaine an Irish Huguenot Son in Spain and Virginia 1710-1719 (Williamsburg: The Colonial Williamsburg, Foundation, 1972) pp. 26-27, 130. For Fontaine's 1752 map see the 1853 ed. Ann Maury, Memoirs of a Huguenot Family.

2. CS, I, p. 434.

3. CS, I, p. 40.

4. CS, I p. 436.

5. Moravian Journals, 1752, VMHB, v. 12, p. 273.

6. Clement, Pittsylvania, p. 45.

7. Ibid. p. 120, Patton to Dinwiddie, July 2, 1754, LCPP, pp. 134-135.

8. Dr. J. Francis Amos, Rocky Mount, Virginia, letter to author, August 9, 1981. In 1768 the Pittsylvania court ordered a "road from Robert Hill's to head of Wiggan to lead to Little River", Clement, Pittsylvania, p. 104.

9. Smyth, Tour, pp. 310-311.

10. Eisenberg, Virginia Lutherans, p. 127.

11. John Mitchell, "Remarks on the Journal of Batts and Fallam in their Discovery of the Western Parts of Virginia in 1671", Alvord-Bidgood, Explorations, pp. 197-198.

12. Baptismal Records of the Evangelican Bruder Gemeine in Lancaster County Pennsylvania, 1743, Laurence Nyberg, Pastor.

13. Eisenberg, **Virginia Lutherans,** p. 27 quoting Henry M. Muhlenberg, **Journal** July 25, 1747.

14. Report of Brother Gottschalk, March 1748, **VMHB**, v. 11, p. 234 and "Diary of Leonard Schnell and John Brandmueller on their Journey to Virginia, October 12-December 12, 1749," **VMHB,** v. 11, pp. 124-125 and v. 12, to p. 82

Chapter XIII

Dr. Thomas Walker
and Christopher Gist Go Exploring

Several months after Schnell and Brandmueller returned to Pennsylvania more visitors arrived on New River. Dr. Thomas Walker, who liked exploring better than medicine, reappeared on the New in March 1750 leading an exploring party. He had been here in 1748 which he mentions in the journal he was now keeping.

On March 13, 1750 Walker records, "We went to William Calloway's (near present New London, Bedford County) and supplied ourselves with rum, thread and other necessaries and from thence took the main wagon road leading to Wood's or the New River. It is not well cleared or beaten yet, but will be a very good one with proper management. . .lodged at Adam Beards. . .afterwards we crossed the Blue Ridge. The ascent and descent is so easy that a stranger would not know when he crossed the Ridge."

By March 16 Walker and friends were at William Ingles' mill on a branch of Roanoke River which "was not much hurt by the fresh" says Walker remembering the Roanoke river flood some months before.

By March 17 they arrived at "very hospitable" Mahanaim "the upper inhabitants on the New River which is about 400 yards at this place. They live on the west side, and we are obliged to swim our horses over. The Duncards are an odd set of people, who make it a matter of religion not to shave their beards, ly on beds, or eat flesh though at present in this last, they transgress, being constrained to it, as they say, by the want of a sufficiency of Grain and roots, they not having long been seated here. I doubt the plenty and deliciousness of the venison and turkeys has contributed not a little to this."[1]

Who Walker found at Mahanaim is uncertain. Israel and Gabriel Eckerlin had returned to Pennsylvania. Samuel sold his part of Mahanaim to Rhinelanders Gerhart and Margaret Zinn, from Memram and

Neustadt respectively. They came to America about 1743, joined the Sabbatarians and followed the Eckerlins to the New.[2]

After purchasing meal and hominy at Mahanaim mill Walker, Ambrose Powell, William Tomlinson, Colby Chew, Henry Lawless and John Hughes went on to Reed Creek where on March 21 they camped at James McCall's. Then they left New River and set off toward Cumberland Gap into Kentucky, the first known Englishmen to enter there.

It was June 28 before they found their way back to New River just below the mouth of Greenbrier. Walker writes, "Powell, Tomlinson and myself striped and went into the New River to try if we could wade over at any point." They found a place where they waded over leading their horses carrying their belongings on their shoulders. Walker comments, "The bottom is very uneven, current strong." Following the Greenbrier they returned home.

At this same time James Patton was expecting a visit from Colonel Joshua Fry, who with Peter Jefferson, had been asked to make a map of Virginia, now they had finished the western boundary across the New. Patton said, "Colonel Fry writes me the Government has ordered him to make out a plan or charte of this country as far as Aligeeaney & my opinion. I expect him here soon."

Patton was having some difficulty with James Burke over Burke's Garden tract which is on a New River tributary and his surveyors were very busy on Reed Creek. He wrote, "McCall's land & John & Robert McFarlands land is returned to the Secretary's office so you cannot run those places again." Patton expected the price of his New River land to boom. "In Conofe (Kanawha) good land will in a few years sell at 10 pounds pr 100."[3] His present price was three pounds per hundred.

On September 1, 1750 Patton made his will dividing his estates between his daughters, Mary, married to William Thompson, and Margaret married to John Buchanan. On New River he left the Thompsons "Spring Field joining where widow Goldman now lives and on which Henry Patton lives containing about three thousand acres." This Back Creek estate has recently been owned by the Farises. Patton left Mary the 3,000 acre "Indian Fields" estate on the Holston where "Samuel Stalnaker and other were "living and has only liberty to crop." Margaret Patton Buchanan received the Anchor and Hope estate on Reed Creek.[4]

The Calhouns claimed that Patton made his will to defraud his creditors. Whether true is questionable. He did hope to strengthen his grasp upon his grant for the powerful Ohio Company had just been formed, claiming 800,000 acres on the Ohio watershed. The same month Patton made his will they sent Christopher Gist into that territory to explore for them.

Gist, the son of Richard Gist who had surveyed the town of Baltimore, had come from Maryland to North Carolina and was the first person to settle in 1750 at Mulberry Fields of Yadkin, present Wilkesboro.[5] The New River headwaters were not far west of Gist's home and it is possible that he had already explored them.

Christopher spent the winter wandering through the Ohio drainage basin. By May 1, 1751, in what is now West Virginia, he came near the Kanawha. From a point N75 E10 he climbed to the top of a very high mountain and through holes in rock could see a "prodigious distance."

"I could plainly discover where the Big Conhaway broke the next high mountain." Gist was seeing the Kanawha or New from the western approach.

Continuing eastward, by May 7 Gist was on the New and spent the night on an island (NE6 min, E10 min) eight miles above the mouth of Bluestone. On May 8 he made a raft of logs and crossed the New.

"The Conhaway or New River (by some called Wood's River) where I crossed it. . .is better than 200 yards wide and pretty deep but full of rocks and falls. The bottoms upon it are very rich but narrow," reports Gist.

He continued 13 miles up the New and came to a "large Indian Warrior's Camp where we killed a bear and stayed all night." Continuing through mountains covered with laurel and ivy thickets he climbed to the top of a "very high mountain upon which was a lake." He had discovered Salt Pond or Mountain Lake in Giles County. Gist says the lake was 3/4 mile long, 1/4 mile wide, with clean gravelly shore and six springs nearby. Heading on east he arrived at Richard Hall's between present Blacksburg and Christiansburg, near the intersection of Routes 114 and 460.

"This man is one of the farthest settlers to the westward up the New River," wrote Gist. At Hall's Gist wrote the Ohio Company telling of his safe arrival back at the settlements and went on home to the Yadkin following the much traveled Indian trail down New River which connected with the Occonee trail near Wilkesboro. [6]

This same week of May 8 Joshua Fry sent a **Report on the Back Settlements** to London, giving information about the New. Fry had planned to get Patton's opinion about the New but either did not or completed the map before he did for there are errors in the Fry-

Jefferson Map that Patton could have corrected. Patton called the river Wood's River but their map is the first to call it New. Youghiogheny is mistakenly shown flowing into the New. Peter Salling on the James is shown as the farthest west inhabitant in Virginia which was untrue and is contradicted by Fry's own report which says, "Beyond the Allegheny or Mississippi Ridge, on New River and its Branches, and on the North Branch of Holston are seated about one hundred families, but the settlements that way with proper encouragement will in a short time greatly increase." Fry also noted, "Below or anywhere on the New River there are no Indians seated."[7] Since this is a correct assessment of conditions on the New River at the time, Fry may after all have visited with James Patton, before he sent off his report to London.

In 1751 John Buchanan and wife Peggy Patton Buchanan went out to settle with their little Molly at Anchor and Hope on Reed Creek. On July 8 Colonel Patton wrote Buchanan telling him about Wood's River Company accounts, mentioning land on Cripple Creek, Lorton's "ould place" and "Litel horse shoe bottom." He explained how land was divided among partners in the company. He sent daughter Peggy "one fine scent Rose, one pr. Sisors, one pc bobing, one pce of moneso pretty, one pce of Silver buttons for my Little Molly."[8]

Attakullakulla, the Little Carpenter (far right) Cherokee chief came often as peace envoy to the New River Valley

(Photo from the Library of Congress)

Before 1750 the Overhill Cherokees in the Tennessee Valley had traded with traders out of South Carolina but as the New River Valley began to be settled their eyes turned toward Virginia as a source of trade. Samuel Stalnaker was already on the Holston trading with them.

In July 1751 a Cherokee delegation led by Attakullakulla or "The Little Carpenter" the Civil Chief of the Overhill Cherokees, left Chota near present Maryville, Tennessee, and entered Virginia by way of the Holston and New. "The Carpenter" was accompanied by Great Canoe, "The Carpenter's Gang" and two traders, Joseph Oliver and Abraham Smith. The entire party numbered about 46. They arrived at Patton's home at Augusta Court House in August.[9] Patton was probably surprised at the appearance of this Cherokee chief who was much smaller than other Cherokees but of "fine personal appearance, very straight, square built, weighing about 145."[10] Patton sent a message to Williamsburg that they wanted to come to discuss trade but Council President Burwell told him to dissuade them. Unable to do so Patton accompanied them down to the capitol. There they had several audiences, were promised trade with Virginia and given some new clothes. On August 14 "the Indians marched in good order with beat of drum through the town and made an handsome appearance in their new clothes."

Reimbursement for Cherokee harassment was made at this time to New River men Sam Stalnaker, Humberston Lyon, Ebenezer Waistcoat and Nathaniel Wiltshire.

After a near-battle with some Nottaway Indians who appeared in town the Cherokees were hustled home by Patton along the road by Hanover Court House into Albemarle where they stayed two days with Dr. Thomas Walker. Then they went through the mountains to the upper James thence along home by New River. Patton charged Virginia fourteen pounds for their food from the James to Reed Creek which he said covered "victuals for 43 Indians from ye 27th August until ye 7th of September — as also for those that was left at my house whilst I was at Williamsburg." The food he provided was 1250 pounds of beef, twenty pounds of butter, one bushel of salt, twelve gallons of liquor, 1 hog, Indian corn and meal.

As the Cherokees wound along through the mountainous terrain of southern Virginia, the gifts President Burrell had given them became burdensome and were discarded. Burwell later said, "I am informed that from an Imprudence not uncommon to Indians, they left the greatest part of them before they passed the bounds of this Colony."[11]

FOOTNOTES—Chapter XIII

1. Walker, **Journal.**

2. Wust, **Saint,** pp. 56-57 and Milton H. Heinicke, **History of Ephrata,** manuscript notes, The Historical Society of the Cocalico Valley, Ephrata, Pennsylvania, p. J1, 32, author's collections.

3. Cumming, **Southeast Maps,** p. 216 and James Patton to Surveyor, 1750, **General John Preston Papers, Perkins Library, Duke University.**

4. James Patton, Will, September 1, 1750, WH,1 QQ pp. 64-66.

5. Hayes, **Wilkes,** p. 6.

6. Christopher Gist, **Journal 1750-51;** Lewis Preston Summers, **Annals of Southwest Virginia 1769-1800** (Abingdon, Virginia: Kingsport Press, 1929) hereafter cited as Summers, **Annals,** p. 28; Pownall, **Description,** p. 198; Lewis Evans, 1755 **Map of the Middle British Colonies in North America.**

7. Fry, **Back Settlements.**

8. James Patton to John Buchanan, July 8, 1751, General John Preston Papers, Perkins Library, Duke University.

9. **VEJ,** V, pp. 414-415 and William E. McDowell, Jr., ed., **Documents Relating to Indian Affairs,** May 21, 1750 — August 7, 1754 (Columbia; South Carolina: Archives Department, 1958) hereafter cited as **SCIAD,** v. II, p. 130; John Blair, **Diary,** W(1) VII, p. 144 and VSL, Colonial Papers, 43/8.

10. **SCIAD,** II, pp. 159-160. President Lewis Burwell to Governor Glen, September 1751; Johnson, **James Patton,** pp. 116-118; **VEJ,** V, p. 351 and James Patton, Cherokee Account, **Colonial Papers, VSL,** 43/8.

Chapter XIV

Moravians on the New

The Moravian missionaries who had visited New River told their brethren in Bethlehem of the rich New River bottoms and others told them of the richness of western Carolina in the Granville District. Bishop August Gottlieb Spangenberg brought a party to North Carolina in 1752 scouting for land. After searching on the Catawba River they planned to cross to the Yadkin headwaters but their guide took them too far west into the Blue Ridge Mountains which they had to climb to find their way out. On December 5, 1752 from a camp in an old Indian field along a stream which was the head of New River Spangenberg writes,

"We have reached here after a hard journey over very high, terrible mountains and cliffs. A hunter, whom we had taken to show us the way, and who once knew the path to the Yatkin, missed the trail, and led us into a place from where there was no way out except by climbing an indescribably steep mountain."

They had followed the main branch of Johns River up through the "Globe" to its head at Blowing Rock, Watauga County, North Carolina. They describe one of the most torturous approaches ever made to New River.

Spangenberg says, "Part of the way we climbed on hands and knees, dragging after us the loads we had taken from the backs of the horses, for had we not unsaddled them they would have fallen backwards down the mountain — this did happen — part of the way we led the horses, who were trembling like a leaf. When we reached the top we saw mountains to right and to left, before us and behind, many hundreds of mountains, rising like great waves in a storm. We rested a little and then began to descend not quite so precipitately."

Men and horses were famished and Spangenberg says, "Soon we found water, and oh, how refreshing it was! Then we sought pasturage for our horses, riding a long way, and well into the night,

Bishop August Gottlieb Spangenberg and Bethabara
the first Moravian Settlement in North Carolina
(Photos by Moravian Archives, Bethlehem, Pennsylvania)

but found nothing except dry leaves. We could have wept for pity for the poor beasts."

Searching for a camp the Bishop says, "It had become so dark that we could not put up the tent, and were oblidged to camp under the trees. It was a trying night! In the morning we went further but had to cut our way through laurel bushes and beaver dams, which greatly wearied our company. We changed our course, and leaving the ravine went up on the mountain, and there in a chestnut grove the Lord showed us a good spring and forage for our horses. He also sent us two deer in our necessity, which were most welcome."

Spangenberg and party were now near the site of present Boone, North Carolina. "Next day," he related, "we went on, and came to a creak, so full of rocks that we could not follow it. . .presently one of our hunters, who had been up on the mountain, returned with the report that he had seen a meadow so we cut our way through the bushes to it, reaching it by evening to the delight of men and horses."

Here at the site of future Boone Spangenberg relates, "We put up our tent, but had barely finished when there came such a wind storm that we could barely stand against it. I think I have never felt a winter wind so strong and so cold. The ground was covered with snow; water froze beside the fire. Then our men lost heart! What should we do? Our horses would die, and we with them."

Their hunters had told them they were on the Mississippi watershed. They knew they were in undiscovered territory miles from any white settlement. Another night was spent by the New and in the morning the Moravians began to scout about.

"Bro. Antes and I rode over the tract," says Spangenberg, " and think that it contains about 5000 acres."

Then he gives an excellent description of New River lands as they were when white man first looked upon them.

"Much of it is already clear, long grass grows here, and it is all low-land. Three creeks united in a river that flows into the Ohio, and into the Mississippi. There are no canes but plenty of grassland. Corn, wheat, oats, barley, hemp, will grow here. Of wood there is no lack; we have included in our tract a beautiful chestnut forest, and fine white pine. The water is clear and delicious. Among the various stones there is a variety which Dr. Antes thinks the best for mill-stones that he has seen in America. Many hundred or thousand wild apple trees, "crab apples" grow here; probably vinegar and spirits could be made from them. From here we can see the Meadow Mountains (the Bald of Rich Mountain three miles beyond the Virginia line) and think they are twenty miles away."

Bishop Spangenberg miscalculating greatly how far west they were said, "We think this place is not so far from Ohio or Alegene one of the largest towns of the Five Nations, though we are not sure." Their error is not surprising considering that in 1752 there existed no maps accurately showing the New River Valley.

The Moravian concluded, "Probably this would made an admirable place for an Indian settlement for it has wood, mast, game, fish and is open in all directions for hunting. The soil is suitable for the raising of corn, potatoes — it is also admirably suited for cattle raising, with an abundance of meadow land."[1]

Even so they concluded they would leave the New River and descend to the Yadkin Valley where they did settle on 100,000 acres which became known as Wachovia or Wachau named for Count Zinzendorff's estate in Wachau Valley, Austria. Here in western Carolina at present Winston-Salem they built the settlements of Bethabara and Bethania which would be of great importance to New River people.

The Moravians did not forget the New River. They surveyed a tract there which they named Freydeck, reasoning, "On New River it is very lonesome, not one man lives there, it is truly a Freydeck." Freydeck was a place in mountaineous Silesia on the Oder River, now in Poland, similar in many ways to the upper New region. News of this American Freydeck rapidly spread so that in 1755 John Mitchell's map showed the upper New near the Moravian's lonely Freydeck.[2]

FOOTNOTES—Chapter XIV

1. Adelaide L. Fries, **Records of the Moravians in North Carolina** (Raleigh: State Department of Archives and History, 1968) hereafter cited as Fries, **Moravian Records,** v. I, pp. 56-57, quoting Bishop Augustus G. Spangenberg, **Diary.**

2. **Ibid.** p. 61 and Dr. John Mitchell, **Map of the British and French Dominions in North America, 1755,** Cumming, **Southeast Maps,** Information given by Irmatraude Hartenstein.

Chapter XV

Patton's Law on the New

While Bishop Spangenberg's party were leaving the upper New in the fall of 1752 Colonel James Patton was hurrying home from Williamsburg where he was being sued by the Ohio and Loyal land companies for the way he was surveying on New River. He rushed to his New River lands from whence he wrote Council President John Blair in January 1753. "I have been on the waters of Missipipia, and on the head of Roanoke since my return from last General Court, where I design to spend most of my time until the end of May. The noise of Mr. Power's caveat has reached the ears of the people here who is very uneasy not knowing but they may have as many proprietors as many of them did in the Jerseys where when they had paid six proprietors was obliged to pay a seventh and turned off in poverty at last."[1]

Patton's reference to the Jersey proprietors is well illustrated by the case of the Clinker Lot Right Men who had derived their titles to land in Jersey from grants made eighty years earlier but after changes in proprietorship were losing title. Some of these came to New River.[2]

Patton had been promised in 1745 that he would get another 100,000 acres when he had surveyed the first and though now under fire he still gambled for the second.

"I mentioned to your Honor when in Town," he told Blair, "I thought I had a just claim for 100,000 acres on Wood's River. I cannot do less in justice to myself than to beg of your honors to give me an order for the 100,000 and that no renewal be given for the (Loyal Company's) 800,000 on the waters of Woods River and Holston's River until I have mine surveyed."

"As to the Ohio who I understand intends to survey. . .to the northward of. . .Woods River, if so it cannot interfere with mine." If the Loyal Company would "settle bounds with me, I should be willing. . .they survey and settle. . .so I may not be prevented from my claim."

Patton explained that he was ignorant of the reason the Ohio and Loyal Companies had sued since "to the best of my judgement I complied with everything I undertook." He would give Blair and friends four-fifths share if he would be given one-fifth.

Then Patton wrote, "I have had some trouble with the Cherokee Indians but has got all differences compromised. I have sent an express to the Governor partly to comply with my promise to the Emperor but principally to quiet our people."[3]

Patton had landed in the midst of a fracas between Indian traders and the Cherokees and found himself bringing justice to New River district in a dual role as the proprietor of a land grant and also as Augusta's County Lieutenant.

The trouble had started between Erwin Patterson and Samuel Stalnaker. Patterson had a trading post at the "Stone House" on Roanoke River where the Carolina Trading Path crossed the Blue Ridge. Stalnaker established on the Holston was much more convenient to the Cherokees than Patterson, so was Patterson's strongest competitor. In June 1752 Patterson went directly to the Cherokee villages with his trading goods. Though warned by trader John Watts that certain rules had to be observed Patterson broke them all — nearly getting himself and the other traders killed.

When Patterson returned home he reported that he had orders from the Governor to run Sam Stalnaker off his land. If Stalnaker refused he was to be taken by Patterson in chains to Williamsburg. Stalnaker was outraged, as well as, said Patton, "all the inhabitants of those waters who has frequently been oppressed by those Fraseling Indians but Stalnaker much more so as he lives 40 miles from our outmost settlement at which place the Cherokees meets our traders."

In March 1752 Stalnaker had sent a subsistence account against these Indians to Williamsburg which the government refused to pay until they cut a road. Stalnaker demanded the Cherokees pay and they refused because they were angry over him taking from them two horses stolen from Andrew Evans and Robert McFarland. Even so, said Patton, the Cherokees liked Stalnaker better than Patterson. At Reed Creek on January 20, 1753 Patton talked with Emperor Ammonscossittee, his wife and his interpreter John Watts who with members of the Tellico Council were returning home from visiting Virginia's new Governor Dinwiddie. The Emperor said Stalnaker's story was true and he wanted to live as friends with Stalnaker if "he would let his people have provisions at the same rate he sold to white people."

The Emperor had a very different grudge with Erwin Patterson. Through his interpreter Watts he told Patton a story which he asked to be sent to the Governor. Watts said, "At Erwin Patterson's house the Emperor of the Cherokee Nation being there was made drunk and afterwards insulted and abused in a very grose mener. Erwin Patterson ordered him to be layed which John Conley did and in so doing, the Emperor was so much abused that the blood gushed out of his mouth and nose. Watts came and relieved the Emperor. He said it was well for him he was there otherwise he believed they would have killed him."

Patterson and the Emperor had many quarrels which was occasioned by an impression the Emperor had that Patterson had "conviveel conversation with his Empress." "Once, said Watts, "he discovered them in the very act and would have shot them both if he had his gun."

John Watts had inquired of the Empress about this. "She acknowledged it to be true," said Watts. "Patterson had debauched her and often was convivial with her and promised to take her for his wife as soon as he would go to the Nations."[4]

John Connolly who had attacked the Emperor was a well-known trouble-maker on New River. This was not the first complaint against him. In 1749 George Draper of Draper's Meadows went out hunting and never returned. It is not known if Eleanor Draper suspected Connolly of harming her husband but the same year he disappeared she complained of Connolly to Augusta Court.[5]

Charles Sinclair also complained that Connolly killed and skinned a deer and left the carcass by his fence. When Sinclair complained Connolly killed his "two find dogs" which guarded his home. Patton now issued a warrant which read:

"Connolly is a vagrant, loose in his morals and worse in his behavior which he has verified for these three years past on New River. During this time he has had no certain place of abode but sulking about pretending to be a hunter and has been very abusive to several of his majesties subjects in those remote parts. The Emperor says unless he has satisfaction he will inform his nation who will have revenge on the white people."

Patton ordered "To all sheriffs and constables and officers of the militia and others of His Majesty's leige people of Augusta but in Particular to Capt. Adam Hermon, Ebenezer Waistcoat, Alexander Sayers, Joseph Crockett, Samuel Stalnaker and Robert Box to make diligent search for Connolly and when found bring him before me. He will be dealt with according to law. I forbid all persons to succor him."

He then notified Williamsburg, "I have sent out warrants against Conolly who has since fled gone to Carolina."[6] Then he had a public announcement read to the Reed Creek settlers that Virginia promised no man would be driven from his land unless convicted of some crime.[7] A full report was sent to Dinwiddie and then Patton sent son-in-law John Buchanan with the Emperor to Stalnaker's to make peace which was successful.

James Patton appears to have done everything possible to keep peace along the New. But forces beyond the Allegheny river would undo his work. Even as he sent off the express to Williamsburg French-paid "norward" Indians slipped in and captured six Cherokees that had been to visit the Governor. These matters were discussed at the Council meeting in April and Dinwiddie notified Patton to attempt "in a friendly manner" to dissuade the northern Indians of the injustice of their orders.

One month later, May 3, 1753, sixty "norward Indians" appeared at George Hoopaugh's place on Sinking Creek. Hoopaugh who had come to Mahanaim with the Eckerlins was now the only settler on Sinking Creek. These Indians burned his house and stable and fifteen bushels of wheat. Other times they had threatened him, burned his corn, killed his best dogs so he had to move and leave his crop in the ground which was then lost. They also killed three horses, two mares and a colt in his field belonging to Jacob Harmon who sworn to the truth of it. Although this happened in the spring of 1753 because New River settlements were isolated Hoopaugh did not get to swear before a law officer until James Patton was on the river in February 1754. After Hoopaugh was burned out he went to live with Valentine Harman until Valentine was killed.[8] Possibly this party of sixty Indians were the ones that rampaged on down through Rowan County, North Carolina in 1753.

Not only Indians passed the New going to Carolina, questionable whites were doing the same. Humberston's Lyon's family on Reed Creek were approached on June 12 by Patrick Gallahur inquiring the way to Carolina. That night Gallahur slipped back to Lyon's where Lyon's son arrested him but he fled again leaving behind his mare and horse, buck skins, saddle and bridle and even his watch and coat.[9]

This same June Henry Grubb was raising a mill on Reed Creek. Hired by John Buchanan to build a saw mill on south fork of Reed

Creek, Grubb erected the frame where Jacob Kettering later had his mill. But the man who was to furnish the iron failed to do so as Grubb reported, "She was not finished." He then started to build a grist mill which also was destined to be unfinished.[10]

This same June in Williamsburg the government was taking action which would have much to do with the settlement of the New. The 800,000 acres granted to Dr. Thomas Walker's Loyal Company was legalized and apparently James Patton became their agent. This meant that the Loyal Company would now be selling the New River land instead of Patton's company.

Several other 100,000 acre grants were made on the New waters at this time, one on the Greenbrier and one in Halifax county from the south fork of Roanoke to the Dan River thence to head of New River. The last was made to John and Francis Willis, John, James and William Maclin, Henry Morris and Charles Lucas.[11]

Several families came to the middle New River settlements in this June 1753. Patton sold to John Bingamin who started a ferry (Pepper's Ferry). The Bingamins had fled from the Ephrata Cloisters and started a ferry. William Leeper (Leopard) arrived at Draper's Meadows and became the road overseer from widow Draper's to Jacob Brown's at Belspring and from Bingamin's (Pepper's) Ferry to Roanoke.

According to the Loyal Company they had nearly two hundred families settled within a year's time. Some others came having nothing to do with the Loyal Company. Andrew Culbertson, for whom Culbertson's Bottom was named, appears to be one of these. He came from Chambersburg, Pennsylvania, to the mouth of Bluestone in 1753 claiming 400 acres in right of settlement and 600 acres in right of preemption. Whether Culbertson bought from the Loyal Company others were paying the equivalent of ten cents an acre, surveyor's fee of $10.42, patent fee of $1.77 and composition fee of $2.22 per hundred.[12]

James Patton probably planned to move to the New at this time for he hired Ben Harrison to build an unusual dwelling resembling a fortified house. Two round log houses with chimney under one roof to be clapboarded with gables was to be built on the place where Charles Hart formerly lived but Patton now claimed as his Springfield estate on Back Creek. This apparition was to be built "on a spot that Henry Patton shall direct". The nearest neighbor was widow Goldman.[13]

So it appears that Patton and Thomas Walker had rosy visions of New River colonization soon to dissipate because of forces far beyond their valley.

FOOTNOTES—Chapter XV

1. Johnson, **James Patton**, pp. 162-163 and James Patton to John Blair, January 1753, **WH**, 1 QQ p. 78.

2. Paula Anderson-Green, "New River Frontier," **VMHB**, hereafter cited as Anderson-Green, **New River**, v. 86, p. 425.

3. Dr. Thomas Walker, **Journal, 1750**, March 24, 1750 and John Watts, **Deposition** sworn before James Patton, January 20, 1753, **WH**, 1 QQ p. 71.

4. James Patton to Governor Dinwiddie, January 1753, **WH**, 1 QQ. pp. 70-73 and David H. Cockran, **The Cherokee Frontier Conflict and Survival 1740-62** (Norman: University of Oklahoma Press, 1962 hereafter cited as Cockran **Cherokee Frontier**, p. 39.

5. **CS**, I, pp. 104, 306.

6. James Patton, Warrant for John Connolly, January 30, 1753, **WH**, 1 QQ p. 70.

7. James Patton, **Memorandums**, **LCPP** Reel 13, folder 3494-3497.

8. Johnson, **James Patton**, pp. 170-173. Colonial Paper, folder 44/9, **VSL: HJ**, 1752-1758, p. 523 and **CS**, II, pp. 124-125.

9. **CS**, I, p. 440.

10. Henry Grubb, **Deposition**, File, Chancery causes 1801-1839, Wythe Court (Wythe County, Virginia, Ketterin vs. Walters Heirs.

11. Clement, **Pittsylvania**, pp. 35, 45.

12. Hark, **Chronicon**, p. 189 and **CS**, I, pp. 62, 440; Memorial to the House of Delegates from the Loyal Company, **VSL**; James Patton, **Accounts**, June 1753, General John Preston Papers, Duke University; Memorial to the House from the Loyal Company; George Wythe, **Court of Chancery Virginia Cases** (Richmond, Virginia: 1795) hereafter cited as Wythe, **Chancery Cases**.

13. **LCPP**, Reel 2, folder 89.

Chapter XVI

Frenchmen on the New

Since the explorations of La Salle and Joliet and Marquette, the French had aspirations to claim the Ohio Valley. From the time of discovery they had been free to sail down it and all the rivers of the Mississippi and became more familiar with the interior of America than any other Eurpoeans. Such was not the case with the English. After Bacon's Rebellion in 1675 when Bacon was hung and his followers dispersed commerce to the western reaches of Virginia among the Indians was discouraged. Nor did North Carolina encourage exploration of the interior. Their ignorance was so blissful that in 1749 when the boundary survey party discovered North Carolina's upper New Governor Johnston said it was "a river nobody ever dreamt of."

On the other hand the French had long known of the old Sault River shown on Moll's 1720 **Map of the French Dominions** and his 1729 map showing the Sault headwaters in Carolina. Upon publication of Fry-Jefferson's 1751 map and Mitchell's 1755 map, Robert De Vaugondy, map-maker to the King of France, quickly made a map **Partis De L'Amerique Septentrionale que comprend Le Cours de L'Ohio** showing the New "a river nobody ever dreamt of" with great exactness giving the correct English names of its tributaries. The Tennessee Cherokee settlements are so clearly shown it is evident the French had great knowledge of the country through which the New and Tennessee flowed.

In 1749 French engineer Captain De Celeron sailed down from Canada along the Ohio planting inscribed leaden plates denoting French possession. He planted Plate 5, at the mouth of the Kanawha claiming all the country it drained including New River Valley as part of New France. Jesuit mathematician Father Bonnecamp made a map labeling the New-Kanawha as Chinondaichio. News quickly spread to the New River hunters. In 1749 Adam Harman swore

Jacob Castle was "going over to the French" and French-paid Indians destroyed Adam's fur cache. This was followed by the news in 1750 that the French were planning to move a thousand families onto New River. Acting Governor Thomas Lee of Virginia sent the news to London saying, "Many of the King's subjects are settled there. . .it will disturb the peace of this colony." To prevent this Lee decided to give the Iroquois a gift to confirm England's right to land along the New but died before he could. When Lewis Burwell became acting governor nothing was done. The next two years on the New brought more French inspired raids. In June 1751 when they wantonly killed a New River woman, Burwell wrote London, "Last June because a poor woman would not with patience see her house robbed of everything in it, they in a most horrible manner murdered her." It was after Patton brought the Cherokee delegation to see Burwell that he sent off this report to London. Apparently Patton impressed upon Burwell the seriousness of the situation because he sent Patton to Logstown that autumn with an invitation to the Iroquois to meet Virginia commissioners in May 1752 to receive a gift and discuss New River land rights. When Patton and the other commissioners met the Iroquois in June 1752 they asked that the murderers of the woman on New River be delivered to the English and that plundering cease. When Patton returned to Virginia he organized the New River militia with Adam Harman and Augustine Price Captain and Lieutenant respectively of a troop of horse and Ebenezer Waistcoat Captain of infantry.[1]

Captain Adam Harman then swore in a deposition to Patton, "Norward Indians has warned our out inhabitants off the land." This was sent to Williamsburg and Patton asked new Governor Dinwiddle "how to manage should these Indians put any of these threats into practice." At this time the northern Indians kidnapped the six Cherokees on Reed Creek.[2]

During the summer of 1753 the French built forts on the Allegheny River moving steadily south toward the Ohio. In the fall of 1753 George Washington and Christopher Gist made their famous visit to the French to tell them to leave the Ohio Valley. When they refused Washington led Virginia troops to drive them out and met defeat at Fort Necessity July 1754.

When news of Washington's defeat reached Virginia Colonel Patton wrote Governor Dinwiddie about conditions particularly on New River saying "From the 10th to ye 20th of June our people on the frontiers of this country was visited by sundry companies of norward Indians who char'g the people to remove otherwise it would be worse for them in a little time.

Hearing of the defeat of our forces by the French has so intimidated them that many of them have moved into our borders with their families and most of their stock leaving their harvest and the remains of their stock a prey for the enemy."

"I have no account as yet what is the fate of our people on the waters of the Mississippia," he continues speaking of the New settlers. "I purpose to set off for that country tomorrow and shall put them in the best posture of defense I can but by the last account I had from there they were almost destitute of ammunition nevertheless of the repeated orders they had from time to time to be equipped as the law directs and to hold themselves in readiness to meet any emergency by what I am informed by our officers even in the strict settlements in this country their men are destitute of ammunition and none is to be bought at any price."[3]

In their desperation to get ammunition some New River people went into North Carolina to purchase it. In August 1755 Governor Dobbs reported, "They don't at present buy lead at our stores, when they buy gunpowder, having enough lead of their own." The stores he referred to were at Salisbury where Buchanan and Hastie had a store, Corbin Town (Hillsborough) where Hogg and Campbell had a store and the Bethabara stores.

By August 1755 the lead deposits had been discovered on New River for Governor Dobbs writes, "There are rich lead mines discovered on New River in Virginia."[4]

Hunter Humberston Lyon lived where the lead mines were later opened and is probably the person who discovered the lead although Colonel John Chiswell gets the credit. It was not a difficult task of discovery, since it was lying around on top of the ground. Even visitors to America had heard lead was there. One traveler in Tidewater said, "There is fine ore, and in plenty, lying above the ground." This account does not agree with the legend that Chiswell discovered the lead while in a cave hiding from Indians. It is even possible Virginians had known of the New River deposits since the 1628 letter to King Charles I, which said, "Four days journey above the falls of James River we are informed certain assurance of a silver mine."[5] Silver was present at the New River lead site so the question arises, could this mysterious 1609 silver mine have been the famous New River lead mine?

Colonel Chiswell's actions indicate when he learned of the lead deposits. This wily mine operator had established himself in Hanover

County in 1743, built Scotchtown, later Patrick Henry's home, and engaged in mining. Elected to the House of Burgesses he seemed well settled as Hanover's representative. Suddenly in 1753 he moved his family and himself to Williamsburg. Although he did become owner of Raleigh's Tavern it is possible his hasty move came because he had learned of the New River lead deposits and wanted to be in Williamsburg where he could more easily market the lead.

Meanwhile out on New River this summer of 1754 Colonel Patton was describing conditions to the Governor in frequent letters. "The French has got command of the Indians," said Patton. "They send them out in parties to ravage amongst us. As we are positively out of ammunition it is not probable we can make any head against them were we ever so numerous in men."[6]

Richard Pearis, a Cherokee Indian trader wrote that the French were already building a fort near Chota and a Frenchman had been among the Cherokees threatening to take Colonel John Buchanan's life.[7] Buchanan, the chief militia officer on New River nearest the Cherokee territory was a prime target for assassination. The French had already given orders to assassinate all the principal leaders of the English frontier settlements such as Lord Fairfax in northern Virgnina, Colonel Thomas Cresap in Maryland and trader George Croghan in Pennsylvania.

On July 25 Patton hurried another letter to the governor. "In case our inhabitants on ye waters of ye Mississippi is attacked unless they have assistans they can't stand it as they're destitute of ammunition. I humbly beg," he pleaded, "for ammunition to be sent us by way of Warwick to Reed Creek."[8]

After receiving the letters of Patton and Pearis Dinwiddie wrote London, "The French are determined to be very troublesome. I am lately inform'd they intend to build forts on Greenbriar, Holston and New River." Frenchmen from Mississippi were to build the forts.[9] Presumably this assignment was given the men at Fort Toulouse sometimes called the "Alabama fort" and the nearest French fort to New River.

Throughout the summer of 1754 Governor Dinwiddie reported "many parties of Indians robbing and ill-treating our people" on the frontiers. These northern Indians were mostly Shawnees described by a trader among them as "tall, manly, well shaped men, of a copper colour with black hair, quick piercing eyes, and good features. All the hair is pulled from their eyebrows and eyelashes. . .faces painted in different parts with vermillion." These fierce warriors now in French employ had "rings of silver in their nose with bobs which hang over their upper lip. The ears are cut from the tips two-thirds of the way round and the piece extended with brass wire till it touches their shoulders, in this part they hang a thin silver plate about three inches in diameter. Their hair is all cut off except a long lock at the top of the head."[10] The autumn brought these Indians through the Holston area homeward bound to their northern camps. Several New River homes were saddened in October when they made good their threats. Stephen Lyon, John Goldman and Benjamin Harrison, all New River men, were killed on the Holston.[11]

Meanwhile in England plans were underway to send an army under General Edward Braddock to America the following spring and politicians sought to prove that the Ohio Valley belonged to England. Commissioned by the government map-maker Dr. John Mitchell made a map of the **British and French Dominions in North America** showing the Ohio Valley and New River. Mitchell shows the extent of English settlements in the Mississippi watershed and in his commentary explains about the Batts-Fallam discoveries on Wood's River in 1671, two years before France explored the Mississippi Valley. He says in the commentary, "Wood's River in Virginia is well-known and well-settled by our people there both above and below the place where these people discovered it."

"We are not only well settled on Wood River but likewise on the Holston," Mitchell announced, hoping the French would get the message.[12]

FOOTNOTES—Chapter XVI

1. Great Britain: P.R.O.: C.O.S.-1327/ p. 357; Lee to Board of Trade, May 11,1750: See De Vaugondy's map, **Special Collections, Newman Library, Virginia Polytechnic and State University Library, CS,** I, pp. 53 and Johnson, **Patton and Colonists,** p. 132.

2. Patton to Dinwiddie, January 1753, **WH,** 1 QQ pp. 73-74.

3. Patton to Dinwiddie, July 2, 1754, **LCPP,** Reel II, folder 134-135.

4. Governor Arthur Dobbs to the Board of Trade, August 24, 1755, **NCCR,** v. 5, pp. 356-357, and James S. Brawley, **The Rowan Story 1753-1953 A Narrative History of Rowan County, North Carolina** (Salisburg: Rowan Printing Company, 1953) hereafter cited as Brawley, **Rowan,** p. 38.

5. Andrew Burnaby, **Travels through the Middle Settlements in North America in the years 1759 and 1760 with observations upon the state of the colonies** London: 1798, reprint (New York: A. Wessels, Company, 1904) hereafter cited as Burnaby, **Travels,** p. 42; **Wilderness Road DAR Address,** February 13, 1975, Author's personal files and A.J. Morrison, "The Virginia Indian Trade to 1673", **WMQ** (2) I, p. 221.

6. Patton to Dinwiddie, July 2, 1754, **LCPP,** Reel II, folder 134-135.

7. Dinwiddie to Pearis, August 2, 1754, **DP,** I, pp. 266-268.

8. Patton to Dinwiddie, July 25, 1754, **LCPP,** Reel II, folder 134-135.

9. Dinwiddie to Earl Granville, August 15, 1754, **DP,** I, pp. 283, and 305.

10. Nicholas Cresswell, **The Journal of 1774-1777** (Port Washington, N.Y.: The Kenikat Press, 1968) pp. 192.

11. **CS,** II, p. 510 **The Preston Register,** hereafter cited as **The Preston Register.**

Chapter XVII

The Massacres — 1755

By June 1755 Braddock's army was marching toward the Ohio. But the presence of a great British army in America did not deter the Ohio Indians. On June 18 Samuel Stalnaker's settlement on Holston River was destroyed. Whether the New River people knew of this before they were attacked is uncertain. On July 3 the Bingeman settlement above Dunkard's Bottom was attacked. **The Preston Register** of killed, wounded and captured on the Virginia frontier in the French and Indian War names the New River victims. **The Chronicon Ephratense** published in Lancaster County, Pennsylvania names the same victims. Those murdered were James McFarland, John Bingeman and wife, Adam Bingeman, John Cook; Henry Zinn and a young child. Wounded were Nathaniel Wiltshire, Dutch Jacob and wife (prisoner escaped), Frederick Stern, Mrs. Bingeman Jr., Mrs. Davies; Bingeman's son and daughter and a wandering stranger. Isaac Freeman, his wife and five children were made prisoners. Margaret Zinn at Mahanaim was wounded and taken to Bethabara. Henry Zinn the same who had begged to come to New River was living with the Bingamins and made no effort to defend himself or them when attacked.[1]

By July 11 the news of the massacre of the Stalnaker family on Holston had arrived in Williamsburg.[2] James Patton was there for the Assembly when he heard the news. This directly threatened Patton's business ventures and family on New River. Stalnaker lived on his land. Dozens had bought from him along the New and his daughter Margaret Buchanan and husband John were at Reed Creek. Hastily he found ammunition and headed for Augusta Court House arriving before July 12. He immediately commissioned nephew William Preston to recruit a ranger company and sent Preston and part of the company toward New River.[3] News of the July 3 New River massacre and the murder on Reed Creek of Lieutenant Wright and two soldiers, part of a detachment of the Virginia Regiment sent by Andrew Lewis, speeded Preston and Patton on their way. Patton sent a last letter to Dinwiddie pleading for more arms. Dinwiddie answered, "I recommend you the the Protection of God."[4]

While the governor was writing from Williamsburg some New River families were already in flight and had gotten to the Moravian settlement at Bethabara, North Carolina near present Winston-Salem. Bethabara means House of Passage and so it would be for New River people. In the next twenty years hundreds of them would pass through Bethabara.

From Bethabara on July 22 the Moravians record, "A so-called Dunkard or Bearded man came to the smithy. He has just come from New River with his entire family, fearing to remain there longer because of the Indians, who are wandering about. Although his home was only about seventy miles from here the journey has taken them three weeks, as they had no other road to take than to the Roanoke. The man told us that some ten weeks ago a man named Stalneckker living on Holston River, about 100 miles from the New River settlement, had been captured by the Indians and his entire family murdered. It was believed that he would be cruelly tortured since the Indians hated him. A few days before the Dunkard left several families had been attacked and part murdered, part captured; and the night before his flight the family of one of his nearest neighbors had been murdered, only three miles from him. So far as the man knew 28 persons had been killed or taken prisoner. When the man reached the Roanoke he found other refugees from New River, but it was no place to stay for the settlers were much alarmed by the news they brought, so this man decided to take his family to the Town Fork."

Town Fork of the Dan, fifteen miles from Bethabara in Stokes County at present Walnut Cove would later be destroyed in the Cherokee war in 1760.[5] This Dunkard coming from New River was probably Gerhart Zinn and family fleeing this first New River massacre of July 1755.

By summer of 1755 many more people had joined the Drapers and Ingles at Draper's Meadows. Most were Germans with names of Moser, Lingle, Bargar, Loy, Cull, Leopard, Sharp and Seilor. These people may have come from Rowan County, North Carolina to the New for Germans named Valentine and Lawrence Lingle, Adam Moser, John Leopard, Martin Loy, George and Henry Sharp and Coonrod Seilor were in Rowan in 1760. The Isaac Freeland or Freeman family captured this summer on the New were probably from Orange County, North Carolina, for a large settlement of this family were in the New Hope area of Orange. Many German names in Haw River area such as Trolinger, Faust, Albright, Sharp, and Ephland were later in the New settlements. It is said that Haw River sent a Reverend Samuel Burgell in 1755 to minister to the New River Germans.[6]

Knowing of the clusters of cabins at Draper's Meadows and other places along the New Patton hurried to join Preston's Rangers. Preston's daughter says Patton and Preston were at Draper's Meadows together while a more contemporary account indicates Patton was alone.

"Colonel Patton, that morning, after having dressed himself in his uniform, and getting his nephew, William Preston, to sew up in the fob of his small clothes thirty English guineas," records Preston's daughter, "told him to go to Sinking Creek, to get Lybrook to help take off the harvest, which was ready to cut. Preston went very early."[7]

An account published in London in the **Gentleman's Magazine** in September 1755 says Patton "rode a little out of the way to see some friends, proposing to overtake the convoy at the end of a few miles, but such was his misfortune, that he fell into the hands of some Indians, who had just murdered his friends and their families, and not discovering his danger till it was too late, he was also inhumanly murdered on the spot."[8]

These accounts of what happened at Draper's Meadows on Strouble's Creek of New River obviously do not concur. The **Virginia Gazette** account published in Williamsburg August 8 is the most contemporary account of what was occurring on New River at this time.

"By an express this morning from Augusta County, we have the melancholy account of the murder of Colonel James Patton who was killed by a party of Indians the last day of July, on the head branches of Roanoke, and eight more men, women and children. Col. Patton was going out with ammunition for the use of the Frontier inhabitants, and stopping at a plantation on the road to refresh himself, the convoy being about five miles before, he was beset by 16 Indians, who killed and stripped him, and then made off with his horse."

William Preston's daughter tells us the names of the other victims of the Draper's Meadows massacre. "The Indians came to (Caspar) Barger's, cut his head off and put into a bag; then came to Ingles' and Draper's, killed old Mrs. Draper and two children of Colonel Ingles, by knocking their brains out on the end of the cabin logs. Took Mrs.

Ingles and her son Thomas, a boy of ten years, prisoners as well as her sister-in-law, Mrs. Draper, who was trying to make her escape with her infant in her arms, but was shot by the Indians, who broke her arm, in consequence of which her infant was dropped. The Indians caught it up and dashed its brains out on the end of the cabin logs. After breakfast Colonel Patton had sat down to his table to write. The Indian warwhoop was raised, and some five or six of them surrounded the cabin and set it on fire. The colonel always kept his sword on the table. He rushed to the door with it in his hand and encountered two of them. Patton was almost gigantic in size. He cut two of them down. In the meantime another warrior had leveled his gun, fired and killed the brave old pioneer. Patton fell; the Indians ran off in the thicket and made their escape before any pursuers could be brought together."[9]

According to William Foote Presbyterian minister writing in the 1840's, William Ingles and the other men were in the fields when the Indians attacked "securing their crop, unarmed and unsuspicious of danger. The savages surrounded the dwelling in which were the women and children and the arms of the families and the men who had come to aid in the harvest. . .Mr. Ingles hearing the noise at the house hastened home in alarm. He approached very near the dwelling before he discovered the Indians; hoping to aid his family he drew still nearer. Two stout Indians discovered him and rushed at him with their tomahawks. He fled to the woods; they pursued, at a little distance from each other, one on each side of Mr. Ingles to prevent his secreting himself by turning aside. He perceived the Indians were gaining upon him, and attempting to jump over a fallen tree, he fell, and gave himself up for lost. Owing to the underbrush the pursuers did not see him fall, and passed by on each side of him as he lay in the bushes. In a few moments he was upon his feet and escaped in another direction. The harvest hands deprived of their arms, believing resistance ineffectual, left the Indians unmolested and secreted themselves in the woods around the meadows."[10]

According to his daughter William Preston arrived with Lybrook back at Draper's Meadows finding those murdered already buried and the whole settlement destroyed.

The Indians were gone, some say down Strouble's Creek, which has a torturous approach to New River. A more logical account by Professor Conrad, once president of Virginia Polytechnic Institute says after the Indians killed Caspar Bargar, they went down Tom's Creek, dragging along the other captives, and went on to the Horseshoe (Radford Arsenal) where they crossed and encamped. "A party of settlers soon pursued," says Conrad, "and coming upon the campfires, found the Indians with the head of poor Bargar upon a staff and they dancing around it with demonical yells. The settlers made the attack but failed to secure the prisoners, though they killed several Indians."[11]

Ranger Abraham Bledsoe killed and scalped two Indians in the chase and asked the colony for the bounty reward for scalps.[12]

The Conrad account saying the Indians went down Tom's Creek with their victims fits a tradition in the Michael Price family. Michael was then living at the mouth of Tom's Creek on New River near Adam Harman's ford. The Price family have said that the Indians who raided at Draper's Meadows passed Michael's cabin, while he was reading his German Bible and threw a tomahawk at him. He shielded himself with his Bible and escaped. Descendants of Michael had the Bible for many years until it was destroyed in a fire.[13]

The Conrad account has the ring of authenticity since it was the custom of the Iroquois and allies to place a skull on a pole called a weelunk or weelin as a warning to proceed no further. This account shows that the Indians placed the weelunk on New River to serve as a warning. The places they did this were known as the place of the skull or weelin. The Iroquois or Delawares did this on the Ohio in 1749 at the mouth of Weelin or Wheeling Creek from which Wheeling, West Virginia, takes its name.[14]

Dr. Thomas Lloyd surgeon, and Colonel Patton's indentured servant, was with Preston's ranger company. Lloyd who had gotten into trouble in England wrote home telling of his experiences on New River. "The French Indians have killed our men and inhabitants all round the camp and they are so much of the nature of a wolf," wrote Lloyd, "that if we don't come on them while at their prey its needless. They lye in ambush and fire on us before we are sensible. My first master Colo. Patton was killed & 12 men close by our camp. We followed them 200 miles but to no purpose."[15]

Either before or after chasing Indians Dr. Lloyd treated Nathaniel Wiltshire of a "wound received from the Indians at Mr. Bingamins on New River." He gave "medicines for 2 women that was wounded in their breasts at Starns on New River" and he "cured James Cull of a wound in his foot when Colo. Patton was killed."[16]

People from New River fled in every direction after this. "Four families on their flight from a branch of New River this minute passed my house," wrote John Madison, Augusta County clerk living in the Roanoke River Valley on August 19, 1755. "Tis shocking to think of the calamity of the poor wretches who live on the Holston and New Rivers, who for upwards of a hundred miles have left their habitations, lost their crops and vast numbers of stock. Could you see, dear friend, the women who escaped crying after their murdered husbands, with their helpless children hanging on to them, it could but wound your very soul."[17]

These refugees from New River followed the Indian Road or Catawba Road down North Fork of Roanoke River to meet the road to Carolina. Or they followed Catawba Valley north toward the James River and on north to the Augusta Shenandoah settlements near Peaked Mountain. The Germans called this "Pinquit Mountdan" on "Chanithor" in "Agoste".

Near the Peaked Mountain settlement Augustine Price, brothers, Henry and Daniel, the Harlesses, Lingles, and others from New River found safety. When aged 80 Augustine testified "he was driven from his home on New River by Indians in the year of Braddock's defeat; he encamped on the land of John Madison." This land was on Cub Run near Elkton, Rockingham County. Madison had a young ward, Thomas Burk, who later came to the New River and would have heard of it from Augustine Price and others when they came as refugees to Madison's land. Certainly Augustine and Jacob Harman were responsible for the orphaned Williams boys, Henry, Philip and Michael, for coming to New River. The Williams were bound to Price and Harman after their father Henry Wilhelm died at Peaked Mountain. Philip Harless was still on Cub Run in 1760. Francis Kerkly, Jacob Shell, Jacob Lingle, Christian, John and Henry Bingamin, all who would live or had lived on New River were added to the tithables of northern Augusta in 1756. [18]

Some fled to the forks of James River near present Buchanan. John Buchanan and Peggy Patton Buchanan returned to Cherry Tree Bottom estate of James Patton in time for the birth of a new baby on December 20, 1755.[19]

Another route of flight was the Warwick Road to Blackwater, Magotty and Pigg River and Hale's Ford (present Smith Mountain Lake). Alexander Sayers, William Ingles and James Newell (who later lived on the New) went to New London in Bedford County where they bought lots. Some Lybrooks went into Bedford County.[20]

For many that was still too close to New River. Large numbers fled to North Carolina, to Bethabara and on to the Town Fork on Dan River. The Moravians report on October 26, 1755, "Three men came today — they are Germans from New River but now living on the Town Fork. Two of them undertake to make us 3,000 shingles in three weeks, the third will fell and trim 100 trees, the pay to be a pair of shoes each."[21]

The younger Jacob Goldman appears in Cumberland County, North Carolina, after he left the New in November 1755.[22] Others went to South Carolina. John Vance once agent for Patton's company left and the Vance heirs were living at the forks of Saluda River, South Carolina, in 1766. The Calhouns went to Long Canes Creek on Saluda.[23]

The Augusta County Court in 1755 noted that a process was "not executed by reason of the murder done on New River by the Indians" and Lyman Chalkley, chronicler of Augusta, claims there was not a single entry in Augusta order books from early in 1756 through 1759 relating to the New River settlements. The valley of the New was once again a no-man's land.

FOOTNOTES—Chapter XVII

1. The Preston Register and Sache, German Sectarians, II p. 357. Sachsa says the Binge- manns were at New Market but New River records establish them at New River in July 1755.

2. Virginia Gazette, July 11, 1755.

3. Johnson, James Patton, pp. 193-198.

4. DP, II, p. 132 and The Preston Register.

5. Fries, Moravian Records, I, p. 133 and Brawley, Rowan, p. 37.

6. Eisenberg, Virginia Lutherans, p. 99 quoting from J.S. Morgan, B.B. Brown, John Hale, History of the Lutheran Church in North Carolina p. 20. and "Germans naturalized in Rowan County 1760's", North Carolina Genealogy, Spring 1972, v. 18, no. 1, p. 2698.

7. Letitia Preston Floyd to Benjamin Rush Floyd, February 22, 1843, Richmond Standard hereafter cited as LPF, RS.

8. Sylvanus Urban, "Jouranl of the War in America," Gentleman's Magazine, XXV, p. 474, September 1755.

9. LPF, RS and Virginia Gazette, August 8, 1755.

10. William Henry Foote, Sketches of Virginia, historical and biographical 2d series, second ed. rev. (Philadelphia: Lippincott, 1856) p. 151.

11. P.N. Conrad, "Early Blacksburg," Blacksburg News, 1881, quoted in Charles Crush, The Montgomery County Story 1776-1957 (Jamestown Festival Committee 1957) hereafter cited as Crush, Montgomery, p. 111.

12. HJ, 1752-1758, p. 460.

13. Crush, Montgomery, p. 44 and CS, I, p. 307.

14. E. Lee North, Redcoats, Redskins and Red-Eyed Monsters, p. 30.

15. Dr. Thomas Lloyd to Edward Hector, October 6, 1755. Great Britain: P.R.O. High Court of the Admiralty. Library of Congress, Manuscript Division.

16. Dr. Thomas Lloyd, Expense Account, LCPP, Reel II, folder 164-165.

17. John Madison to Col. James Madison, August 19, 1755, Kegley, Virginia Frontier, p. 213.

18. LCPP, folder 164; CS, II, pp. 36, 445; CS, I, p. 74, 81; CS, III, p. 364 and WMQ (1) v. 13, p. 249.

19. Buchanan Family Bible in possession of John W. Walker, Letter to author.

20. Map of Franklin County, **1976,** Gertrude C. Mann and George Kegley, compliers; J.R. Hildebrand, cartographer. The Historical Society of Washington County, Virginia, Publications. Series II, no. **8,** July 1970, Agnes S. Riley, "James Newell" p. 16

21. Fries, **Moravian Records,** I, pp. 133, 139.

22. **CS,** I, p. 71 and **CS,** II p. 62.

23. Milling, **Red Carolinians,** p. 299.

Marker in Memory of Draper's Meadows victims and Colonel James Patton, killed on New River 1755.

(Photo by Walter L. Johnson)

Chapter XVIII

Cherokees Defend the New

As Dr. Lloyd reported, William Preston led his rangers in the chase after the Indians for many miles. Then he returned to New River and John Buchanan, now the ranking militia officer on New River, sent him to Williamsburg with the news of the Draper's Meadow massacre. Preston arrived August 8 and the **Virginia Gazette** immediately published the news. The report was repeated in the **Maryland Gazette** on August 21 and Governor Horatio Sharpe sent word to England. "Col. Patton of Augusta County a very active and worthy man was lately scalped as he was proceeding to command a party of Rangers on New River. The inhabitants who dwelt in the distant parts of Virginia on New River and that called Green Brier have left their plantations."[1]

In western North Carolina on August 24 while touring defenses Governor Dobbs received news of Braddock's defeat. "That night having letters by a messenger of an incursion on New River near the frontiers," he ordered out militia under new arrival from Ireland, Captain Hugh Waddell to protect Rowan County and build Fort Dobbs near present Statesville.[2]

Virginia Regiment Captain Peter Hogg sent word to George Washington, "As the inhabitants on Green Brier, New River and Holstons are all scattered from their plantations and have left the best crops of corn in the colony it will become a settlement for the Indians during the winter if more companies are not sent up to protect the farmers while they gather their corn, and by building forts on the two first of these rivers."[3]

Governor Dinwiddie reported to the Bishop of London that 40 people had been killed in the back country. More than half these casualties were on New River. He said he had ordered seven ranger companies to the front. These companies were Hanover Rangers commanded by Samuel Overton; Amelia Rangers by Henry

Anderson, Branch Tanner, and George Farley; Lunenberg Rangers commanded by Nathaniel Terry; Bedford Rangers by John Phelps; Augusta Rangers by William Preston. How many of these actually ranged in the New River Valley is questionable. Preston's men were in the valley in August when they bought a hog from the widow Bargar. [4]

The last weeks in August Cherokee Emperor Old Hop's son accompanied by trader Richard Pearis and other Cherokees came through New River Valley on their way to Williamsburg where Old Hop's son told Governor Dinwiddie, "I was greatly concerned to find the inhabitants on the frontiers had deserted their plantations, left their corn on the grounds, and found many killed."

"If you will supply a small number of men with arms and ammunition and build a fort on Holston's and New River, I will engage our assistance," said the Cherokee, "to recover the land and preserve the grain left by the inhabitants. I believe 100 men in each fort sufficient."

The Cherokees also advised launching a retaliatory attack from the New River. They told the governor, "It is not so far to the (Shawnees) as you imagine. We can go there in seven nights." [5]

Dinwiddie thanked the Cherokee for "your great concern for the murders and devastation made on Holston's and New River. I shall be glad if your nation will send some of your warriors to Holston's and New River to remain there this winter to protect your brothers against the barbarities of the French Indians and the Shawnees. I have ordered forts to be built on Holston's and New River where your brothers will receive you kindly." [6]

On September 6, the same day he talked with the Cherokees Dinwiddie wrote Captain John Smith, who since mid-July had been building a fort at Looney's Ferry on James River. "I recommend forts to be built on both Holston and New River for the safety of the inhabitants and the accomodations of the Indians." [7] It is this author's opinion that John Smith now came to New River to build Fort Frederick. Historian Lewis Preston Summers says George Stalnaker built Fort Frederick but gives no authority for his claim. Samuel Stalnaker was a captive at this time and a George Stalnaker has not surfaced in New River records.

John Smith's family were active in the Cherokee trade, he was in the area with a crew building forts and would be the person naturally assigned this task. William Preston and his rangers did not build Fort Frederick for he was ordered to roam the woods and ended up down on Catawba Creek where his company at this time were building Fort William or Fort Preston.

In September as Preston marched past Ephraim Vause's plantation at present Shawsville he observed Vause's efforts at building Fort Vause and bought beef "for my men returning from Fort Frederick."

Dinwiddie told Preston, "The grain on the ground forsaken by the inhabitants may be gathered in support of the rangers. You may press tools for the building of the forts." We see thus there was more than one fort Preston was concerned with building. [8]

Dinwiddie was angry that the people had left their farms and asked Overton of the Hanover ranger company to make a list of all those who had left their places. He wanted to know the number of men Smith and Preston had which they said was 30 each but he thought was "few or none."

"I expect 150 Cherokee Indians into New River in six weeks," he told Overton. "Remain out to meet them, join with your men and use them well." [9]

Judging from Governor Dinwiddie's letters it appears that Captains Overton and Woodson from Hanover combined with what few men John Smith had are the people who built Fort Frederick at Dunkard's Bottom on New River. It appears to have been completed by November 20 when Dinwiddie wrote Woodson that he hoped the people would "take care of the fort built by Captain Smith and return to their plantations, as they have forts to retire to in any distress." He tells Augusta militia Colonel Stuart, the commissary, he should have supplied Smith. "Captain Smith says you knew where he was building a fort and there was the place you should have supplied him." Stuart wanted Smith to leave the fort he had built and come in to safety. Smith answered, "What use will the fort be if left?" [10]

None of this correspondence mentions Fort Frederick on New River by name yet the implication is it is speaking of it.

Fort Frederick built at Dunkard's Bottom on New River was never more than a makeshift affair. The lumber and timbers probably came from the deserted Dunkard homes. In February 1756 a contemporary says, "There is a trifling fort on Jackson's River, another more trifling at Dunkard's Bottom. . .which have kept the neighboring settlements tolerably well together." [11]

To the newly built Fort Frederick in November came a new group of Indians — Cherokees. Eighty-two warriors and trader Richard Pearis showed up to defend the settlers against the Shawnees. Pearis was lucky to be alive. When he had returned to their villages after visiting Williamsburg he had a surprise awaiting. While away the Carolina traders had turned the Indians against him, though he had a Cherokee wife and had lived among them. They threatened to kill him and only by quick "palaver" and turning over his property of nearly 2000 pounds of deerskins did he save his neck. That he was able to do this as well as persuade them to accompany him back to New River speaks highly for his diplomatic finesse. And he had a big fish with him. Leading the Cherokees was "The Great Warrior", or "Man-Killer", Antossity Usteneeka called by the English Outacite or Ostenaco. Greatly respected among the Cherokees for having dispatched many enemies he would later visit King George in London.[12]

During the late fall Outacite and his warriors ranged from Fort Frederick on the New to Fort Preston on Catawba Creek. Dinwiddie described Outacite as "a brave sensible Indian". William Preston bought rum for them from Richard Hall who Christopher Gist had visited. For the Cherokees Preston purchased three dozen pipes and "an extraordinary fine tomahawk for a Cherokee warrior" probably for Outacite. On one occasion they were entertained at Fort Preston.[13] They camped around Pearis Mountain overlooking Ellett Valley near present Blacksburg. Pearis Mountain commanded a long view of the New River and today stands as a mute reminder of the winter Richard Pearis, Outacite the "Man-Killer", and Cherokee warriors guarded the New River Valley for Virginia.

Meanwhile plans were proceeding for an expedition against the Shawnee villages on the Ohio. Everyone was really encouraged when in November a miraculous thing happened.

One day Adam Harman in his field near Gunpowder Springs by present Eggleston found Mary Draper Ingles alive but near death. After the Draper's Meadows massacre the Indians had taken Mary, her son Tom, Betty Robinson Draper, and other captives down New River to the Kanawha thence to their villages near present Chillicothe. They had put Mary to work making salt and sent Betty and Tom to other villages. After several months Mary escaped in company with "an old Dutch woman who was taken from the upper part of the Ohio." Following the Kanawha-New system through many harrowing experiences they finally arrived back at the white settlements.

This same trek made by Mary and the Dutch woman was later made by Hannah Dennis and Jennie Wiley. Mary's trip was made at a crucial time, however, for the Virginians were planning a retaliatory expedition following the same route. If two women with no provisions could do it men certainly could.

When Mary returned William Ingles took her to a fort in Bedford for safety and then went to see the governor. He told Dinwiddie, "A great many people will go volunteers" against the Shawnees. George Washington told them such an expedition would prove "abortive" because he had heard the Shawnees had left their towns. Dinwiddie answered, "Two women who were taken prisoners and made their escape mention they being in their Towns and did not hear of their intention of moving.[14]

Dinwiddie appointed Andrew Lewis, "a person well acquainted with the woods and in good esteem with our people," as commander and told him to rendezvous at Fort Frederick. Outacite and his warriors encamped at the fort in January 1756 to await Lewis. From there William Preston, John Smith and Richard Pearis sent a letter to the Catawbas in North Carolina asking them to join the expedition. Two Catawba children, taken from the Shawnees, being cared for by the Cherokees at Fort Frederick would await their arrival. Kerorostekee who once lived with the Catawbas and George Pearis,

Outacite, "The Man-Killer", leader of the Cherokees
who guarded the New River, 1755-56
(Photo from the Library of Congress)

Richard's young brother, and the man for whom Pearisburg on New River takes its name, were sent to the Catawbas with the letter.[15]

The Robert and James Donald Company, merchants originally from Glasgow, Scotland, brought goods to Fort Frederick as did Robert Hastie and John Pearce.[16]

William Preston kept a journal of the activities of this force gathering by the New. After spending the night at Richard Hall's his company marched to Fort Frederick where they saluted the Cherokees with a volley which was returned "in great joy." Then the Cherokees honored them with a war dance. Guards were put at the river crossings, provisions gathered, sermons preached by Presbyterian ministers John Craig and John Brown. By February 12 Andrew Lewis bringing men from Washington's Virginia Regiment arrived to take command. He called a troop review for noon. Three hundred and forty men marched past and had a good look at their

Major Andrew Lewis led the Sandy Creek
expedition from New River against Shawnee
towns on the Ohio in 1756
(Photo by Virginia State Library)

commander. Lewis was already considered one of the best soldiers in Virginia having suffered with Washington at Great Meadows and Fort Necessity. He is described as a "tall, heavy formed man, full, florid with a fine countenance, dark brown eyes, austere and reserved and seldom known to smile."[17] This man who would meet with much misfortune would become the greatest military leader of western Virginia in the colonial era.

Lewis gave captain's commissions to Yellow Bird and Round O, Cherokee warriors. Soon after James Burk who had settled Burke's Garden in Tazewell arrived saying Indians had driven him out and he had found Robert Looney murdered on Reed Creek. Looney's son, Absalom and family settled on Bluestone and in 1754 Robert sent word to them to leave and come back to the James River settlements. Probably Robert was on his way to see them when killed. [18] Because of Looney's murder Lewis sent a hundred men to scout along Reed Creek for the main force which moved out February 18 leaving a skeleton crew at Fort Frederick.

There were approximately 350 men who marched on this expedition in the companies of Overton, Woodson, Smith, Preston, Pearis, Breckenridge, Alexander, Montgomery, Dunlap and Hogg. Among the men was one Turk Weybrand, a snow-haired old man from New River who claimed he had been born in Amsterdam in 1642 which if true would make him an incredible 110![19] His story surely ranks him as New River's first flamboyant tall-tale-teller.

The first night out the men slept on the floor of William Sayer's barn in present Draper's Valley. Captain Preston whipped a soldier for swearing which incensed the Cherokees who did not even whip children. Some deserted and Lewis, Pearis and the interpreter had to follow them to John Buchanan's place on Reed Creek to persuade them to rejoin the force. From Reed Creek the force marched by the Holston and Burke's Garden to Big Sandy Creek. [20]

Many doubted their success including Reverend James Maury who knowing of the region's vulnerability asked for a fort to be built immediately at the "Horseshoe on the New." As Maury anticipated enemy Indians did attack the Harmans in February. Jacob Harman and son were killed. Valentine and Daniel with Andrew Moser were attacked. Valentine was killed before his nephew Daniel less than a foot from him. Daniel and Moser who had worked for Jacob Castle were carried off prisoners. Daniel Harman eventually escaped the Indians but Moser is said to have died. [21]

As the Harmans were being murdered on New River, Andrew Lewis's force was following Sandy Creek (present boundary between

West Virginia and Kentucky) to starvation and death. Other than capturing several Frenchmen making their way from South Carolina through the woods to the French on the Ohio, nothing was accomplished. An army of skeletons staggered back into the James and Roanoke settlements in April. [22]

Lewis and some Cherokees went to Williamsburg to report to the governor. Fourteen of the Cherokees did not go to Williamsburg but headed home by way of New River. Here occurred a tragic postscript to the Cherokee attempt to help the white man. Andrew Burnaby, an English traveler in America tells the story. "About the year 1756," writes he, "some Cherokees who had been out upon a military expedition in our behalf against the French were treacherously murdered by an Augusta militia captain under pretence that they had pilfered some of his poultry. He had received and entertained them as friends; and when they took their leave of him to return to their own country, he placed a party in ambush, murdered several." Later "he attempted to defraud the government by claiming the premium assigned for the scalps of hostile Indians." The Cherokees who escaped arrived home just as Dinwiddie's embassy to them, Col. Randolph, William Byrd III and Mr. Campbell were winding up an advantageous treaty. Upon hearing the news the Cherokees seized the ambassadors and only the intervention of Little Carpenter saved their lives. [23]

Randolph and Byrd had agreed to build the Cherokees a fort in exchange for the help they had given on the Sandy Creek expedition. In May Governor Dinwiddie ordered Andrew Lewis to enlist a company to build the fort.

FOOTNOTES—Chapter XVIII

1. Virginia Gazette, August 8, 1755, and Patricia Givens Johnson, William Preston and the Allegheny Patriots (Pulaski, Virginia: B.F. Smith and Co., Printers, 1976) hereafter cited as Johnson, William Preston, p. 20.

2. Maryland Gazette, August 21, 1755; Governor Horatio Sharpe to Cecilius Calvert, Maryland Archives VI, Sharpe Correspondence, I, pp. 273-277; Governor Arthur Dobbs to the Board of Trade, August 24, 1755, NCCR, V p. 357 and Brawley, Rowan, pp. 23-26.

3. Stanislaus M. Hamilton, ed., Letters to Washington and Accompanying Papers (Boston: Houghton Miflin Company 1898) hereafter cited as Hamilton, Washington, I, p. 93.

4. Dinwiddie to the Bishop of London and Thomas Robinson, DP, II, pp. 161-163 and William Preston, Expense Account, September 3, 1755, LCPP, Reel II, folder 164.

5. Old Hop's Son to Dinwiddie, September 6, 1755, DP, II, p. 188.

6. Dinwiddie to Old Hop's Son, September 6, 1755, DP, II, p. 189.

7. DP, II, p. 190 and Johnson, James Patton, p. 196.

8. Dinwiddie to Preston, September 15, 1755, DP, II, p. 200; Johnson, William Preston, pp. 25-27 and LCPP, Reel, II, p.164.

9. Dinwiddie to Overton, September 20, 1755, DP, II, p. 211.

10. Dinwiddie to Woodson and Stuart, **DP**, II, pp. 279, 288.

11. Reverend James Maury to Philip Ludwell, **Virginia's Frontier Defense**, February 10, 1756, **VMHB**, v. 19, p. 297.

12. **SCIAD**, III, p. 210; Letter to author, April 16, 1975, William L. McDowell, and J. Ralph Randolph, **British Travelers Among the Southern Indians**, 1660-1763, (Norman, Oklahoma: University of Oklahoma Press, 1973) hereafter cited as Randolph, **British Travelers**, pp. 143-144.

13. Johnson, **William Preston**, p. 28 and **LCPP**, Reel II, p. 164.

14. **LPF**, **RS**; **DP**, II, pp. 295, 325. For the complete story see Hale, **Trans-Allegheny Pioneers**.

15. **SCIAD**, III, pp. 98-99 and **DP**, II, p. 306.

16. **HJ**, 1752-1758, pp. 369, 395, 425-426.

17. Patricia Givens Johnson, **General Andrew Lewis of Roanoke and Greenbrier** (Blacksburg, Virginia, Southern Printing Company, 1980) hereafter cited as Johnson, **Andrew Lewis**, p. 47.

18. **CS**, I, p. 497.

19. Fries, **Moravian Records**, I, p. 286.

20. Johnson, **Andrew Lewis**, p. 47; William Preston, Sandy Creek Journal, **WH**, 1 QQ pp. 96-123 and Johnson, **William Preston**, pp. 33-44 for an overview of the entire expedition.

21. **CS**, II p. 124; The **Preston Register**; **LCPP**, Reel II, folder 64 (Moser) and **VMHB** v. 19, p. 297.

22. Dinwiddie to Washington and Governor Dobbs, April 8, 13, 1756, DP, II, p. 382.

23. **VEJ**, VI, p. 8; Burnaby, **Travels**, p. 196; **DP**, II, pp. 382, 446 and **VMHB**, v. 13, pp. 226, 262 and **VMHB**, v. 37, p. 303.

PAYTAKOOTHA, Flying Clouds
Shawnee signer of Treaty of Greenville
1795

KISHKALWA
A Shawnee chief who took part in the battle of Point Pleasant, 1774.

Shawnee Warriors of the 1770's painted by Charles Bird King.

Chapter XIX

Strange Land by the Sinking Sun

In May while Andrew Lewis was gathering his company to march to Cherokee country, Dunkard's Bottom people were communicating with Conrad Beissel at Ephrata with a view to returning to Lancaster. It appears that John Miller who had bought Peter Schaefer's land on Mill Creek when Schaefer left in 1754, Henry Miller and Gerhart Zinn had returned to New River and Beissel addresses the following letter to Johannes Mueller.

> Ephrata
> The 17th of the 5th month
> 1756

Love and joy, blessings and salvation from God and His rich plentiful grace. It cannot be denied that a certain memory lingers on with me since you were with us the last time, but since the opportunities for spiritual action have been out of our hands, very little could be done between us. This opportunity to write presented itself for several causes both from letters from you and from others as well as my mental disposition. If I can shed light on your distress with my words my letter is well served. My affection remains unchanged towards all the souls who originally were enlightened. . .but were frightened to flee into a **strange land by the sinking sun** dwelling in darkness of bad dreams and nocturnal ghosts, although you were reminded; remain in the land make an honest living. You have spiritually and physically suffered ill fortune through a certain deviation from the eternal goodness and because you turned your countenances from Jerusalem to Jericho and **fell among murderers** and thus you will again turn your eyes from Jericho back to Jerusalem; I believe you could bring yourself, without any conditions, to come back here as though nothing had happened. You could absolve yourself from all the past low deeds and could return to your God-given heritage. With greetings and kisses again in spirit, I remain faithfully yours. Peaceful in earthly non-ownership.

P.S. I can tell you that I am certain of my special esteem of you and as far as you are concerned I scarcely believe that you will ever be at peace without coming back here. I learned from your cousin that he has indicated to return in the spring with his kin. . .

P.P.S. It is a tremendous burden on my heart concerning the grace of your wife, because her physical mother left something with me when she still lived here and since she was very young then it has been with me until now. I think if she could be brought to be baptized I could be relieved of my oath. . .she could attain her grace and be saved. Please give my regards to her mother and tell her she has not been forgotten and neither have we. Concerning George Hartmann, greetings none the less and especially his beloved wife Maria who is ever in my fondest memory. As far as your brother (Heinrich Miller) is concerned though he is on very friendly terms with the congregation he has not regained his brotherly rights. In addition and finally special greetings to all especially Gerhart Zinn. I recall having received greetings from Emanuel Eckerlin, please return in kind when you have a chance.''

Beissel also sent a letter to Gerhart Zinn revealing more of the venom he felt toward the New River apostates. Addressed to Gerhart the letter says,

My best wishes to you all. I don't really know with what rational I should meet you or write to you since I don't know the reasons for your leaving the Christian church in such a shameful manner. Especially since the shameful action towards God, his people and his church have become known to others, especially since such shameful manner oppresses. The other gross injustices I will report later. When the miracle hand of the Supreme Being has done its interventions and has sought to save its honor instead of the evil over all mankind has been presumed to be steered so that they are obliged to apostatize and flee the land from which nobody has chased them; you set out and joined the same procession, just as though you were people who had the injustice and became partners in their sin which afterwards resulted in the desertion of the Lord.''

Beissel rambles on giving the impression he was much angrier with Zinn than with Miller. Finally he says that Zinn had gone "to live among swindlers and rogues" and if "you have stayed with us everything would have been all right." [1]

The Zinns had lost a family member, their neighbors had been murdered and carried to captivity and they lived among Shawnee destruction yet Conrad Beissel mentioned not these misfortunes, nor condoled with them. His thoughts concerned their insubordination to his authority. The Zinns soon left the Sabbatarians forever and joined the Moravians at Bethabara. Nor did Emmanuel Eckerlin and Henry Miller return to Ephrata. Eckerlin went to South Carolina and established a Sabbatarian colony. Miller was still in Anson County North Carolina in 1762. [2]

Whether these Sabbatarians were still at Mahanaim or Dunkard's Bottom when Major Lewis marched into the New River Valley in June is unknown. Lewis was leading fifty axmen with Captain Overton and Lieutenant Gunn as junior officers. He stopped long enough at Fort Frederick to relieve Captain John Smith sending him down to command Fort Vause. [3] Then he marched on toward the Cherokee country where he would be all summer engaged in building a fort for the Cherokees Overhill.

Meanwhile Sam Stalnaker who had been captured in the New-Holston raids the previous summer, escaped from the Shawnee villages and returned to Halifax County in June bringing bad news. While prisoner he had seen six French officers and 1,000 Indians come through the Ohio villages heading for Fort Duquesne. They intended to attack Virginia's frontier that summer.[4]

Stalnaker had no sooner gotten this news to Governor Dinwiddie than John Smith was attacked at Fort Vause. While Andrew Lewis had been marching a company away from the New River Valley a large French force was approaching it. Captain Picot De Belestre, commander at Fort Miami arrived at Fort Vause leading 205 Miamis, Shawnees and Oyatonons with 25 French Canadians. He reported he came by an unknown route into Virginia apparently along New River at some point. Later it was said these French had a camp "in the gap of a mountain beyond New River." Months before Shawnees disguised as Cherokees had come through Virginia spying. Guided by their intelligence De Belestre planned to penetrate deep into Virginia within 60 miles of Williamsburg to "Wanock" (Weynoke?).[5]

If successful this would have been a demoralizing stroke by the French deep into the interior of Virginia. But on June 25 at Fort Vause John Smith "made a valiant stand" according to George Washington. After a day-long seige Fort Vause fell, Smith's son was burned before his eyes and the fort was burned. Smith who had once commanded Fort Frederick on the New and the other captives were taken to Ohio.[5]

According to Smith, in the villages of the "Putsataways" whose language he could speak, he got their promise to help him take Fort Duquesne, if he escaped and brought back a body of Englishmen. After eleven months as prisoner which included being sent to France, capture enroute by the English and an audience with William Pitt in London, Smith returned to Virginia. He approached Washington about his plan to attack the Ohio villages apparently using the New--Kanawha system as a route of attack.[6] Nothing came of the plan.

News of the burning of Fort Vause reached the Moravians at Bethabara by July 2 when a Dunkard came and asked if several families might come to Bethabara for protection. The Moravians met in conference and decided they could if they built their own log cabins and brought their belongings and cows with them.[7]

In February Reverend James Maury had urged Virginia to build a chain of forts calling especially "for one at the Horseshoe on New

River."[8] In September Dinwiddie ordered a hundred pounds given Samuel Stalnaker to raise a company and "build a little stockade fort at Draper's Meadows." Stalnaker raised 15 men but it is uncertain whether he built the Draper's Meadows Fort.[9] This might well be the fort known as Bargar's Fort near present Shadow Lake, Blacksburg, Virginia.

FOOTNOTES—Chapter XIX

1. Conrad Beissel to John Miller, May 17, 1756 and to Gerhart Zinn, May 17, 1756, **Beissel Letterbook, The Historical Society of Pennsylvania**, pp. 80-83 129-130.

2. Wust, **Saint**, p. 57, 116.

3. Johnson, **Andrew Lewis**, pp. 57-62.

4. Dinwiddie to Governor Horatio Sharpe, June 21, 1756, **DP**, II, p. 447.

5. Johnson, **William Preston**, pp. 49-52 and Vaudreuil to the Ministry, September 19, 1756, Canada: Public Archives: Archives of Colonies, F3, v. 14, folio 343.

6. Isabel M. Calder, **Colonial Captivities, Marches and Journeys** (Port Washington: Kennikat Press, Inc., 1967) pp. 137-139.

7. Fries, **Moravians Records**, I, p. 169.

8. Maury to Philip Ludwell, Febraury 10, 1756, **VMHB**, v. 19, p. 297.

9. Dinwiddie to Colonel Clement Read and Captain Peter Hogg, September 8, 1756 and Dinwiddie to Andrew Lewis, December 17, 1756, **DP**, II, pp. 503-504, 567.

Chapter XX

Halifax and Bedford Defend the New

Since the valley of the New was deserted and some of its people refugees in Bedford and Halifax Counties in November 1756 Virginia ordered three forts built on the Halifax frontier. Indian arms would be stored at Bedford Courthouse and Captain Nash of Halifax and Captain Peter Hogg were ordered to rebuild Fort Vause, the fort nearest New River with a garrison. When Colonel Buchanan and others wrote from Bedford to Governor Dinwiddie about the terrible murders committed in Bedford, Dinwiddie answered, "I am sorry for so many murders and captives the enemy have made" but suggested abandoning Fort Vause!

Now when Shawnee war parties came into the New River Valley they found little so continued over the Blue Ridge into the Smith River settlements or those on the eastern slopes in Halifax and Bedford. By summer 1757 it was not only Shawnee war parties but Cherokees wandering and snooping. Colonel Clement Read, Colonel Peter Fontaine Jr., Colonel Matthew Talbot tried to arouse the people against these Indians and Captain Dillard was given command of another ranger company to protect the people.[1]

Colonel Fontaine had surveyed across the New in 1749 and knew the region and conditions. Now as County Lieutenant of Halifax he wrote in June 1757 that many who had escaped the Shawnee were in Halifax and remarked, "Such cruelties they practice upon our people that all had rather perish than be taken alive."[2]

No eye-witness descriptions exist of how the Shawnees behaved when attacking on New River but we do have these from Halifax where many New River people had taken refuge.

Shawnee warparties are described as leading as many as forty pack horses when they came through. They plundered houses, carried off women. "Bed ticks" were ripped open and feathers scattered all over the house and yard. Often they would catch a white man, strip him naked of his clothes, take his horse and leave him helpless wherever they happened to find him, just as they had James Patton at Draper's Meadows.[3]

Halifax men gave depositions in June 1758 about how the Shawnee prepared for war. The whites had followed the Shawnees trying to regain stolen horses. They found the horses tied to some bushes and the "Indians painting, some black, some red but mostly black." Old William Verdiman approached the Shawnees on foot calling to them, "We come in a brotherly manner to ask you for our horses."

"The Indians gave a kind of grunt," began stripping themselves, threw out the priming of their guns, fresh primed, and cocked. Some struck their tomahawks into trees. Angrily they yelled for the whites to fight, all the while edging around them pushing them into a half-circle. Most accounts of face to face encounters with the Shawnees tell of them manuevering their white opponents into a "half-moon" after they had stripped to fight.

While old man Verdiman and the others were pushed into a half-circle they kept their faces to the Shawnees, backing toward the trees, then sprinted for cover. The Indians threw their tomahawks, narrowly missing them. One would have hit old Verdiman but he parried it with an elder stick he had in his hand because he had no gun. From the trees the whites began firing and drove off the Indians. They scalped the ones they had killed and threw their bodies in the river.[4]

Because of the repeated raids by the Shawnees into Halifax and Bedford Captain Robert Wade's 35 rangers marched to the New August 12, 1758 from Fort Mayo, Halifax, present Martinsville. Some were Carolinia men, notably the Clapps, probably from Ludwig Clapp Mill on Big Almance Creek, Rowan County.[5] Wade's rangers were one of many companies coming from Halifax, Pittsylvania and Bedford into the New River Valley in the next decades, yet they are the only ones who left a detailed record of their activities while on New River written by John Echols.

"We crost Little River & went to Francis Eason's plantation where we continued that night. Our hunters brought a plentiful supply of venison. Next morning (August 15) we marched to Richard Rattlecliff's plantation on Meadow Creek where we continued that night."

The next day they sent out spies to search for the enemy while the company waited at Ratcliff's. Several days later the spies returned saying they had seen signs of Indians at Draper's Meadows where they had been catching horses that day. Then they had "gone on a straight course for Blackwater." They had missed the Indians, who were on their way to the Blackwater settlements in Bedford County, so decided to pursue the Indians the next day but were delayed because one man did not return. "Captain Wade said he and some men would go see what they could discover. The Capt., William Hall, Adam Hermon and two or three more went off and left the men under my command," writes Echols.

While the company waited five Indians appeared. The rangers surrounded them which startled them for "there was 20 guns presented at them."

Echols relates, "They said they were Cherokees. I made signs to them to show me their pass but they had none. They had with them 5 head of horse kind & skelps that appeared to be white men's."

The rangers believed them to be Shawnees. When Captain Wade returned he passed the "sentence of death upon them." However hunter Abraham Dunkleberry said they were Cherokees and urged Wade to let them go. This "displeased the Carolina men" who argued, "It is very hard for us to be compelled to range & then let the enemy have liberty to kill some of use before we dare kill them. At that rate we may all be kill'd and never kill an Indian, for if there is enough of them to oversome us, then they are enemy, but if we are too numerous for them they are friends."

"Captain Wade told them to be easy and after Dunkleberry was gone we would go after them and kill them," Echols continues. "Dunkleberry packt up his skins to go off & we marcht after the Indians. They were going toward New River."

The rangers followed and laid an ambush at "each ford". Echols and Wade were at the upper ford, another party at the lower. Wade's orders were to fire at them as they crossed the river. But the Indians separated so Wade "concluded to ly by awhile and let them all get together and then follow them and kill them."

"The Captain's order," said Echols, "was for 12 of the best men to follow them and kill them and the remainder of the company to go to the Dunker fort which was about half a mile below us."

From Echol's description it would appear that the following incidents happened around Fort Frederick near present Claytor Lake. After Wade took part of the company to Fort Frederick, Echols, Adam Hermon, Daniel Hermon, William Hall, Richard Hall, Jr., Tobias Clapp, Philip Clapp, Joseph Clapp, Benjamin Angel, David Currie, Richard Hines and James Lyon went after the Indians.

"We followed them and overtook them at a peach orchard," says Echols, "jest as they were leaving it — fired at them and followed them up till we killed 4 of them and wounded the other — we skalped them that we killed. . .followed the other — he bled very much — he went into the river and to an Island — but we could not find where he went out. . .we sercht the island till late in the afternoon & when we came to the Fort the Capt. and men were a handling the Indians goods."

Here at Fort Frederick Captain Wade had the men swear a false oath. "The Capt. told me we were all to be sworn," says Echols, "so we tarried there that night — next morning we packed up in order to march homeward, for signs of Indians was plenty & we had but little ammunition but before we left the fort we were sworn. . .not to tell that we ever heard them say that they were Cherokees."

Wade's company then left Fort Frederick, marched to Little River, thence to Blackwater, then to Robert Jones's plantation on the head of Pigg River then to Goblingtown and home to Fort Mayo.[6] We have no description of Fort Frederick on New River but we do have a fort description in the Fort Mayo vicinity. English traveler J.F.D. Smythe about twenty years later, writes,

"This was what is called a stockaded fort. . .it resembled a quadrangular polygon inclosed with large timber, and cuts of trees split in two, about twelve or sixteen feet high above the ground, standing erect, and about three or four feet in the earth. . .close together, with loop holes cut about four or five feet from the ground."

"There was also something like a bastion at each angle. . .and a log-house, musket proof, on each side of the gate. Within the area, nearly in the centre was a common house framed and boarded, filled in, to the height of six feet, with stones and clay on the inside, as a defence against small arms; it was covered only with shingles made of pine, which could be easily set on fire as well as every other part of the whole structure," Smythe relates, after he crept into the fort through a "wicker gate."[7]

The homeward March of Captain Wade's company appears to have followed the Warwick Road route either through Pine Spur Gap or Nearway Ridge. This route today would be from Basham to Terry's Fork to Check to Calloway.

As seen in this account of Wade's rangers the Indians had taken horses from Draper's Meadows then headed straight for the Blackwater, the route used by the company returning home. Several years later Indians using a similar route along New River to Little River over the crest of the Blue Ridge, raided settlements east of the mountains. They raided a German family, stole cooking utensils and captured wife and mother of Captain Henry Harman who overtook and recaptured the women.[8]

Captain Wade's escapade on New River did not escape official notice. Governor Fauquier wrote John Buchanan, Augusta's County-lieutenant, that he had heard of "Captain Wade's ugly scrap with the Indians. They are not to be molested while hunting," Fauquier ordered.[9] As a result of these scraps tension between the whites and Cherokees in western Virginia steadily increased.

FOOTNOTES—Chapter XX

1. **DP**, II, pp. 557-558, 589, 613, 620, 677-678, 685.

2. James Fontaine, **Memoirs of a Huguenot family**, ed. Ann Maury (New York: G.P. Putnam and Company, 1872) p. 357, 368, Randolph, **British Travelers**, p. 74: H.H. Hardesty, **Excerpts from Hardesty's Historical and Geographical Encyclopedia** (New York: H.H.Hardesty & Co., Publishers, 1884) p. 4.

3. Clement, **Pittsylvania**, pp. 83-84, 86 and **Virginia Gazette**, August 8, 1755.

4. Clement, **Pittsylvania**, pp. 80-85.

5. "Germans Naturalized in Rowan County, 1760", **North Carolina Genealogy**, Spring 1972, v. 18, no. 1, p. 2698, and Lefler, **Orange 1752**, pp. 15, 58.

6. John Echols, "Concerning a march that Captain Robert Wade took to the New River, August 12, 1758", **CVS**, I, p. 255.

7. Smyth, **Tour**, pp. 281-282.

8. Colonel William Harman, **CSA, Account of Harman family**, told to author by Harman family member.

9. Fauquier to Colonel John Buchanan, November 14, 1758, **WH**, 2 **QQ** p. 11.

Chapter XVI

Cherokee War

By 1760 war had broken out with the Cherokees from Virginia to Georgia. One New River family attacked on February 1 at Long Canes Creek, South Carolina was the Calhoun family who had fled New River in 1756. Many of the family were killed including Mrs. Patrick Calhoun, grandmother of John C. Calhoun. She had fled Shawnees on New River only to be murdered by Cherokees in South Carolina.

The beautiful spring brought wandering Indians along the New. Fearfully the people sent Mr. Hamilton with a petition to Williamsburg asking the colony to protect them. Although the Cherokee uprising in South Carolina was well-known Governor Fauquier considered their fear "ill-grounded."

"It is a shame," said he, "for men to talk of deserting a country and their growing crops because 10 or 11 Indians have been seen."[1]

Fort Loudoun on the Tennessee was beseiged and Colonel William Byrd III was placed in command of an army sent by way of New River to its relief. All summer Byrd gathered supplies at Fort Lewis (Salem, Roanoke County). As he started for New River he received news that his estranged wife had killed herself by pulling a wardrobe upon herself. Under the shadow of personal tragedy Byrd led his troops on to New River rendezvousing at Dunkard's Bottom where his commissary was located. Merchants hoping to make money from the campaign brought their goods there. Joseph Ray and William Chandler of Bedford agreed for Chandler to deliver 100 pounds of goods to Ray which he would sell at 6% profit to Byrd's troops. The goods were not delivered so Ray could not supply Colonel Blagg's company as promised.[2] John Hamilton was more successful in trading at his Dunkard's Bottom Store selling to Colonel John Smith, Lieutenant Hansley, John Lucas, John Cotrel, Stamp Evins, Richard Dodd, Thomas Diggs and Richard Newport.[3]

Byrd's army crossed the "Great Kanawha" as he called New River on September 3 where he says, "I met with four men just starved to death, who had made their escape through the Indians from Fort Loudoun. They informed me that the garrison was in the utmost distress subsisting on four ounces of horse flesh a day."

Byrd immediately sent Major Andrew Lewis with 300 active fellows and thirty days provisions to scout about Fort Loudoun and save as many people as possible."

But Byrd was too late. As he waited in "Camp 30 miles to the west of Kanawha," Sayer's Mill (Wythe County), the Fort Loudoun garrison was massacred. Captain Demere, the commmandant, had been "scalped alive, made to run about bareheaded for the diversion of the Indians; then they chopp'd off his legs and arms and left him to himself."

Soon Andrew Lewis returned bringing along "The Little Carpenter", who had smuggled to safety John Stuart, later British Indian agent for the Southern colonies, Stuart's servant, an old doctor, two squaws and three other Indians. Byrd immediately wrote the Cherokees the following:

Camp on the Kanawha, 16 September 1760

To the Standing-Turkey, Ocunnastotah, and the Rest of the Headwarriors of the Cherokee Nation

My good brother the Little-Carpenter, has delivered me Capt. Stuart and three others of my countrymen; who have informed me of your treacherous behavior to the garrison of Fort Loudoun, and have told me of the many English prisoners now in your nation, which I am determined to chastise you for, unless you immediately deliver them all up to me; for Virginians and Carolinians are the same people. As you know I always wished your nation well and never told you a lie in all my talks with you. I will now tell you my situation; and what you may expect from me, if you persist in your own obstinacy to bring destruction on yourselves, your women and children. I am now encamped on the waters of Kanawha with a powerful army of Virginians; and can have as many more men as I please; and as many Indians as I want, from the Ohio and Sir William Johnson, now we have drove the French out of Canada and their forts to the Northward. I am building forts all the way, and propose soon to be in your nation; when I will not leave one Indian alive, one town standing, or one grain of corn, in all your country, if I do not find all the white people well when I go there. I tell you this truth, because I am not afraid of you; and wish for nothing more than to fight with you, if you still desire war; for my men have beat all the Indians to the Northward, and are not to be frightened by your yells. But, as I once loved you like my brothers and still wish to see you happy, hear what I have to say to you, and think on your own miserable situation. King George's armies have drove the French from the Northern parts of America, and the Indians there are now begging for peace. We have nothing to do now, but drive the French from the Southward. Then what will become of you? Who will supply you with goods to keep yourselves and your families warm? Who will let you have ammunition to kill deer, or knives, or salt, or any necessaries of life? Our people know the way into your nation: They are as numerous as the fish in the sea; and will go every fall into your towns, and kill you if they find you; and if they cannot find you (because you run away) they will destroy your corn in your granaries, and will build forts in your hunting grounds: and at last drive you into the South-Sea. Think of these things, Cherokees, and think of all my straight talks, and believe what I now say; for, 'tis for your own good. Call in all your warriors directly; come down, and talk with me, and bring me in your prisoners; and you shall be safe and go home when you please; and I will be your friend and brother again; and will procure you a good peace. Tom will tell you how I used him; and the Little-Carpenter will be with you as soon as he has refreshed himself with me; and they will all tell you what I say is true. If you have a mind for a peace, come in directly; and depend upon it, I will not detain you, but let you go when you have a mind: You shall meet with good usage, and not a hair of your heads shall be hurt, for I do not want to destroy your people: Send in a runner before you, and the path shall be clear. Be sure to have a good interpreter, that he may tell you all I say: I would send you Dick Smith (Richard Smith, interpreter) but I do not know how you would use him.

Given under my hand, at the camp of the waters of Kanawa, September the 16th, 1760

William Byrd, commanding an army of Virginians.

P.S. If you refuse my offer now, my guns shall talk of war, and not of peace.[4]

While Byrd waited for an answer from the Cherokees he continued work on the fort he had begun called Fort Chiswell. Sometimes in old records this name is written Chissel, the way it was pronounced. Located on the "Great Road" it was described as a "big fort" by Louis Philippe, Duke of Orleans, later King of France, when he visited the New River valley in 1797. Partially torn down when the Duke saw it, later it was described as without a stockade, containing ten double log cabins with loop holes, with a stone chimney to each two cabins, a mess hall, stables, powder mill, smith and wagon shops.[5]

Fort Chiswell was originally constructed as headquarters for Byrd's army but later was looked upon as protection for the Lead Mines down on the river some miles away.

Thomas Jefferson gives the best contemporary description of these New River mines. He locates them "opposite to the mouth of Cripple Creek."[6] During the French war Chiswell had done little on the mines but had managed to enter a partnership with Governor Fauquier; with his own son-in-law John Robinson, Speaker of the House of Burgesses and Treasurer of Virginia and with William Byrd III.

Just months before Byrd's army arrived on the New, on May 6, the Council granted Chiswell permission to survey 1,000 acres on both sides of New River beside Humberston Lyon. Chiswell was now in charge of getting arms for Byrd's army and probably returned to New River at this time. Chiswell's family were living in Williamsburg but he was spending much time on the New so built himself a clapboard house, the first of its kind in Wythe County, which stood well into the 1800's.[7]

The partners had much difficulty getting the mines started. Byrd's mother wrote, "I long to hear some good tidings of the led mine."[8] When they were ready to start they found Dr. Thomas Walker and the Loyal Company had a prior claim so they had to pay him two thousand pounds to clear title. Chiswell had to take ore samples to England where the assays did prove the worth of New River lead. Miners and materials had to be gathered to bring to Virginia. Then Governor Fauquier dropped out of the partnership doubting, he said, "lead would bear the expense of so long a land carriage as is necessary to bring it to market. The mine is certainly rich in Lead and contains...a considerable quantity of silver, but...not sufficient...to extract." Upon Fauquier's default John Robinson had to furnish more than his agreed share of money leading to bankruptcy.[9]

Meanwhile Byrd waited at Fort Chiswell until November 3. The Little Carpenter returned with ten of Captain Demere's men and said Cherokees were willing to accept Byrd's plans. Virginia told him he had no authority to negotiate since it was an inter-colonial affair to be handled by the British regular army. As news of the Fort Loudoun massacre spread across Virginia public opinion was aroused against Byrd. Because of this and because his hands were tied in negotiating with the Cherokees, he resigned his command and left New River bound for Philadelphia to take a new wife.[10]

As Byrd had waited at Camp Sayers he was able to procure the release of Katherine Bingamin captured when the Bingamins were attacked in 1755. Most of the family were killed but Katherine was captured losing "all she had when carried into captivity." Byrd paid for her release and Katherine petitioned the House of Burgesses to repay Byrd which they did.[11]

In the wake of Byrd's army people began to drift back into the New River Valley. However as the French war wound to a close the government in London wrote Governor Fauquier that certain western lands must be left to the Indians. Fauquier questioned if they meant to include the "lands on Green Bryar, New River or Kanawha River as lands not to be patented. These rivers have been tolerably seated for sometime. The settlers abandoned their plantations," he noted, "but are now returning and applying for new patents."[12]

After Byrd resigned Major Andrew Lewis, Captains Thomas Bullitt and William Fleming were stationed at Fort Chiswell throughout the winter. Lewis, senior officer, was allowed three meals a day while Bullitt and Fleming got along with one.[13]

During this winter of 1760-61 Andrew Lewis surveyed around the Lead Mines for Colonel Chiswell. As early as February 7 Captain Bullitt wrote from Fort Chiswell that Cherokees bringing in prisoners were expected soon. John Chiswell and Dr. Thomas Walker were appointed to go commissioners to Fort Chiswell to purchase the prisoners.[14] By April 13 a Cherokee peace party of two hundred with prisoners camped near Fort Chiswell and during the night they were attacked by what was presumed to be northern Indians. Six Cherokees were killed and many wounded. The next day the warriors left fifty women and children to Andrew Lewis's care while they went scouting to find their assailants.[15]

Shortly after this William Byrd was again commissioned to lead another expedition through New River Valley to punish the Cherokees for the Fort Loudoun massacre. He was to join Colonel James Grant's British regulars now crossing Carolina into Cherokee territory. Due to poor communication Byrd knew nothing of Grant's activities. Grant's well-equipped, well-fed army bounded through South Carolina trouncing the Cherokees and devastating their villages before Byrd ever marched.

Unawares of what Grant had done Byrd gathered a little army of about seven hundred many of whom deserted for lack of food. Governor Fauquier and General Amherst were slow to aid Byrd with supplies. Delayed by lack of food, arms, powder, wagons and tents, Byrd sent all over Virginia on his own credit buying supplies. Dunkard's Bottom on the New was again the rendezvous point for supplies.[16]

This same year William Ingles got a license to operate a ferry "over New River to the opposite shore, the price of a man three pence and for a horse the same."[17] Ingles' Ferry kept busy, though records are very sparse for this campaign telling us only a few who helped him at New River. John Milton worked as a wagon driver all summer, Samuel Cowdon and company hired Thomas Davis to ferry twelve wagons twice at New River at five shillings nine pence per crossing. James Leister ferried horses over the New. These supply wagons gathered at Dunkard's Bottom may have come into New River Valley by way of the Warwick Road. The road from Ingles Ferry to Fort Vause thence into Roanoke Valley, the modern route 11, was not petitioned for until 1767.[18]

Byrd arrived with his second army for the second time on New River on June 30, 1761. From Camp at Fort Chiswell, July 1, he wrote General Jeffery Amherst, "I have done everything in my power to forward this expedition."

"I arrived yesterday at this our most advanced post, without the least assistance from the contractors, having myself taken the trouble to engage all the provisions & carriages for the march & to forward up the necessary stores and tools. We are now advanced three hundred miles from Winchester," Byrd reported.

"We have about a months provision with us, which will enable me to proceed with five hundred men to Stalnaker's where I must remain till a magazeen can be formed," he wrote.

"I propose to leave Lt. Col. Stephen here with the remainder of the regiment to escort the flour & cattle to that place, when it comes up."

Regarding supply problems he wrote, "Notwithstanding the orders your Excellency & General Monckton were pleas'd to give the contractors to supply me, it was the 10th of June before they agreed with Doctor Walker at Philadelphia to act for them. I never saw one of their commissarys till the day before yesterday."

Regarding enlistments he wrote, "I inclose Sir a return of the regiment & am sorry to tell you we have had very little success in recruiting."[19]

In this letter which Byrd wrote from New River we see capsulized the extent of his problems. Certainly he deserves better press than history has given him.

By July 9 Byrd wrote General Monckton from Fort Chiswell that he had only 650 men fit for duty, 250 miles yet to march, roads to cut, posts to garrison, escorts to furnish.

The North Carolina regiment was still recruiting and the Virginia militia would not come up to the fort though they had been ordered to do so.

"When I reach the Cherokee Nation I shall have five times my number to engage," said Byrd. However he would go ahead with 500 men to the Holston. He dispatched this letter to Monckton by Adam Hoops the commissary from Philadelphia.[20]

By July 10 Byrd had marched from Fort Chiswell and by July 19 was at Sam Stalnaker's outpost on Holston at present Chilhowie. Here he learned that Grant's army had attacked the Lower Cherokees in South Carolina which made his job more difficult since refugee Cherokees fleeing from Grant would re-enforce the Overhill Cherokees.

Collett's 1770 Map of North Carolina showing New River
(Photo Courtesy of Virginia Polytechnic and State University)

After cutting themselves a road known as the "Island Road" Byrd's force got to the Great Island of the Holston where they built Fort Robinson at the site of present Kingsport. Byrd's mother writing him mentions "the sad situation of your encampment," "dews that fall like rain" and "musquetas and stinging gnats. 'Tis no wonder that your army are so sickly." Byrd. harassed beyond endurance, resigned, August 1, 1761, turned over command to Adam Stephen and went to Philadelphia to see his sick wife.[21]

Meanwhile as late as August 10 North Carolina's force of 500 men were still at Fort Dobbs waiting for orders to march to join Byrd. Finally they marched through the Moravian settlement where it was reported, "Four hundred soldiers arrived, on their way to New River and the Cherokee. They camped several days by the mill. Some of these troops mutinied not wanting to be marched out of Carolina. They were punished but luckily none put to death."

"We furnished much meal to the troops on New River, 500 men on horseback carried it across the Blue Mountains," said the Moravians.[22]

These troops, commanded by Colonel Hugh Waddell, among whom was Daniel Boone, marched to the Holston in September. Adam Stephen reported from Fort Chiswell that Waddell had 374 men and 52 Indians armed with 50 stands of arms. He told Waddell to hurry to his men as fast as they were armed. Leaving a serjeant and 25 men guarding Fort Chiswell and New River "crossing" Stephen advanced to the Holston complaining, "The first of July Colonel Grant with 3600 troops had been within 100 miles of Chota. Why was not peace then made?" Waddell and Stephen joined forces at the Great Island and accomplished little except building Fort Robinson and the "Island Road" joining the New with the Holston. Peace was eventually made with the Cherokees and for a long time Waddell loudly criticized Byrd for wasting time building roads and blockhouses.[23] The one thing this dismal attempt against the Cherokees did was to provide military experience for men later to fight in the Revolution. Robert Howe commanded some of the Carolinians so for a brief moment in time three future generals of the American Continental Army, Robert Howe, Andrew Lewis and Adam Stephen, shared in a military campaign.[24]

London was already taking action that would push the colonists, particularly on the frontier, into rebellion. Just as Byrd's army was disbanding and colonists were struggling back to their New River homes, London sent plans to Virginia that all trans-Allegheny land was eventually to be given to the Indians, the same Indians that had done so much to defeat the English colonists.

Before Christmas Governor Fauquier answered London, "I immediately consulted His Majesty's Council in relation to the claims of the Indians on New or Wood's River."

"Consideration of the question was postponed till General Court in October," Fauquier reported.[25] This would give New River colonists another year to settle back in their homes.

After peace was made with the Cherokees in the fall of 1761 life began to return to normal on New River. The farmer returned to the harvest and the hunters to the trails. John Chiswell finally had the lead mine producing for the Moravians report, "This year work was begun in a lead and silver mine on New River about 80 miles from here."

According to Thomas Jefferson, "The metal is mixed. . .with earth and rock, which requires the force of gunpowder to open it and is accompanied with a portion of silver." The lead yielded was "from fifty to eighty pounds of pure metal from one hundred pounds of washed ore. The veins are sometimes flattering, at others they disappear suddenly and totally.[26]

Fort Chiswell was becoming a hub of activity. The Cherokees wanted it rather than Stalnaker's as the place to trade. In April Outacite, Austenaco and Uschesees, The Great Hunter, passed with Lieutenant Henry Timberlake on their way to London to see King George who snubbed them. Their landlord Caccantropos charged admission to see them undressing, Sir Joshua Reynolds painted them and Oliver Goldsmith wrote about them in his **Animated Nature.** [27]

War left unpleasantness in its wake, one being a band of robbers operating in the mountains behind the Yadkin settlements between them and New River. The Moravians reported in August 1762 that much was being heard about these robbers who had built a stockaded fort beneath a cliff in the mountains and from there sallied forth to rob and plunder. Whether New River visitors to Bethabara were attacked we know not but on July 19 the Moravians reported, "The Virginia Colonel Chiswell Inspector and Partner of the mine on New River, came from there with a small company to see our settlement, for they get their bread or meal from here."[28]

When a young girl was kidnapped by the robbers North Carolina raised companies to go against them. Daniel Boone commanded one company. The fort was stormed, the robbers captured and taken to Salisbury jail. But this would not be the last that would be heard of robbers in the mountains between the New and Yadkin. The upper

New folk would yet be terrorized by the gang of "Plundering Sam" Brown alias Martin.

Another problem this spring of 1762 was the hunger among the people. Bethabara Moravians came up to New River to see about their land and upon returning "had much to say about the scarcity of food" along the New.[29]

FOOTNOTES—Chapter XXI

1. Milling, **Red Carolinians**, p. 299 and **FP**, I, pp. 381-382.

2. Tingling, **Three Byrds**, II, p. 702 and **CS**, I, pp. 343, 493.

3. **CS**, I, p. 490.

4. Tingling, **Three Byrds**, II, pp. 703-705. Byrd to Capt. James Abercromby, Jr., Sept. 16, 1760 and **FP**, I, p. 413. William Byrd to the Cherokees.

5. Louis-Philippe, King of France, **Diary of My Travels in America** (New York: Delacorte Press, 1977) hereafter cited as Duke of Orleans, **Journal** p. 52 and Colonel Joseph Kent Gordon, Letter to Goodridge Wilson, Southwest Corner **The Roanoke Times**.

6. Thomas Jefferson, "Notes on Virginia" (written 1781, published 1784) in Albert E. Bergh, **The Writings of Thomas Jefferson** (Washington: The Thomas Jefferson Memorial Association, 1903) hereafter cited as Jefferson Notes, v. II, p. 33.

7. **VEJ**, v. 6, pp. 158, 166; Mays, **Pendleton Papers**, II, p. 706, **FP**, II, p. 1015, p. 25.

8. Maria Byrd to William Byrd III, July 2, 1761, Tingling, **Three Byrds**, II, p. 738, **FP**, II, p. 1015.

9. John D. Mays, **Edmund Pendleton, 1721-1803** (Cambridge: Harvard University Press, 1952) hereafter cited as Mays, **Edmund Pendleton**, v. I, p. 203 from Lidderdale v. Robinson's Administrators and Robinson's Adm. v. Byrd. Ended Files 136-137 U.S. District Court, Richmond also U.S. Circuit Court Record Book 20, pp. 274-464.

10. Johnson, **Andrew Lewis**, pp. 111-113.

11. F.B. Kegley, "Shot Tower at Jackson's Ferry," **Journal of the Roanoke Historical Society**, v. 3, p. 2 and HJ, 1758-1761, p. 239.

12. Fauquier to the Board of Trade, December 6, 1760, **HJ**, 1758-1761, p. 290, in **FP**, I, p. 439.

13. Rations for Fort Chiswell Officers, 1760-61, **Fleming Papers**, Z-12-1, **WL**.

14. **VEJ**, v. 6, pp. 182, 189, **FP**, II, p. 472.

15. **Ibid.**, v. 6, p. 184 and Colonel Adam Stephen to Colonel Henry Bouquet May 12, 1761, **The Bouquet Papers** (Pennsylvania Historical Commission) Series 21634, p. 247.

16. **VEJ**, v. 6, p. 186, 189 and Tingling, **Three Byrds**, II, p. 609.

17. Hening, **Statutes**, VII, p. 588.

18. **CS**, I, pp. 132, 327, and 477.

19. Colonel William Byrd III to General Jeffery Amherst, July 1, 1761, Tingling, **Three Byrds**, II, pp. 741-742.

20. Colonel William Byrd III to General Robert Monckton, July 9, 1761, Tingling, **Three Byrds**, pp. 745-747.

21. Tingling, **Three Byrds**, II, pp. 751-752, 761.

22. Fries, **Moravian Records**, I, pp. 234, 249.

23. **FP**, II, p. 569. Stephen to Governor Fauquier, September 7, 1761. Reuben G. Thwaites, **Daniel Boone**, Williamstown, Massachusetts: Corner House Publishers, 1977 hereafter cited as Thwaites, Boone., pp. 49-50.

24. Andrew Lewis to George Washington, January 18, 1776, Washington Papers, UVA.

25. Fauquier to the Board of Trade, December 1761, HJ, 1758-1761, p. 295.

26. Fries, Moravian Records, I, p. 234 and Jefferson, Notes on Virginia, v. 2, p. 33.

27. Randolph, British Travelers, pp. 143-144. Milling, Red Carolinians, pp. 307-308 an v. 6, p. 215.

28. Fries, Moravian Records, I, p. 249 and Thwaites, Boone, p. 62.

29. Ibid. and Johnson, William Preston, p. 240; Deposition Captian John Cox, July 16, 1779 in Betty-Lou Fields and Jene Hughes, ed. Grayson County: A History in Words and Pictures (Independence, Virginia: 1976) p. 39 and Fries, Moravian Records, I, p. 246.

Old building at Fort Chiswell burned in 1901
(Photo courtesy Dr. W.R. Chitwood)

Chapter XVII

The Long Hunters

Even during the war with the Cherokees the men that would be known as Long Hunters were already scouting the wilderness along the upper New and west of it. Some had lived on the New since the 1740's never leaving during the French or Cherokee wars. When peace reigned again they continued their hunts. About 1760 Daniel Boone left his home on the Yadkin and along with other hunters wandered in the wilderness of western North Carolina where the New heads. Most are unkown but the names Meat Camp Creek, Butcher's Creek and Trapper's Meadow, attest to their presence.

How far west the Long Hunters had gone along the New River and beyond at this time is unknown. It is claimed that the Harmans had built a hunter's cabin on John's Creek of Levisa River about 1755. This is in present Johnson County, Kentucky, far west of New River.[1]

These hunters came principally from the upper counties of North Carolina or Yadkin country and from Halifax and Bedford in Virginia. Daniel Boone, Bazel Boren, Obadiah Terrell and William Blevins were Yadkin men. Bazel Boren and Obadiah Terrell were neighbors in Orange County, North Carolina on North Hico Creek and neighbors of Christopher Gist at Mulberry Fields. The Judds, Wards, Wallens, Blevins, and Coxes were from Halifax or Pittsylvania County. The Harmans, Packs, Scaggs, Lyons, Pitmans, Drakes and Aldridges lived on middle New River. The first three families were there in the 1740's. Henry Scaggs, leader of the New River group, "a man of very great truth and high sense of honor, enterprising and fearless" was physically a six-footer dark-skinned and bony.[2] James Aldridge was "dark haired, heavily built, stoop-shouldered but with a spritely mind."

The Wallens, Blevins, Coxes and others lived as squatters in western Pittsylvania (later Henry County) on land owned by speculators. 1767 Pittsylvania County tithables, later New River hunters were, John Ward, Joseph, Thomas and Elisha Wallen, John Cox, Rowland and Nathaniel Judd, Thomas, Charles, Richard Calloway, Charles Scaggs and the Elkins brothers, Ralph, Jesse, Richard and Nathaniel.[3]

The Wallens (Walling, Walden) lived on Smith River at the "Round-About" at present Martinsville. William Blevins, originally from the Yadkin but in Pittsylvania in 1767 with Dan and Peter Blevins, was Elisha Wallen's son-in-law. Elisha Wallen, leader of the Smith River hunters, reportedly helped Byrd build Fort Chiswell in 1761 as well as the Long Island Fort. Elisha is described by Major John Redd as "a dark-skinned, very course featured man," weighing about 180 pounds and having "an ordinary intellect."[4]

John Wallen (probably Elisha's brother) and brother-in-law Lewis Hale had come from Bedford to the New River before 1760 where they learned that the Indians were restless so Hale stayed on the New while Wallen continued to Wallen (Walden) Ridge where he was killed. Learning of Wallen's fate Hale decided to stay on New River starting "Hale's Settlement" on Grayson's Elk Creek.[5]

The Long Hunter who is described as "the most venturesome" going alone on hunts was William Carr from Albemarle County, Virginia. An Albemarle long hunter was also a mulatto.[6]

The 1761 Long Hunt was led by Elisha Wallen, Henry Scaggs and William Blevins accompanied by Charles Cox, Jack Blevins, William Newman, William Pitman, Uriah Stone, Michael Stoner, James Harrod, William Carr and others. They crossed the Blue Ridge at Flour Gap, New River at Jones's Ford and Iron Mountain at Blue Spring Gap. In Powell's Valley they were at Wallen's Creek, Scagg's Ridge, Newman's Ridge. In Tennessee they established "The Blevins Settlement" in present Sullivan County.[7]

In 1764 Daniel Boone and Sam Calloway went into the Cumberland area to hunt and sometimes hunted with Captain William Bean.[8]

The Long Hunters gathered along New River and later at the head of Holston near present Chilhowie about the last of September. Each man was equipped with two horses, traps, a large supply of powder and lead, a small hand vise, bellows, files and screw plates for fixing guns. They set off in groups of two or three since small parties were less likely to excite the Indians and were also more succussful in capturing game. A good Long Hunter could bring back skins worth nearly seventeen hundred pounds, an immense sum. They departed the first of October and returned the first of April.[9]

We question, "What did the Long Hunters do with their pelts? Who bought them?" By 1769 the William Donald Trading Company had a store in Prince Edward County where they paid various New River hunters one pound sixteen shillings three pence for four beaver fur, for sixteen beaver skins fifteen pounds and for one hundred and four deerskins, twenty six pounds thirteen shillings.[10] Also the Bethabara Moravians bought skins. On February 9, 1765 there arrived at Bethabara two hunters out of Virginia named Blevins, bringing 1600 pounds of skins and furs. Two weeks later two Harmans brought into Bethabara eighty pounds of deerskins. The Moravians said the Harmans "had been into the Shawnee country this time but seen nothing of the Indians." These skins went on to Charleston.[11]

The Harmans had a station camp on the Levisa River definitely in Shawnee country. A station camp usually was a three-sided structure of poles covered with puncheon or bark. The front was open with a fire and a puncheon floor sloped toward the back so snow would melt and drain out.[12]

In 1767 Benjamin Cutbirth (pronounced Cutbaird), married to Daniel Boone's niece Elizabeth Wilcoxen, went with John Baker, John Ward and John Stewart across the Blue Ridge in North Carolina to the Mississippi. In autumn 1767 Daniel and William Hill left the Yadkin, climbed the Blue Ridge, crossed New River and went into the Holston Valley thence to the Prestonburg, Kentucky area. The same year Michael Stoner (George Michael Holsteiner) with Isaac Bledsoe, Kaspar Mansker, John Montgomery and Joseph Drake were on the Cumberland River and had a station camp in middle Tennessee. Several of these were New River men. Cotterill in his "Kentucky in 1774" says Boone and Stoner, close associates, had first met on New River.[13]

In May 1769 Boone, John Finley, Joseph Holden, James Mooney, William Cooley, crossed Iron Mountain into Cumberland Gap to present Estill County, Kentucky. It is said they went by Three Forks of New River (present Boone) over the mountains into Kentucky. On the Boone-Finley trip the hunters were gone so long that Squire Boone set out to find them. He was joined on New River by Alexander Neely, possibly at Fort Chiswell where Neely was a tailor. Upon finding Daniel they continued with him until John Stewart was lost. Neely returned to Fort Chiswell.[14]

On June 2, 1769 twenty men from New River, Rockbridge County, Virginia and North Carolina, met on New River eight miles from Fort Chiswell on Reed Creek. Kaspar Mansker, Bazel Boren, Elisha Wallen, Obadiah Terrell, John Raines, Abraham and Isaac

Bledsoe, Joseph and John Baker, Joseph Drake, Uriah Stone, Henry Smith, Ned Cowan, Robert Crockett, William Carr, James Dysart, Thomas Kilgore, Jacob Harman, William Crabtree, James Aldridge, Thomas Gordon, Humphrey Hogan and Castleton Brooks were in the party. Known as the "wanderingest party" they went through Cumberland Gap to Wayne County, Kentucky and Summer County, Tennessee, naming Bledsoe's Lick and Mansker's Lick. Some returned to New River for supplies but others went to the Ozarks finally returning to New River through Georgia and the Carolinas. Most were home by spring 1770.

This was possibly the Long Hunt most publicized. Most of the hunters were from the New River settlements in Virginia. John Raines had come from Culpepper County to the New and lived to be ninety-one on the Cumberland. The Bledsoes were from Culpepper. Abraham was one of Preston's Rangers in 1755. Anthony Bledsoe was his son and a surveyor on New River in 1765. Joseph Drake lived near Buchanan's Anchor and Hope Plantation on Reed Creek. He married Margaret Buchanan and went to Kentucky in 1777. William Crabtree born in Baltimore County, Maryland in 1748 married Hannah Lyon, sister of Humberston Lyon (Jr.?) and later Katherine Starn, both New River girls.

In the fall of 1770 Joseph Drake, Henry and Charles Scaggs, some of Stone's party with forty hunters from the New and Holston headed for Kentucky to Knob Licks, where they saw thousands of buffalo and elk licking the earth. After a winter's labor when their large cache of skins was robbed by Cherokees, one of them carved on a tree "1500 skins gone to ruination." The initials of each member of the party was signed beneath. Staying on to get more skins, they returned home after two years absence and in Powell's Valley Northwest Indians attacked and stole all their skins again. They returned home completely empty-handed.[15]

FOOTNOTES—Chapter XXII

1. Henderson, Old Southwest, p. 132 and Connelley, Harman's Station, p. 27.

2. Redd, Reminiscences, v. 6, pp. 338-340 and v. 7, p. 249, 250; Arnow, Seedtime, p. 160; Kerry R. Boren, The Boren Family of Southwest Virginia, Historical Sketches of Southwest Virginia Publications hereafter cited as Boren Family no. 10, p. 39; Emory Hamilton, The Long Hunters, manuscript hereafter cited as Hamilton, Long Hunters, quoting letter of Col. William Martin to Lyman Draper July 7, 1842.

3. "Tithables of Pittsylvania, 1767," VMHB, v. 24, pp. 180-192; Hayes, Wilkes, pp. 420-424 and Mary Kegley, New River Tithables, 1770-1773 (Roanoke, Virginia: Copy Cat, 1972) pp. 6, 19.

4. Redd, Reminiscences, v. 6 pp. 338-340 and v. 7, pp. 249-250.

5. Benjamin F. Nuckolls, Pioneer Settlers of Grayson County Virginia (Baltimore: Genealogical Publishing Company, Inc., 1975) hereafter cited as Nuckolls, Grayson Pioneers, pp. 106-108, 111.

6. Redd, Reminiscences, v. 6, p. 339 and v. 7. p. 249.

7. Ibid. pp. 338-340; Haywood, Tennessee p. 45; Henderson, Old Southwest, p. 119; and Hamilton, Long Hunters.

8. Hayes, Wilkes, p. 17.

9. VMHB, v. 7, pp. 248-249.

10. Humberston Lyon, Jr., Account with William Donald Company, July 31, 1769, Fincastle County Records, no. 13, Montgomery County Courthouse, Christiansburg, Va.

11. Fries, Moravian Records, I, pp. 300-301, 304.

12. Hamilton, Long Hunters, pp. 69, 73, 78-81.

13. Thwaites, Boone, p. 90 and The Filson Club, Quarterly, I, p. 24.

14. Boren Family and Thwaites, Boone, p. 90.

15. Hamilton, Long Hunters, quoting Lyon's Will, Washington County, Virginia, 1784 Henderson, Old Southwest, pp. 123; Thwaites, Boone, p. 92-93. "The Bledsoe Family of Virginia and Tennessee, "The Historical Society of Washington County, Publications, II, no. 2 p. 3.

Chapter XVIII

Pontiac's War

In January 1763 Governor Fauquier reported, "The proprietors of the lead mines are now beginning to work it." As the world lay frozen on February 6, the Moravians noted, "There was a company here from New River where many are settling." And again in March, "Mr. Terry from New River and several other gentlemen were here. The whole day there was a heavy storm." The Samuel Cecils, another family settling at this time bought Jacob Harman's Neck Creek place where Moravian missionaries had preached in 1749.[1]

Later in March Dr. Thomas Walker asked the Virginia Council for permission to make another exploring trip into the western country to the Great Island of the Holston. He wanted to go down New River to the Ohio, down the Ohio to the Tennessee then up it to the Great Island. The Council gave him permission to do so not knowing that war fire was ready to ignite the western country.

The French and Indian war was over. France had surrendered her claim to all of North America and the French had sailed back to France leaving their defeated and disgruntled Indian allies. Where once the blue and white fleur-de-lis had fluttered from Canada to Florida the Union Jack now rippled. The French could sail away but the English were still on the land of the red man. Now came to the fore a great chieftain who believed he could rid the land of the English forever. Pontiac, chieftain of the combined Chippewa, Potowotomi and Ottawa tribes in the Great Lakes region, whose influence extended the length of the Mississippi, believed now was the time to drive the English into the sea. He organized the greatest confederacy of Indian tribes in American history involving all tribes in the Mississippi Valley. In early summer he unleashed his warriors, arranging for each tribe to attack the nearest English fort. Then they would wipe out the surrounding settlements. The earliest raids against Virginia were made on the Greenbrier tributary of the New.

The escape of Mrs. Hannah Dennis from the Ohio villages back down the New is believed to have initiated the attacks on Greenbrier. Hannah was an outstanding woman among the Shawnee. She had been captured on Purgatory Creek of James River near present Buchanan, Virginia, in July 1757. The Shawnees killed her husband, Joseph, and child, and took Hannah to the Ohio. In order to survive in the Shawnee towns she became one of them, painting herself, learning their language and attending the sick. Recognizing their superstitious nature, she declared herself a prophetess, pretending to practice witchcraft. In 1763 she escaped but badly cut her foot so she could not run. In desperation she hid in a hollow sycamore. After the Indians gave up the pursuit she nursed her foot for three days before starting for home. She crossed the Ohio at the mouth of the Kanawha on a log of driftwood. Traveling only at night she followed New River subsisting on roots, herbs, green grapes, wild cherries and river muscles. Exhausted she got as far as the Greenbrier River where she was found by Thomas Athol and others from the Clendennin settlement, She had been twenty days on the journey alone.[3]

Many people thought it was Shawnees in revenge for the escape of Hannah Dennis that soon struck the Greenbrier and Muddy Creek settlements. This raid led by Cornstalk marked the beginning of Pontiac's War in western Virginia.

Word of this June raid rapidly spread through the New River settlements. By June 30 the Bethabara Moravians reported, "All settlers on Holston's River have fled. On New River the settlers are building forts."[4]

The forts known to be built on New River at this time, other than Fort Chiswell and the Dunkard's Bottom Fort, were Fort Hope built by William Ingles near Ingles Ferry; Fort Lookout, an unknown site and Harman's Fort, probably at Gunpowder Springs (Eggleston). David Robinson commanded at Fort Lookout and William Thompson's "Springfield fort at Back Creek." Alexander Sayers rotated his militia between Fort Chiswell and Springfield.

As in 1755 many were afraid to rely on forts and fled. William Preston reported, "All the valleys of Roanoke River and along the waters of the Mississippi are depopulated, except Captain English (Ingles) with a few families on New River, who have built a fort, among whom are Mr. Thompson and his family alone remaining."

"They intend," continued Preston, "to make a stand until some assistance be sent. Seventy-five of the Bedford militia went out in order to pursue the enemy but I hear the officers and part of the men are gone home and the rest gone to Reed Creek to help in the family of James Davies and two or three other families that dare not venture to travel."[5]

Again as in 1755 New River people fled toward Carolina and Bethabara. On July 25 the Moravians reported, "During the last days several families from New River have fled thither. Today another man, Hamilton by name came with his family. He brings news that the Indians have declared war and everybody has left New River." The next day other New River families arrived including the George Loesch family. They "brought more terrifying reports of the Northern Indians who are said to have joined the Southern Indians."

The Hamiltons and Loeschs were followed by the Harmans. "Peter Harman from New River passed our mill," writes the Moravian, "and reported the Indians had killed many families on Roanoke (we later learned it had happened on James River); also that a few days before he himself had been in a fight with Indians at Trapper's Meadow, and had shot one whose tomahawk he had with him. More families of refugees arrived next day."

Another man from New River came to have the Moravians cure a wound received from an Indian. "He brought a letter from our friend, the elder Herman which said that since the last alarm they had seen no more of the Wild Men. The Hermans had built a fort, where they and several other families were living together and expecting a guard of 100 men from Virginia."[6]

Though the Harmans had seen no more of the "Wild Men" William Ingles' men discovered a party returning from Smith River with prisoners and horses encamped on Little River where Ingles attacked on September 13.

"After exchanging about seventy shots we got possession of the ground and plunder. We kild two. We had two men wounded and one very mortal. The men all behaved like good soldiers and the Indians was as loath to give way. The Battel lasted more than half an owor," wrote Ingles.

"The shouts of boath parteys could be heard I dare say neer two miles. We are informed by one of the prisoners that there is another party of Indians gone down the Maho River. We are to follow those," Ingles reported to his commander, William Preston.

"Mr. Robinson can give you the particlers as he came up just as we had drove them off. I sent you a shot pouch that we tuck in the plunder which I believe was the captain's. I beg you accept it as a small trophie of our victory."

"I hope sir you will indever to purswed Colo Lewes to cintinew me at this post as I find I can be of great sarves to the settlements both of Hallafax and yours for I find that they go within a little ways of this place when they go to Smiths River and we ly as handy to the Narrows as of aney other place."

Colonel Phelps of the Bedford militia was supposed to aid the New settlers but Ingles aid, "Phelps refused to comply with your orders and would not send any of his men with Mr. Cloyd but would go with his own men where he thought fit." Finally Ingles persuaded Phelps to give him men, one of whom was shot in the battle.[7]

In October fifty Delawares following the Big Sandy came to New River where they separated, one party going toward Roanoke and the other toward Jackson's River. Their trail was discovered by hunters, Swope, Pack and Pitman trapping on New River and they hurried to warn the settlers. Pitman headed to Jackson's River running all day and all night. He met a search party led by Captain Paul from Fort Young (Covington) saying the Indians had already killed one man. Paul's party continued to search and met with the second Indian party that had just raided on Roanoke. They were discovered about midnight camped on the north bank of the New opposite an island at the mouth of Indian Creek.

Bluestone Lake, The ancient Indian warcamp near Indian Creek was in this region.
(Photo by Peggy Powell, West Virginia Governor's Office of E.C.D.)

This area was a traditional camping place for Indians traveling the New. Hieroglyphics in this vicinity are silent reminders of the multitudes buried on Indian Creek.

Paul's men fired killing several, one of whom drowned himself in New River to save his scalp. The rest fled downstream. As Paul's men took the camp they nearly killed a woman sitting by the fire before they discovered she was Mrs. Catherine Gunn taken captive on Catawba a few days before when her husband and two children were killed. Questioned why she had not cried out she replied, "I had as soon be killed as not — my husband is murdered — my children are slain— my parents are dead. I have not a relation in America, everything dear to me here is gone. I have no wishes — no hopes — no fears. I would not have risen to my feet to save my life."

Paul's men followed the Indians down the New. Upon discovery they took careful aim and would have killed all except for John McCallum calling, "Pull steady and send them all to Hell." This scattered the Indians so a few escaped.[8]

Meanwhile Captain William Christian and Captain Hickenbotham with 25 Amherst militia were also following these Indians after their attack on Roanoke and Catawba. On October 12 advancing along the New Christian says, "We marched on their tracks until two hours before sunset when we heard some guns and soon afterwards discovered three large fires on the bank of Turkey Creek (Indian Creek) where it empties into New River." Christian's men advanced, found them on an island, fired on them and forded the stream. The Indians killed Jacob Kimberlain a prisoner and fled. Christian seized the Indian's plunder and followed a party of about twenty.

"By the tracks of blood we imagined several of them very wounded," wrote Christian from Roanoke later.[9]

Once again the Indians had proof that the New River was the River of Death. The whites had reason to know the same and named Kimberlain Creek for the unfortunate Jacob.

While William Christian was chasing Indians on lower New River Colonel Chiswell was holding forth at his Lead Mines. He had enough workers that he had to buy flour from Bethabara. In November the Moravians report, "People from the Hollow (meaning Carolinians from below the Blue Ridge) bought 1200 pounds of meal at our mill and started with it to Col. Chiswell on New River. A still larger quantity has been ordered for him and lies ready in the mill."[10]

A path had been beaten between Bethabara and Wachovia to the New settlements. The gap through which the flour trains passed was called Flour Gap and is present Low's Gap between Piper and Fancy

Gaps. Sometimes it is called Flower Gap but its name came from the flour trains transporting flour by packhorse over the Blue Ridge to New River. For years this was the only place for crossing the mountains between the New and North Carolina.

Although difficult of access the settlements in North Carolina were actually near New River. This can be seen from the comments of an English traveler J.F.D. Smythe who climbed to the top of Wart (Bull) Mountain to see chasms where the Dan, Mayo, Smith, Bannister, Blackwater and Staunton Rivers flowed eastward.

"On the northeast you will observe with great astonishment and delight the tremendous and abrupt break in the Allegheny Mountains through which the mighty waters of the New River pass," wrote Smythe. To the south he could see the Catawba, the Yadkin and the Haw.[11] And it was from these Carolina river settlements that a new wave of settlers would come up through Flour Gap to New River.

For years the Moravians had done everything possible to help the New River people, from giving food, medical attention and shelter to sending meal to them. Now evil rumors began against these good people. At Christmas 1763 they reported, "There is a false report current among the people about us that we were supplying the Indians on New River with ammunition, sending it to them by white people."[12]

These rumors were a natural result of feeling against King George III for his western land policy. His commissioners had just met with the Cherokees at Augusta where Little Carpenter said, "The land towards Virginia must not be settled nearer the Cherokees than southward of New River. Hunting is their Trade and they have no way of getting a living."[13] Sentiments like this had long been sent by the Indian subjects to London. So word came before Christmas that King George III proclaimed that the Indians were not to be molested on land reserved to them as hunting grounds. No governor could grant land beyond the heads of the rivers which fall into the Atlantic ocean. Everything west of the Allegheny divide belonged to the Indians. The New River was beyond the Allegheny divide.

"We strictly require all persons whatever, who have either wilfully or inadvertently seated themselves upon any lands within to remove themselves," proclaimed the English king.

The lands which the New River people had struggled for years to colonize, bled and died for during the recent French war and were still struggling to secure against Pontiac's minions were to be taken away. All would be turned back to the very Indians that had been French allies thus cancelling their victory against the French. Though their country had won the victory, they, suffering colonists of that country who had done most to hold the land for England, were to win nothing.

The buyers of James Patton's grant lands on the New and Holston, the buyers of the Loyal Company, as well as the buyers of John Lewis on the Greenbrier and Jackson Rivers, and all other settlers were affected.

In February 1764 David Robinson, writing from Fort Lookout, told William Thompson at Springfield, "I am sorry that your provisions are expended. I fear we shall scarcely be able to supply you from this place. Capt. Sayers is at the mines, at his return we shall try to contrive you some. If your beer is not exhausted as well as your beef, I believe I shall call upon you sometime next week and condole with you in your late misfortune. Colo. Preston desires me to assure you that Colo. Buchanan is going to London to redress his Grievances, and that he will attempt the same Embassy for you, provided, you pay him for his trouble."

"Captain Sayers has been damning this month about the Loss of Dunkard's Bottom and is not yet reconciled," continues Robinson, speaking of Alexander Sayers. "'Tis a great Mercy that Roanoke has not in like manner been given as a compliment to our good Friends and faithful Allies, the Shanee Indians ."[14]

Robinson's letter well expresses the bitter predicament of the New River colonists. John Buchanan of Anchor and Hope and William Thompson at Springfield were large landholders on the New. Besides these estates they claimed other lands as sons-in-law of James Patton. They could afford to fight for their lands. The plight of the smaller owners was expressed by a Harman, "By spring there will be no families left on New River, for by the King's Declaration, the lands must be returned to the Cherokees."

The Moravians at Bethabara again gave the New River fugitives sanctuary. "From New River came our friend the elder Herman, and his son Adam," the diarist reported on February 10. "The rest of their families will follow next week." By February 16 the Harmans camped by Wachovia mill. They were assigned land to settle upon at the southeast border of Wachovia. And all was not sadness among these people who had to leave New River. Easter weekend brought all the Harmans for a wedding of Daniel Harman to Billy Bughsen's daughter by Justice Loesch. "About forty people had to be cared for in the Tavern at Bethabara but all went with reasonable quiet," the Moravians reported. On Easter Sunday a special baptism was held for the little sons of Adam and Henry Harman, grandsons of the elder

Harman. Remembering Valentine killed on New River in 1756, Adam's son was named Valentine. The other child was named Henry.[15]

FOOTNOTES—Chapter XXIII

1. Fries, Moravian Records, I, p. 269; Smith, Pulaski, p. 12, FP, v. 2, p. 1015, Governor Fauquier, Report, Jan. 30, 1763.

2. VEJ, v. 6, p. 249.

3. Withers, Warfare, p. 89 and Johnson, William Preston, p. 78.

4. Fries, Moravian Records, I, p. 272.

5. Preston to Reverend John Brown, July 27, 1763, Kegley, Virginia Frontier, pp. 284-285.

6. Fries, Moravian Records, I, pp. 273-274. and Smith, Pulaski, p. 41.

7. William Ingles to William Preston, Setpember 13, 1763, WH, 2 QQ p. 43.

8. Withers, Warfare, pp. 96-99. Withers says the date was October 1764 but contemporary documents show it to be 1763.

9. Captain William Christian to ?, Roanoke, October 19, 1763, Withers, Warfare, p. 99.

10. Fries, Moravian Records, I, p. 276.

11. Smyth, Tour, p. 53.

12. Fries, Moravian Records, I, p. 278.

13. NCCR, V, pp. 356-357.

14. David Robinson to William Thompson, February 18, 1764, WH, 2 QQ p. 44.

15. Fries, Moravian Records, I, p. 285.

Chapter XIX

The Welsh Mines

In order to get the Lead Mines operating Colonel Chiswell, William Byrd and John Robinson had sent in Welsh miners and negro slaves as workers. Chiswell, native of Wales, naturally got his countrymen as miners when he took the lead samples to England for the assays. He employed as supervisor a skilled Welsh ironworker, William Herbert.

William Herbert brought with him his son David Herbert, his father David Herbert, his mother and his wife. Other Welsh that came were Charles and Nancy Devereaux, John Jenkins and probably Philip Dutton. Herbert was well trained in mining and may have been from the great Herbert family of the Welsh border country. Herbert is an ordinary and numerous name in Wales but also the name of a powerful Welsh family who built Powis Castle on the border between Wales and England and exercised great influence in that region. In the English Civil War they were Royalists supporting the Stuarts. When the last Stuart King James II was overthrown the Herberts lost everything. The last scion of the family was named William Herbert. It is possible there was a connection between this William Herbert and the man who brought Welsh miners to New River about 1764. Certainly New River William was acquisitive, owning ten New River plantations before he died.

So many Welsh arrived that they began to call the Lead Mines the Welsh Mines. Little is known of these Welsh miners yet their presence and that of the negroes adds two more racial strains to the German and Sctoch-Irish colonists that predominated. As usual when newcomers arrive in a community some view them suspiciously. During the Revolution the mines were operated by Colonel Charles Lynch of Lynch law fame. He did not like the Welsh. This conflict was mentioned by Nancy Devereaux who siad, "There is a misunderstanding between Colonel Lynch and the Welsh in general." [1]

When the King's proclamation became known Herbert wrote William Byrd,

Wilsh Mines, 6th March, 1764

Your favour of the 7 of last month came safe to hand lickwise the Negroes came all safe & well.

It will be the greatest plesuer to me to have it in my power to oblidg you in any respect. Moreover acquainting you of the state of the mine which is a duty incombent on me for which I shall take particuler care to acquaint you by every feavorable opportunity.

The account which I gave of the mine is in my opinion such as it desarves that is the aparance of the vain at the surfuis is such as I never had seen before all tho I have seen most mines of note in His Majestys Uropean dominions but as your mine is not as yeat tryd in depth no man can give you certain accounts — tho at the same time there is all the prospect that we can expect that it will be a good workes in depth.

I am in hopes that we shall make good somers work this somer tho we are badly off in regard to conveniance espesialy a god streem of water. The wether is so sever hear in the winter that our people has not bin able to do but little espishally out of dor work — I have not bin able to kip the furness in above one fortnit since the coale has bin gon for want of wether to wash the ore.

All the people that lives heearabout are laving thayer places. Some or gon & others preparing to go & with out any hopes of retourning any more for since they hard of His Majisty late Proclamation concarning the lands upon these waters they seem to be left without hopes of ever enjoying thayer lands hear any more. Oppon this alarm of our nabours moveing away our people began to be verey angry for tis' heear reported that the land is abseluty given out & that whoever stays shall be without protection & all the argument that I had to make use of in preswading our people to stay was till such time as the militia should be cauld in — & if it should be so that they will be cauld in I shall be under the necessity to hiear men to stay or otherways leive the place. But you may depend I will do all in my power to prevent our leaving the mine & all the care which is layd upon me shall be faithfully maniged by

Sir you most Obedient humble servant,

Will. Herbert[2]

That Herbert was successful in getting the Welsh to remain on New River is seen when George Loesch arrived on June 4 at the Wachovia store bringing 300 pounds of lead from the mines.[3] This lead produced under primitive conditions while Indians were roaming about and the laborers were in an uproar is indicative of the Welsh miner's skill.

John Chiswell sometimes lived at the mines supervising construction. He had the miners dig out lead by the open cut method, wide gashes in the hills around Austinville revealing the cuts. He worked only galena which cropped out near the river. This was smelted with a common air furnace which in 1790 was reported still smelting one and one half tons of lead. It was lined with firebrick possibly brought from England.[4]

Jefferson describes the furnace in 1781 which apparently is the one installed by Chiswell and the Welsh. "The present furnace is a mile from the ore bank and on the opposite side of the river. The ore if first wagoned to the river, a quarter of a mile, then laden on canoes, and carried across the river, which is a mere two hundred yards wide, and then again taken into wagons and carried to the furnace. This mode was originally adopted that they might avail themselves of a good situation on a creek for a pounding mill on the same side of the river, which would yield water without any dam, by a canal of about half a mile in length. From the furance the lead is transported one hundred and thirty miles along a good road leading through the Peaks of Otter to Lynch's Ferry or Winston's on James River where it is carried by water about the same distance to Westham."[5]

A cupel furnace was found which was used for refining silver. It became a legend that Chiswell made and buried silver coins at the mines. Chiswell sunk one horizonal shaft into the base of a high cliff through 25 feet of dolomite before abandoning the project. This is Chiswell's Hole.[6]

At the same time the Welsh were starting to mine parties of Delawares and Shawnees were at New River threatening the forts. An unnamed woman prisoner captured seven years before and now with them escaped. "She says the Delawares are stronger now than before the war because of the young people whom they have captured and who are more cruel in killing than the Indians themselves."[7]

Many prisoners held among the Indians would be released later in the year and as can be seen from the prisoner list some were New River people. By August Andrew Lewis commanding defense of the Virginia frontier ordered Preston to put Francis Smith, William Christian, David and William Robinson with Capt. McDowell over defense of the New River region. They were told to get lead from Chiswell.[8] David Robinson dreaded going to Chiswell for the lead since he was finding this Tidewater aristocrat a hard man. Robinson confided, "Our great Colonel Chiswell has descended so far as to be angry with me tho' I conscious I never did any thing which justly merits his displeasure but on the contrary did everything in my power from the beginning to humour him. He is determined to stop a number of the company's pay for no reason than that they are inhabitants in the county; and he is now gone to Town to address the House on this head. I find to my great mortification that I am no ways capable of insinuating myself into the Good Graces of the Great."

While Chiswell was in Williamsburg Robinson said the New River region was enjoying quiet. "We enjoy a deep respose in this part of the world & scarcely ever dream of an enemy."[9]

As early as August Mr. Wiltshire and others from New River told the Moravians that Little Carpenter and his Cherokees had left New River and returned to their nation. "It was believed generally" that the Cherokees "would make no claim to that section still less take possession of it." People were also returning to Holston.[10]

One reason for the lull in Shawnee raids was "certain intelligence" that Andrew Lewis had from the Shawnee villages that "the poor rascals were dying very fast with ye small pox, they can make but little resistance and when routed must perish in great numbers."[11] Another Birtish army was marching against the Ohio villages led by Colonel Bouquet. With it went Augusta men raised by Andrew Lewis who wanted to send them by way of New River claiming it was nearer than through Maryland. Lewis reasoned that the army could then "fall in with the Shawnees" who habitually followed the New to attack Virginia and thus "save their settlements." Other officers told Bouquet it would be easier to march men by the New and join him at the mouth of Kanawha rather than Pittsburgh but Bouquet did not agree. Augusta men were sent by way of Fort Pitt to Shawnee towns on Muskingum River where peace was made ending Pontiac's War. Prisoners captured years before on the New, Holston, Greenbrier, Roanoke and James began to come into Fort Pitt. The known New River people on the prisoner list following are starred. Those taken at Fort Vause are double-starred.

A List of Prisoners at the Lower Shawana Towns, November 1764

Robert Puzy
John Potts
John Cotter
Samuel Huff
Abraham Ormand
John Freeland & 3 children*
  & wife
Daniel Cowday
Jacob Good
Dutch John
Thomas Cabe
Gower Sovereign &
  4 children
Margret Bard & 5 children
Mary Pringer & 2 children
Dutch Garrah & 3 children
Sarrah Barnett & 1 child
Vanny Barnett
Aley Cincaide & 3 children
Mary Burke & 2 children

Betsy Robinson*
Hannah Densey*
Betsy Snodgrass
Betsy Medley**
Dutch Girl
Nansey Miller
Betsy Jamison
Nely Fulerton
Mary Moore
Susanna Voss**
Molly Gould
Jean Macrakin & sister
Ann Folkison
Wm. Medley**
Nansey Rancok her sister
  & four brothers
James Stewart
John Guthrey
Lezy Bingiman*
John Martin

William Days
Benjamin Robertson's
  Son
Lodick
Solomon Carpenter
Margrett Cartmill
Saley Boyles &
  Brother
Joseph Ramsey
Moly Cristopher
Molly Moore

List of Prisoners going to Fort Pitt November 15, 1764

John Wiseman	Eve Harper	Nancy Davison
John Donehoo	Mary Campbell	Molly Davison
Soremouth	Ann Finley	Magdalenor Pagothow
Crooked legs	Elizabeth Slover	Mary Craven
David Bighead	Elizabeth Slover, Jr.	Catherine Westbrook
Clem	Mary Cath. Lengenfield	Molly Metch
James Butler	Kitty Stroudman	Whitehead
Micheal Cobble	Betty-black eyes and hair	Margaret Yokeham*
Pouter or Wynima	Eliz. Franse	Mary McCord
Charles Hermentrout	Peggy Baskin	Eliz. Gilmore
Ebenezer	Mary McIlroy	Eliz. Gilmore Jr.
Mordicai Batson*	Sour Plumbs	Florence Hutchinson
Henry Bonnet	Christiana House	Mary See*
James	Mary Lowry	Barbara Huntsman
Tommy Wig	Jane Lowry	Susannah Fishback
Michael See*	Susan Lowry	Margaret Fishback
George See*	Peggy Revneck	Peggy Freeling
John Huntsman	Mary Lanciaco & child	Peggy Cartmill
Solomon Carpenter	Mary Greenwood Sore knee	Molly Cartmill
John Gilmore		

Lezy Bingiman and Hannah Densey had already come home, Susanna Voss was brought into Fort Pitt Oct. 26, 1763 by "Wide Mouth" a Shawnee Indian at the Treaty of Lancaster.[13]

The Moravains had told of a band of robbers operating on upper New River and now as Pontiac's War was ending a band of counterfeiters was discovered on Middle New River. Upper class families were involved. The activities of this group might never have come to light had there not been an election pending for a coveted Assembly seat. One of the contenders was William Preston hoping to unseat incumbent Israel Christian. Both had connections with the New River. Both were seeking the New River vote. William Preston as the nephew of James Patton had always enjoyed an influential position in the area while Israel Christian noted merchant at Big Lick on Roanoke had long exerted an influence on New River affairs. Christian had been a merchant for years in Staunton and in the late 1760's had established a trading post at the crossroads of the "Trading Path" to Carolina near present Roanoke. He had bought the "Stone House" belonging to Cherokee trader Erwin Patterson and had supplied goods for Byrd's army on the Cherokee expeditions through the New River Valley. William Christian had led the militia through New River Valley during the recent Indian troubles. And it was William, Israel's son, who was the most active person in spreading the counterfeiting story threatening to involve William Preston. Christian was reading law in Patrick Henry's office and would become Henry's brother-in-law. He wrote Henry telling the counterfeiting story trying to implicate Preston through association with his relative William Thompson, planting and distilling on Back Creek.

Though Christian did not mention Thompson's first name his "impartial account" is of Preston's kinsman. According to Christian, Mrs. Thompson passed two counterfeit bills which fell into the hands of Captain Ingles. Thompson asked Ingles to return the bills, claiming they were paid by Israel Christian to Commodore (Cornelius?) Brown as soldier's wages. Ingles was advised to trace the bills. He took them to Colonel Chiswell who sent them to Israel Christian. Thompson was arrested, tried and his case went to Williamsburg. The weather was bad so Thompson did not go. Then he changed his story, pleading that counterfeiters had broken into his desk, took Brown's good money and replaced it with bad. Thompson "denied a letter in his own hand" to several counterfeiters. To thicken the plot, counterfeit bills from the same mint had been passed and another man brought to trial for the same crime had been allowed to escape by Colonels Buchanan, Preston and Breckenridge, all kinsmen of William Thompson. Thompson was tried and heard in his own defense on March 22, 1765. The Augusta Court ordered him tried at Williamsburg and put under a thousand pound bail. New River men, William Ingles and Daniel Goodwin were called as witnesses. John Buchanan, Thompson's brother-in-law, was later also accused of passing counterfeit bills.[14]

The trouble caused Thompson and Buchanan by William Ingles may be the reason John Buchanan sued Ingles to keep him from getting a road built to his New River ferry. By 1768, Edmund Pendleton, Buchanan's lawyer was seeking arbitrators to settle the affair.[15]

Meanwhile William Preston was trying to defend New River. Though war was over and militia companies disbanding, he still had the responsibliity for the watch on the New. Andrew Lewis urged him to send scouts along the river, Mathew Arbuckle and Charles Lockhart scouting the east side of the river and men of Preston's choice the west side below Culbertson's Bottom.[16] The warpaths on both sides of the New were to be watched with vigilance. Probably now was the time Arbuckle traveled the entire length of the New and Kanawha.

While militia scouted and counterfeiting plots unraveled, up river at the mines William Herbert was ill. On January 10, 1765 he visited the Moravians whose doctor at Bethabara was the nearest the New. They reported, "Mr. Herbert, a superintendent in the mine on New River came to the doctor. He has a swelling over the whole body but as there is no suitable lodging for him for so long a treatment as this would require he was advised to return in the spring when the weather was good."[17]

Herbert's illness slowed progress at the mines and soon neighboring Reed Creek settlement received a blow. Their militia captian, Alexander Sayers, long a resident, who had so recently cursed over the loss of Dunkard's Bottom, was drowned with another man while crossing the New.[18]

Then came another shock. In late April a party of Overhill Cherokees passed Fort Chiswell on their way to Fort Cumberland, Maryland, to go on the warpath against the Ohio Indians. The Cherokees got as far as Staunton where Andrew Lewis gave them permission to travel. "I had them provided with proper colours and a pass fastened to the colours," said Lewis, "to let everybody know they were our brothers the Cherokees."

That night they slept in John Anderson's barn five miles from Staunton. At daybreak, May 8, a party of whites, "The Augusta Boys", brutally murdered five of the Cherokees. The ones that escaped fled to the forest and did not leave Virginia before they murdered a blind man and his wife in revenge.

Immediately Lewis imprisoned the murderers and wrote Governor Fauquier that "villaneous bloody minded rascals" had murdered the Cherokees. He wrote a peace letter to the Overhill chieftains, sending the letter to Colonel Chiswell at Fort Chiswell to send on quickly.[19]

Because of all the past Indian troubles, public opinion in Augusta was on the side of the "Augusta Boys". The jail was robbed at Staunton and the murderers released. Andrew Lewis and other law officers were much put upon to preserve the law. Lewis's greatest fear however was "in consequence of what they have done our frontier inhabitants who are innocent of the crime may be cut to pieces by a nation of Indians who otherwise would have lived in amity with us."[20]

The frontier inhabitants who would be cut to pieces would be the New and Holston people since they were nearest the Cherokees. Abraham Smith immediately took the peace message to the Overhill Towns, one month passed with no news. The silence was ominous. The people at Fort Chiswell braced for attack.

Then one hot July day people around the fort looked out to see a Cherokee peace party numbering fourteen approaching on foot. Leading it was that mender of breaks, the Little Carpenter, Attakullakulla. He and John Watts, his interpreter had come once again to Fort Chiswell to mend a breach between whites and Indians. Well does he deserve the name Little Carpenter!

Leaving most of his party at Fort Chiswell, the Carpenter, Watts and another Cherokee, went on to Williamsburg. On July 8 they had a private conference with Governor Fauquier who Thomas Jefferson said was the best governor Virginia ever had proven now by the pains-taking care he exercised to mend the breech with the Cherokees.[21] To Fauquier as well as Andrew Lewis the New River people owed gratitude for staving off an Indian war.

Little Carpenter in company with Colonel Chiswell had left Williamsburg to return home when they received word that forty men from the Hot Springs in Augusta were going to intercept the Carpenter's party. Chiswell and the Carpenter were told to halt at New London till the Council could decide what to do. Then they sent word for the Carpenter to go home by way of North Carolina rather than New River.

New London was the county seat of Bedford where Colonel William Calloway was County-Lieutenant. Calloway saw Chiswell off to his New River fort and the Carpenter off to Carolina. With Chiswell was the German missionary, John Daniel Hammerer of Strasbourg, Alsace and companion Thomas Crowley. Hammerer had arrived in Virginia on the **Madiera Packet** from England. At Colonel Peter Randall's he had joined Chiswell who conducted him to the Lead Mines. Hammerer planning to go as a missionary to the Cherokees was still at Fort Chiswell in mid-September with some of the Carpenter's company. After outlining his work to William Herbert Hammerer headed to the Cherokees where he was well received in his attempts to establish an Indian school.[22]

1766 would be a bad year for the Lead Mine owners. John Robinson died leaving an estate in debt over one hundred thousand pounds much illegally taken from the treasury of Virginia. Some had been given to John Chiswell and William Byrd to develop the New River mines which were in debt to Robinson's estate to the tune of eight thousand pounds. It would take years to clear the debt. An uproar went up in Virginia over this scandal among the Tidewater oligarchy. This financial wrongdoing would ultimately lead to the deaths of Byrd and Chiswell. Byrd's end would be several years in coming. Chiswell's would come immediately, his mine ownership sparking the chain of events leading to his death.

Shortly after Robinson's funeral Chiswell stopped one night at Cumberland Court House. While dining at Eppingham Tavern he began bragging about his New River mine. Since the mines were deeply in debt Chiswell's boasting was an understandable attempt to promote business. A man in the tavern named Robert Routledge challenged Chiswell's claims. Routledge was drunk and unarmed. Chiswell called Routledge "a fugitive rebel and Presbyterian fellow." A heated argument ensued. Chiswell sent for his sword and killed Routledge on the spot.

As later reported, "Chiswell was under the influence of nothing but his passions." Routledge lay dead at Eppingham Tavern. Chiswell was arrested and taken to prison at Williamsburg, but released on bail raised by William Byrd and others. Public opinion was so intense against Chiswell that his friend the Attorney-General fled the colony rather than try the case. Three months after the stabbing of Routledge Chiswell died. His doctor testified his death was the "result of nervous fits caused by constant uneasiness of mind." The verdict of history is that he killed himself.[23]

A lurid footnote follows. Public opinion was so aroused over his actions and those of John Robinson that the populace believed Chiswell's death had been faked. So a mob raided his coffin and took out the body to be sure an imposter was not in his coffin with Chiswell gone scot-free!

Edmund Pendleton had been appointed to administer the Robinson estate and told Byrd the Lead Mines would get no more money. It was agreed to deliver to John Esdale at Warwick all the lead to be shipped or sold. Esdale would pay the expences of the works. Slaves and everything would be sold to turn into money. Byrd himself bought the 36 mine slaves for 2,000 pounds and Pendleton agreed work could continue at the mines "if they could continue it without calling on us." So with Byrd's backing and Herbert's supervision the mines continued to operate under private ownership. However in the ten years before the state assumed control in 1776 the mines did not realize a profit, leading to Byrd's bankruptcy and suicide.[24]

William Herbert established himself well on New River in these years. He bought the Bingamon-Stanton tract on New River known as Poplar Camp, one of his ten New River plantations. The county records of extinct Fincastle County indicate that he also had a trading post near the Lead Mines.[25]

William Ingles was building a handsome estate on New River and came by Bethabara on his way to Georgia to see Valentine Zinn about buying Gerhart Zinn's land at Dunkard's Bottom. Ingles brought New River news in this spring of 1767 that a party of Indians, probably northern, had shot cattle belonging to white people and robbed a house. Capt. Thompson and some of his company had gone to the nearest camp to speak to them about it but the Indians took to the woods, and believing that the soldiers meant to take their goods shot at the soldiers, killed the Captain and wounded his cousin." Ingles confirmed the report saying the Indians killed Captain Thompson's cousin not the Captain. The Moravians also heard now of the death of "our old friend" Adam Harman. Adam's place near his New River ford would become the Kent and Cowan estate.[26]

FOOTNOTES—Chapter XXIV

1. Dr. W.R. Chitwood to author, Letter, February 3, 1976; Col. Charles Lynch to William Preston Aug. 17, 1780, WH 5 QQ p. 57; Nancy Devereaux to William Preston, 1780, WH 5 QQ p. 58 and Johnson, William Preston, p. 250.

2. William Herbert to William Byrd III, March 6, 1764, Tingling, Three Byrds, I, p. 768.

3. Fries, Moravian Records, I, p. 288.

4. "Lead Mines Virginia," N and W. Magazine, November 1947, p. 598 and C.R. Boyd, "The Wythe Lead and Zinc Mines, Virginia," Engineering and Mining Journal 1893, v. 55, p. 56.

5. Jefferson, Notes of Virginia, p. 34.

6. "Lead Mines Virginia", N and W Magazine, Nov. 1947, p. 598.

7. Fries, Moravian Records, I, p. 289.

8. Colonel Andrew Lewis to Colonel William Preston, Aug. 4, 1764, WH, 2 QQ pp. 46-48.

9. Robinson to William Fleming, October 22, 1764, WLFP.

10. Fries, Moravian Records, I, p. 289.

11. Lewis to Bouquet, Sept. 10, 1764, Bouquet Papers, no. 50, II, Series 21650, pp. 126-127.

12. Johnson, Andrew Lewis p. 126.

13. Bouquet Papers, British Museum, Add MSS 21655, f. 296 D and "The   urnal of James Kenny 1767-63" PMHB, v. 37 p. 178.

14. William Christian to Patrick Henry, February 28, 1765, WH, 15 ZZ pp. 1-2 and Augusta County Order Book, IX, p. 252 and Captain George Moffett to William Preston, WH 2 QQ 122 and LCPP 618, 674.

15. May, Pendleton Papers, I, p. 40.

16. Col. Andrew Lewis to Col. William Preston, March 23, 1765, WH, 2 QQ p. 91.

17. Fries, Moravian Records, I, p. 304, 311.

18. Ibid. I, p. 302 and CS, I, p. 358.

19. Johnson, Andrew Lewis, pp. 132-133.

20. Lewis to Fauquier, June 5, 1765, P.R.O.:C.O. 5:1331, p. 65.

21. VEJ, July 29, 1765, v. 6, p. 277 and Johnson, Andrew Lewis, pp. 133-138.

22. Fries, Moravian Records, I, p. 304, 311, and Milling Red Carolinians, p. 309 quoting South Carolina Records, P.R.O. 32: 79, 108.

23. Jonathan Daniels, The Randolphs of Virginia (Garden City, New York: Doubleday & Company, Inc. 1972) pp. 75-76 and Tingling, Three Byrds, II, pp. 611-612.

24. Edmund Pendleton to William Preston, February 6, 1768, WH 2 QQ pp. 102-104; Mays, Edmund Pendleton, I, p. 203 and Mays, Pendleton Papers, I, p. 36.

25. Will of William Herbert, 1776. Southwest Virginia Enterprise, May 1, 1945.

26. Fries, Moravian Records, I, p. 357 and Wust, Saints, p. 116.

Chapter XX

Treaties Place the New in Botetout

In March 1768 Governor Fauquier died at the palace in Williams-burg. Lord Botetourt arrived from England in a 74-gun ship and was installed as governor with much pomp. Wearing a coat of gold thread he drove to the Capitol in an elegant coach drawn by six white horses.

Governor Botetourt immediately took steps to solve the question of western lands. His actions would be particularly important to the New River settlers. He believed the best way to settle Virginia's western boundary problem was to buy the land. In the summer of 1768 Botetourt sent Commissioners Andrew Lewis and Dr. Thomas Walker to Fort Stanwix, New York, to buy the land between the Alleghenies and the Ohio from the Iroquois. Lewis and Walker were successful but at the same time they were buying the land John Stuart British Indian agent in the South, the same who had escaped from Fort Loudoun to Fort Chiswell in 1760, was negotiating with the Cherokees to settle the boundary between them and Virginia. He told the Cherokees to meet the Commissioners at Chiswell's Mines on October 25 to run the boundary. And he wrote Virginia to prepare to meet the Cherokees but soon changed the meeting time to November 10. The government ordered Israel Christian to rush Cherokee Gifts to Chiswell's. Laced hats along with powder and shot were all to be sent by way of Calloway's in Bedford on to New River. Meanwhile since Lewis and Walker were taking longer with the Iroquois at Fort Stanwix than expected Lewis was told to leave Walker and start for New River. He made the journey of over nine hundred miles in seventeen days.

"After a most fatiguing journey, I arrived at this place on November 2," Lewis wrote from the mines. He immediately made contracts with Captain Ingles and Israel Christian, now establishing trading stations on New River, to provide the provisions for the Cherokees when they arrived at Fort Chiswell.[1]

Meanwhile unknown to Lewis and the Virginians, John Stuart had concluded a treaty with the Cherokees at Hard Labour, South Carolina, recognizing a Cherokee boundary giving them claim to land Lewis and Walker had just bought from the Iroquois — land hundreds of years under Iroquois jurisdiction. When Governor Botetourt received this news he sent word to Lewis at Fort Chiswell telling him to go to Bedford and tell Calloway to hold the Cherokee present. Israel Christian was told to dispose of his "perishables" the best way he could.[2]

The Hard Labour Treaty gave the Cherokees the territory west of the New River to the confluence of the Kanawha with the Ohio. It took away land along New River from settlers who had been there for years. The council said some surveys could continue on New River using Fort Chiswell as a point between whites and Cherokees but the surveyors were told, "Do not go further than the mines or Reed Creek."[3]

Early in 1769 Lewis and Walker went to Charleston, South Carolina to meet with Stuart and unravel the mess. Little was accomplished but that did not stop Walker. That spring he opened a land registry office for the Loyal Company at Ingles Ferry with Ingles, Robert Doak and Arthur Campbell taking subscriptions. He directed surveyor William Preston to survey "between Culbertson's (Bottom) and Big Island on the Holston."[4]

Naturally the people west of the New clamoured to change the boundary. In 1770 Virginia arranged with the Cherokees to have yet another treaty to resolve the dispute. A meeting with the Cherokees was appointed at Lochaber, South Carolina. On September 20 Colonel Donelson coming to survey the boundary with his surveying party arrived at Bethabara saying the King had agreed to "buy all of New River and part of Holston from the Cherokees." The Young Warrior had gone to receive gifts valued at twenty-five hundred pounds.[5]

However even after the Treaty of Lochaber the headwaters of the New in Carolina lay in Cherokee territory and were not legally the white man's until the Watauga Purchase in 1775 when the Wataugans bought the entire Watauga Valley and the headwaters of the New from the Cherokees.[6]

After these treaties settlers poured into the New and Holston country. A traveler says, "We arrived at New River. . .crossed it in safety though with great difficulty and hazard of being carried down with the stream" and describes the land the Loyal Company was selling.

"The low ground on the New River is narrow, but exceedingly rich and fertile; the high land is also very fine in many places but excessively broken, rocky and mountaineous. The timber on the high land is very large and lofty and that on the low ground is almost equal to the prodigious heavy trees on the Roanoke."

"On the New River, the upper part of the great Kanawha, not

Smithfield (1772) New River home of William Preston
(Photo by Walter L. Johnson)

William Thompson at Springfield on the New Advertises in 1764
(Author's Collection)

being navigable, the extreme roughness of the country and difficulty of access to it, the roads or rather paths being not only almost impassable but totally impossible even to be rendered tolerable by any human efforts will not only greatly retard the settlement of this country but will always reduce the price and value of land be it ever so rich."

Soon however the region was populous enough to be made into a new county. As a way of thanking Lord Botetourt the new county formed in 1770 with Fincastle Town as county seat was named Botetourt. It stretched from the Blue Ridge to the Mississippi, with New River a boundary. William Preston became the County Lieutenant and County Surveyor. [7]

Shortly Preston would begin construction of a house, known as Smithfield, named for his wife Susannah Smith, on Patton lands at Draper's Meadows. Smithfield stands beautifully restored today and is one of only a few structures built in the New River Valley in the 1770's still remaining. Built by slaves and Preston's nephews it had a basement used as quarters for the Smithfield garrison, a secret tunnel, wide chimneys, carved mantels, paneled drawing room, and a Chippendale staircase. Though it looked more like Raleigh's Tavern than a Tidewater mansion it was a grand house for the mountain wilds. The old Draper's Meadows community which the Prestons moved to was well known to William but not to Susannah. She found her many neighbors to be Germans, speaking German and keeping to themselves. The family living between Smithfield and New River were the Prices, Walls, Barragars, Lybrooks, Shulls, Harmans and others. They had cleared the land, fought the Indians, run from them, and returned again and again to plow the fertile New River bottoms and hunt the abundant game.

Philip Lybrook (Leibroch), serving with the Smithfield garrison, told how people along the river went "fire-hunting." They set fire in canoes, letting them drift downstream at night. The curious deer would come to the river to see the fire. When the hunters could see their shining eyes they knew they had a sure shot. At age thirteen Lybrook killed the largest panther ever seen in the area, measuring fourteen feet from nose to tail. It had been standing upright in a tree when he shot it through the heart. Lybrook would become a great New River hunter, during his lifetime killing 600 bears, 3,000 deer and 100 panthers.

A panther incident was remembered years later on the Cumberland in Tennessee when a woman said, "I heard the Panther answer when the woman down on New River called her eaten child."

Anyone searching for their New River ancestors from 1770 to 1772 should seek them in Botetourt County records at Fincastle or in Montgomery County at Christiansburg, where a few Botetourt records are found. For example on February 14, 1770, Botetourt records show that William Herbert had established a ferry on the New, later known as Jackson's Ferry, and he was appointed road surveyor from his ferry to the Pittsylvania County line. Herbert also took the tithables, a colonial type census, from Cripple Creek on the east side of the New up to Hamilton's store at Dunkard's Bottom.[8] Herbert was now living in a large log house in a bottom at Poplar Camp near the Poplar Camp Furnace. The area around the Lead Mines was becoming well populated. Hanover Presbytery records show that on April 13, 1769 Reverend John Craig reported a church had been organized at Boiling Springs on Lower Reed Creek with 42 families enrolled. William Herbert, David Sayers, William Sayers, Nathaniel Wiltshire, and Robert Montgomery were elders.[9] The Montgomerys were leaders in establishing the Presbyterian faith on New River. Robert's brother James helped organize New Dublin church and brother Samuel organized Unity on the Holston.[10]

Before 1765 James Addair and John Taylor had settled near present Radford on the "upper Horseshoe". Taylor built his home "Rockford" where an old Indian trail crossed the New near a rock visible above the surface when the river was low enough to ford. By 1767 Samuel Pepper had located on New River resuming Bingamin's ferry operation where Route 114 bridge spans the river today. He was a constable and Pepper's Ferry crossing would become as famous as Ingles Ferry up the river. Robert and George Pearis brothers-in-law to Pepper joined him. George in 1756 had taken a letter from Fort Frederick to the Catawbas and would establish at the present town of Pearisburg.

One section that received many settlers at this time was Back Creek. In the summer of 1767 Joseph Howe with wife Eleanor Dunbar and six children came from Hampshire County, Virginia, to Back Creek. James Hoge would come to the adjoining plantation, marry Elizabeth Howe and build a log house called "Hayfield" later the site of the brick mansion "Belle-Hampton" home of Governor James Hoge Tyler.[11]

By 1769 the Cloyds had settled on Back Creek. Colonel Joseph Cloyd gave the land on which the New Dublin Church would be built. William Thompson and Henry Patton with their families had been settled for years on Back Creek. The Thompsons sold land to the Cloyds.

—179—

Other families were arriving on the Middle New. The Pierces who would later own the mines were represented by Jeremiah who was appointed constable near the mines. James Carr was appointed constable on Mack's Run and Joseph Apperson on Little River. Philip Dutton on Cripple Creek was clearing title to his land. However the settlers were poor having little ready currency so petitioned the House of Burgesses to be exempted from payment of taxes a few years longer.

In the autumn of 1770 the Israel Christian family moved to Dunkard's Bottom. William Christian accompanied his father and at Christmas 1770 his wife Ann wrote from New River, "We are now settled in our new habitation. Mr. Christian is highly delighted with Mahanaim." They intended to celebrate by going to a ball at John Madison's at present Shawsville.

The Triggs, in-laws of the Christians, located on the New at this time. The Christians and Ingles and possibly others of this group had been merchants in Dublin, Ireland and it was these families who gave the name New Dublin to a tiny village on New River where James McCorkle established a store. The New Dublin Presbyterian Church was founded about 1769 by Joseph Howe, Samuel Colville, John Taylor, Samuel Cloyd and James Montgomery.[12]

The Duke of Orleans when traveling through Virginia and crossing New River in 1797 writes, "We dined two miles on the other side with some Irishmen who have given the name New Dublin to a shanty they've been living in for six years."[13]

The Irishmen may have been living in the shanty only six years, but the name New Dublin had been attached to this settlement considerably longer.

The Christians became a leading force on New River. They opened their doors to travelers and even to Baptist preachers who were openly persecuted in Virginia at this time. "Simon the Baptist" had been at Mahanaim "twice preaching, for want of a better minister," said Ann Christian. "He has done much good among the poorer sort of people, as I don't doubt but his intentions may be good."[14]

An even better insight into New River activities at this time comes again from the marvelous Moravian records. In June 1773 George Frey or Fry of the Sinking Creek community near present Pembroke on the New went to Bethabara. Fry was acquainted with the Moravians for they wrote, "In all these corners of the earth there are people who crossed the ocean with the Brethren, or once lived in their neighborhood, or who went to a country school with them and so have known the Brethren well.

On June 22 Frey, "who once lived near Lititz and knew many of the early Brethren there, came to ask for a visit, as they would like to have a pastor and school-teacher. The poor people feel the lack of God's word in their neighborhood. He said they lived like Indians."

The Moravian centers in Pennsylvania were Lititz, Nazareth and Bethlehem in Lancaster County which had fed people to New River. The Hauck-Fry Cemetery of Lancaster holds the remains of Frys who stayed in Pennsylvania.

The best the Moravians could do for George Fry that June 1773 was to promise "If possible some one would come to him. Adam Hartmann, his brother-in-law offered to go as a guide." Adam Hartmann had been wanting to move to Fry's on New River but his wife would not consent."

True to their promise in October the Moravians sent Brother Utley, the Wachovia minister, "to New River in Virginia having been invited by residents to visit and preach there. The path thither was almost impassable, the land very rough, with a little farm here and there between high rocks and steep mountains. He found one opportunity to preach to the Germans, and preached twice to the English and not without making a blessed impression."

"The land on New River is much broken," said Brother Utley, "Here and there. . .little plantations with fertile fields and meadows and then more frightful mountains."[15]

Just after this Lutheran minister "P. Schmid who serves in Orangeburg, South Carolina," passing Bethabara "stopped on his way to New River."

Orangeburg on the Edisto River a far distance from New River was where a Peter Schmidt had recently been involved with the Weberites claiming he was Jesus Christ. The Weberies had murdered several people in their services. One man who they claimed was the Devil they put in a bed, piled pillows upon him which they sat on and stamped with their feet. When the man was dead they burned his body. The Weberite leader had been executed in Charleston in 1761. Afterwards Peter Schmidt's family disappeared gone to some place unknown.[16]

The settlers mentioned to this point on New River have been largely middle New River settlers. We will now see what was occurring on the upper reaches of New River toward Carolina.

FOOTNOTES—Chapter XXV

1. VEJ, v. 6, pp. 297-304; Andrew Lewis to Botetourt, December 14, 1768, P.R.O.C.O.:5: 1435, p. 45; CVS, I, p. 297; Dr. Thomas Walker, Deposition, P.R.O.:C.O. 5:1347, pp. 43-44 and John Alden, John Stuart and the Southern Colonial Frontier, A Study of Indian Relations, War, Trade and Land Problems in the Southern Wilderness 1754-1775 (Ann Arbor: The University of Michigan Press, 1944) reprint (New York: Gordian Press, 1966) pp. 273-275.

2. VEJ, v. 6, pp. 306-307.

3. Thomas Lewis to William Preston, January 14, 1769, WH 2 QQ p. 106.

4. Petition of Montgomery and Washington County to the House of Delegates, 1782, LCPP; Walker to Preston 1769, WH 2 QQ pp. 116-117 and David Robinson to William Preston, May 1, 1769, WH 2 QQ pp. 109-111.

5. Fries, Moravian Records, I, p. 415 and II, 614.

6. Max Dixon, The Wataugans (n.p.: Tennessee Bicentennial Commission 1976) p. 82.

7. Johnson, William Preston, p. 101 and Smyth, Tour, pp. 310-312.

8. Philip Lybrook, Narrative, WH, 31 S p. 431, Arnow, Seedtime, p.3 Botetourt County Order Book I, February 14, May 10, 1770.

9. "Captain William Herbert Helped in Early Development of This Section," Southwest Virginia Enterprise, April 1945.

10. Agnes Riley, "John Montgomery, 1717-1802" Historical Society of Washington County Publication, Series II, no. 5 p. 7.

11. Smith, Pulaski, pp. 46-47.

12. Ibid., p. 52; WH 2 QQ p. 128, Robert Doak to William Preston, November 20, 1771; Petition, 1770, WH 2 QQ p. 115; Hanover Presbytery Minutes, April 13, 1769 History of the New Dublin Presbyterian Church 1769-1969 (Dublin: Dublin Presbyterian Church 1969) pp. 4, 6-7. Ann Christian to Ann Fleming, December 4, 1770, WLFP

13. Duke of Orleans, Journal, p. 51.

14. Ann Christian to Ann Fleming, January 31, 1771, WLFP.

15. Fries, Moravian Records, II, pp. 752, 758, 761, 782.

16. Ibid., p. 889 and G.D. Bernheim, History of the German Settlements and of the Lutheran Church in North and South Carolina from the earliest period (Spartanburg, S.C.: The Reprint Company, 1972) pp. 202-203.

Rockford built by John Taylor on New River 1765 near present Radford.
(Photo courtesy Mrs. Radford C. Adams)

Chapter XXI

First Settlement on the
Upper New in Virginia

Between 1765 and 1770 the Middle New River bottoms filled with settlers so prospective buyers now headed for the lower or upper New. Since the lower New followed an inaccessible gorge through savage filled mountains, the small bottoms of the upper New were more inviting, especially when the boundary disputes with the Cherokees were settled in 1770. Settlers then began to go to the area now Grayson County, Virginia, and Watauga, Ashe and Allegheny Counties, North Carolina where only hunters had gone before. Thomas McGimsey first court clerk of Ashe wrote in 1811, "Capt. John Cox informs me he recollects where there was but two or three hunters cabbens from the Lead Mines to the head of Watauga."[1]

Because of the great Blue Ridge barrier in North Carolina this region of the New was first settled mostly out of Virginia, settlers filtering south along the New. The courts were far away in Botetourt's Fincastle Town and later when Fincastle and Montgomery were formed, at the Lead Mines. These mines and Fort Chiswell were a rendezvous point where settlers rested and geared up to continue upstream to the vacant river bottoms. The John Cox family, later influential on the upper New, was at Fort Chiswell in February 1763 where son James was born.[2]

In the summer of 1765 when Daniel Hammerer came from Germany to the Lead Mines to go as missionary among the Cherokees, newly-weds Rosamond Jones (relative of John Paul Jones) and William Bourne of Hanover County, Virginia, had come to Fort Chiswell by wagon. They would continue on pack horse across Iron Mountain to Knob Fork of Elk Creek near present Fries, Grayson County. The first Grayson court would be held in a barn on their place where nearby they are buried. This barn still standing is made of unhewn V-notched logs, a double corncrib structure, a style also used in local dwellings.

Elk Creek was the first place along the New in Grayson to be settled. There were only eight settlers, Lewis Hale from Bedford being one of the first on Elk Creek in 1760, founding Hale's settlement, Hale's Ferry (Blair's Ferry) and the first church in Grayson called Hale Meeting House.[3]

When the Bournes came to Elk Creek they brought a mahogany clock made by Aaron Willard of Boston, thought to be the first clock on the upper New. In order to work the iron ore discovered near Peach Bottom they later built forges and were partners in Matthew Dickey Point Hope Furnace built at Peach Bottom falls near present Independence. Major Minitree Jones and William Jones, kin of Rosamond Jones Bourne settled on Elk Creek and between the mouths of Elk and Meadow Creek where there was an island in the New. A road was made passing Jones' place and a ford crossing the river at the island became Jones Ford. Later it passed to son-in-law

Map of the State of Virginia (Facsimile) by Herman Böy 1825-1859
(Photo courtesy of Carol Newman Library, Virginia Polytechnic and State University)

Isaac Garrison and became Garrison's Ford. For years it was the region's only ford for crossing with wagons.[4]

In 1765 when the Bournes settled on Elk Creek other settlers were moving into Peach Bottom Tract near the Virginia-Carolina line surveyed for Dr. Thomas Walker, Peter Jefferson and Thomas and David Meriwether on March 16, 1753 as Loyal Company land. Andrew Baker from the Yadkin is said to have been there in 1754 buying from the Loyal Company but was driven out by Indians. His first permanent settlement was in 1765. The John Cox, Ephraim Osborne and John Hashe families accompanied Baker on his return in 1765, Cox settling opposite Baker. George Collins and George Reeves from Drury's Bluff below Richmond arrived at Peach Bottom in 1767. Baker soon sold land to Jeremiah Harrison, James Mulkey and James, John and Samuel Blevins. The Hashes located where Bridle Creek enters the New. The Osbornes located between Bridle and Saddle Creek opposite the Bakers.[5]

John Cox son of Joshua and Mary Rankin Cox of McDowell's Mill near present Fort Loudoun, Pennsylvania, had been captured when seventeen by Delawares on February 11, 1756, with brother Richard and John Craig. The Indians stripped them stark naked, stretched their limbs to the utmost, tied them to trees and in this condition left them all night. They were forced to watch Paul Bradley tortured to death and then made to burn him. Nearly starving for six months, John escaped to Fort Augusta with dangerous swellings on his body. He came to Winchester, served in Preston's Rangers, then with brother David (who had settled on Kerr Creek) came to the upper New in 1765. David settled at Cox's Ford ten miles from Grayson Courthouse and John later moved to North Carolina to his "Roundabout" at the mouth of Cranberry Creek of the New's South Fork. In 1778 the Coxes built the first Peach Bottom Fort at the mouth of Peach Bottom overlooking the river. Enoch Osborne who settled on Bridle Creek built in 1780 the second fort where Ancella Post Office would later be. Supplies for these forts were packed in on pack horses from the Lead Mines along a trail that could be seen even recently.[6]

The Osbornes originally from Pennsylvania had come to the Yadkin and then to the New to establish the "Osborne settlement." The father was Ephraim Osborne, a fur trader in the Yadkin Valley and furs brought them to the New. A family hunting story involving Enoch, Solomon and Ephraim tells how they had gone from the New hunting on Watauga, got wet and hung their clothes to dry when attacked by Indians. Solomon was killed. Ephraim and Enoch escaped and got home but Enoch arrived minus all his clothes.

Ephraim was a relative of Caleb and Alexander Osborne, New Jersey men who had migrated to the Carolinas. Alexander established a classical school in his home in Rowan County and had been in Hugh Waddell's company when they marched to New River. They brought ideas of seaboard life style with them to Carolina and on to the New. Just as Alexander Osborne was a leader in Rowan Enoch Osborne led in the foundation of a middle class society on New River. It was most natural that Bishop Francis Asbury riding up the mountain from North Carolina on March 22, 1792, stopped at Enoch Osborne's home. "Here we were generously entertained," says Asbury, "after talking and praying together we were guided across the river, for which I was thankful."[7]

One daughter of Enoch Osborne, Eleanor, married William Hashe and her brother Enoch married a Hashe. The Hashes included John, his second wife, sons William, Thomas and John, grandson Richard Hall and sons-in-law Francis Sturgill and Enoch Osborne. According to tradition the Hashes and Osbornes had lived near each other in Philadelphia and traveled south together which is substantiated by land and tax records of Pennsylvania. Hashe and Osborne names are in the townships of Upper Dublin and Whitemarsh, Philadelphia County, along with other names, Cox, Phipps, Livesay and Howell that later appeared on the New.[8]

Caleb Osborne had been involved in a famous colonial real estate litigation case. On April 13, 1745 a petition was filed in New Jersey Chancery Court by which East Jersey landholders including the Earl of Stair tried to oust settlers around Elizabethtown, New Jersey. The settlers known as Clinker Lot Right Men had derived their titles from grants made eighty years earlier. They signed a petition in their defense to be sent to England. Caleb Osborne signed. Many surnames on the New Jersey petition later show up on the New including Halsey, Sturgis, Young, Wright, Williams and Whitehead. The relationship of Caleb Osborne and Ephraim who later moved to New River proves a definite link between the New River frontier and the Elizabethtown petitioners.[9]

It was to these "Jersey" people that James Patton referred when in 1753 he was being sued.

As well as coming from New Jersey some New River settlers came from the Delaware River Valley which in colonial times was a "single economic province and a single cultural area." As well as Quakers and Presbyterians in the region there were New England

Puritans, newly arrived Scotch-Irish and French Huguenots. According to Paula Anderson-Green, many New River families were located in New Jersey counties of Essex and Burlington, in Philadelphia County, Pennsylvania and Delaware.

These families moved by steps into the Cumberland and Susquehanna Valleys, then to Shenandoah, Roanoke and the New. Some went to North Carolina then back-tracked to New River.[10]

Flower Swift who figured prominently in New River defense in the 1770's came to the New from North Carolina, paid for his land on the east bank by the sale of a lady's side saddle. Another boundary of land on the west bank was bought with a flintlock gun. Swift settled near the place first selected for the Grayson Courthouse. He and Charles Nuckolls of Cripple Creek donated one hundred acres to build the court house and public buildings of the county. The county seat was first named Greenville. Swift married Mary Bedsaul, built a puncheon floored cabin with a board roof weighted on with logs.[11]

The Andersons, Carricos, Currins, Dickeys, Dickensons, Livesays, and Philips later settled along the upper New in Virginia but their settlement was beyond the time frame of this book so will not be discussed. We would note one Africa family, slaves of William Bourne, which came directly from Africa to the New River.

When William was in the legislature in Richmond he took a wagon loaded with New River fur skins and sold them. A negro woman and little girl were on the block for sale. He bought them and sent them home by a wagon going back to New River. The woman became known as Granny Beck and the little girl as Aimy. One night in Africa Granny had been called to a neighbor's home. When she and Aimy arrived two men rushed into the house, caught them, tied clothes over their mouths and dragged them from the house. They were sold to a slaver which brought them directly to Virginia where Bourne found them on the auction block. From them descended a large African New River family.[12]

FOOTNOTES—Chapter XXVI

1. Newsome, Carolina Counties, p. 420,

2. James Cox, Deposition, 1832, Betty-Lou Fields and Jene Hughes, ed. Grayson County A History in Words and Pictures (Independence, Virginia: Grayson County Historical Society, 1976) hereafter cited as Fields-Hughes, Grayson, p. 43.

3. Ibid. p. 20 and Nuckolls, Grayson Pioneers, pp. 17-22, 45, 111, 163; Laura B. Nolen, "Courthouse of Grayson County," Virginia Cavalcade, Spring 1976.

4. Nuckolls, Grayson Pioneers, pp. 155-156 and Fields-Hughes, Grayson, 153.

5. CS, II, p. 143, Case of John Cox vs. James Newell; Nuckolls, **Grayson Pioneers,** pp. 23-24, 176 and Paula Anderson-Green, hereafter cited as Anderson-Green, **New Frontier,** 'The New River Frontier Settlement,'' **VMHB,** v. 86, p. 420.

6. Ibid. pp. 418-419 and Fields-Hughes, **Grayson,** p. 171; Grayson County Deed Book I, p. 40; Colonial Records of Pennsylvania v. 7, pp. 241-243.

7. Anderson-Green, **New Frontier,** pp. 419, 421; Elmer T. Clark, ed.. **The Journal and Letters of Francis Asbury** (Nashville: Abingdon Press, 1958) v. I p. 710; Robert W. Ramsey, **Carolina Cradle Settlement of the Northwest Carolina Frontier 1747-1762,** (Chapel Hill. The University of North Carolina Press, 1964) p. 198.

8. Anderson-Green, **New Frontier,** pp. 419, 421; John Hashe, **Will,** Montgomery County, Will Book B, Clerk's Office, Christiansburg, Virginia.

9. **Ibid.** p. 425.

10. Anderson-Green, **New Frontier,** pp. 425-426.

11. Nuckolls, **Grayson Pioneers,** pp. 65-66, 98-101, 142, 168.

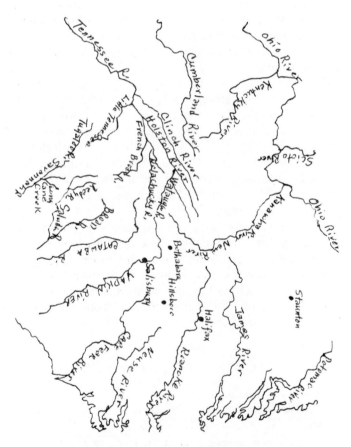

The New in relationship to other eastern rivers

(Map by Patricia Givens Johnson)

Chapter XXII

First Settlement on the
Upper New in North Carolina

The area in North Carolina where the New branches into North and South Forks is today in Ashe, Allegheny and Watauga Counties. In 1750 this was Anson and in 1753, Rowan, with county seat at Corbintown later Hillsboro. During the 1754-65 war years it did not matter that Rowan's county seat was far east of the New. No one lived on the New in North Carolina. When settlers began to arrive after 1765 albeit illegally the western part of Rowan became Surry in 1771 with court at Richmond, later Dobson, and Wilkes in 1778 with court at Mulberry Fields (Wilkesboro). Wilkes' extreme western part where flowed the New was made into Ashe in 1799 and later Watauga in 1849 and Allegheny in 1859. People searching Carolina New ancestry should look in these various court records.

To avoid confusion in this book the New River region south of the Virginia boundary and west of the Blue Ridge will be called Ashe, the same which was called the "Lost Provinces" of North Carolina due to its dependence on the railroad at Marion, Virginia.

The Virginia-Carolina boundary which crosses New River in Ashe was first surveyed October 1749 by Peter Jefferson, Joshua Fry, Daniel Weldon and William Churton. They crossed the New's crooks and turns several times in running the line but left no record of their experiences.

One of the surveyors was named Wilson. When he died his body was buried on a creek bank hence Wilson's Creek. Later the town Mouth-of-Wilson grew here near the boundary. A man named Fulcarson may have been with the survey party for South Fork of the New was first Fulcarson's River so-called at least until 1770 when Captain John Collett's Map of North Carolina was published. This map was based upon twenty years work by William Churton in western Carolina. Collett also shows upper New creeks named H. Day and Farenell.

Fulcarson may have been Frederick Fulkerson living in 1755 on the Rowan County line, meaning the Virginia boundary. In 1767 he was in Pittsylvania and in 1783 was paid for supplying four hundred pounds of beef to American troops and sending corn to General Sumpter in South Carolina during the Revolution. This patriot may have guided the 1749 boundary surveyors over the Blue Ridge to South Fork thus getting it named for him.

On their 1751 Map of Virginia Fry and Jefferson showed the boundary they had just surveyed and labeled Wilson Creek, Butcher's Creek and Fulcarson River. The French anxiously watching English activity on the Mississippi watershed needed a map showing this region. This was made in 1755 by Robert De Vaugondy. His map copied from Fry-Jefferson shows all the details known of the upper New at this time.[1]

The same year the surveyors were running the boundary across the New Dr. Thomas Walker's Loyal Land Company was given permission to survey 800,000 acres on the New and other western waters. His surveyors ran the Peach Bottom survey in 1753 and began sales in the region.

In 1755 Governor Arthur Dobbs of North Carolina reported "lead mines discovered on New River in Virginia near our line and I am told also within our line."[2] If lead was discovered in the Ashe area certainly people would try to get to it. Thomas McGimsey, Ashe County clerk, writing in 1811, says, "That tract of country called Ashe County was first settled in 1755" and Ashe people were noted for longevity, living often over one hundred. However, he continues, "the first hunters were much oppressed by the Shawnees and Cherokees until the end of the Revolution."[3] During the French war, the Cherokee war and Pontiac's war which lasted until 1765 when settlers began to return to New River few came to Carolina's upper New since the entire region was considered Cherokee hunting grounds. Both the Hard Labor and Lochaber treaties left the region in Cherokee hands. However treaties were made to be broken.

About 1765 the Coxes, Bakers, Collins, Reeves and Blevins appeared at Virginia's Peach Bottom and then spilled over the line into Ashe. William Wallen, William McLain and David Helton from Virginia settled in Ashe in 1771. Helton Creek on North Fork was named for Helton.[4]

The adventures of the "much oppressed" hunters of Ashe is lost to us. One surviving story concerns Benjamin Cleveland of Mulberry

Fields on Yadkin hunting up on New River. Cleveland was a huge man weighing over 300 pounds and a patriot of the upper New. Reubin Stringer, a noted woodsman of the upper Yadkin, took Cleveland elk hunting among the herds at the head of New River. Pursuing a wounded elk to a rocky point in the river Cleveland suddenly found himself surrounded by a large number of coiling rattlesnakes, hissing and rattling. The only way to avoid a horrible death was to instantly plunge into the river. Cleveland did and saved himself.[5] He lived with pounds intact to figure prominently in coming events on the upper New.

A number of these upper New hunters were associated with the Cherokees in trading and cohabitating. The Judds came from Pittsylvania to establish a hunting camp on the New. A Judd was captured by the Cherokees before 1752. Ready to be executed he was saved from death by Outacite who was then called Judd's Friend. Judd brothers were in Ben Cleveland's company at King's Mountain in 1780. Before the battle Cleveland asked if anyone wanted to drop out. John Judd said he would stay behind "to hold the horses". Rowland Judd "to redeem the honor of his family went forward into battle."[6]

The Wards were early hunters in the area. There is a Ward's Gap on the upper New between Carolina and Tennessee and a Ward's Gap in present Carroll County, Virginia, where an early road crossed from Carolina to the New. Whether these gaps are named for the same hunter is unknown. John and James Ward were early living on the upper New in Cherokee territory. John Ward went in 1767 with Ben Cutbirth, another New River man, down the Mississippi. Cherokee princess and Beloved Woman, noted friend of the whites, was named Nancy Ward after she married Brian Ward.

Some hunters like the Maynards from Surry who lived awhile on New River moved on when it got "too crowded."[7]

The white man was not in Ashe long before he began naming places. One of the first was "Old Fields" on South Fork, a rich meadow, naturally open, where there were never any trees. Here where Gap Creek empties into South Fork was once the home of a wandering Cherokee band. It was early claimed by Ben Cleveland. Other early landmarks were Pennington's Mill, Nathaniel Judd's Camp, John Coxes Roundabout on Cranberry Creek of South Fork, William Ray's Mill, Ward's Gap, Blevin's Crossroads and Elk Crossroads.[8]

When Wilkes County land office opened in 1778 the following are some on the upper New on Elk Creek: Beverly Watkins, Enoch

Osborne, Barnabas Evans, William Maxwell, James Mulkey. On New River were Moses Tolliver, George Gibson, William Sturdie and Daniel Richardson. On South Fork were Christopher Maynard, John Ayers, Daniel Yarnell, John Green, James Tompkins, Benjamin Cutbirth, Jesse Council, Andrew Baird, Rowland Judd, Garret Hendrick, William McLain and Andrew Baker.

Others on South Fork were George Morris near William Ray's Mill, William Humphries, Timothy Perkins, Royal Porter, Samuel McQueen, John Johnston, Samuel Wilcoxen, William Sperry, William Nall, Spillsberry Tribble, John Dick, Hugh Smith, Thomas Calloway, Mathew Sparks, Isaiah Cass and Ben Cleveland. Nathaniel Judd's Camp was on Beaver Creek. William McNeill, David Smith, Nathaniel Vannoy, George Reaves, William Colvard, Morris Baker, Jonathan Courtney, Martin Gambill, Thomas Payne, Thomas Massey, John Church, Benjamin Herndon, George Collins and William Howell (in their old cabins) and John Cox on the Roundabout were other South Forkers. On North Fork were Abel Pennington, Joshua Neaves, James Ward, Osaac Weaver, Paul Henson, Zack Wells and Benajah Pennington at the mill. On Helton Creek were William Huff, J.P. Fletcher and Elisha Baldwin. Joseph Herndon was on Horse Creek.

At the 1778 Wilkes Court at Mulberry Fields Meeting House a new road was ordered across the mountain to the ford on South Fork of New River and to Pennington Mill on North Fork. Reubin Stringer was to be road overseer to the Old Fields on New River and Andrew Baker overseer of the bridle path to William McLain's.[9]

By the time of the 1778 court these landowners were not so neighborly. Some were American Patriots but others were Loyalists. Such was Timothy Perkins who with brother Joseph were tax collectors for the Crown in Massachusetts but because of political persecution at the beginning of the Revolution fled in 1776 to "Old Fields" New River where Timothy was killed in a Tory skirmish. [10]

For skirmishes there were, the most famous involving Patriots Ben Cleveland, Ben Cutbirth, Richard and Joseph Calloway, Berry Toney, Samuel McQueen, Benjamin Greer and John Baker opposing Loyalist Captain Riddle aided by New River man Zachariah Wells. This involved kidnapping Cleveland, assaulting females, a wild chase to a mountain peak ending with Cleveland hanging Zack Wells on the banks of the Yadkin.[11] Another Tory gathering occurred at Round Meadows (present Baywood) on the New. But the Patriots won, the New even having its own Paul Revere in Martin Gambill aided by Enoch Osborne.[12]

After the Revolution a settlement called "the Jersey Settlement" on the Yadkin, then Rowan now Davidson County near Linwood fed settlers to the upper New. Nathan Horton, a member of the guard at Major Andre's execution, brought his family from New Jersey or Chester County, Pennsylvania, to the "Jersey Settlement" about 1785 and up to New River. Their second child was born on New River August 15, 1786. Appalachian State University displays the grandfather clock the Hortons brought from New Jersey to North Carolina, then over the mountains to New River.[13]

Many of the early settlers on upper New River were of Quaker stock from such heavily Quaker areas as Loudoun County, Virginia; Chester County, Pennsylvania and Burlington County, New Jersey. A Quaker meeting established on the New River by New Jersey Quakers about 1785 sent their records to Deep River Monthly Meeting in North Carolina and later to Mt. Pleasant-Chestnut Creek Meeting in Grayson County, Virginia.[14]

The extreme upper reaches of the New that is today Watauga County was formed from Ashe in 1849 and is at the river's highest altitude on Grandfather Mountain of 5900 feet. Eight other mountains nearby which feed the New are over 5000 feet.[15]

Watauga was visited by Bishop August Gottlieb Spangenberg and other Moravians on December 6, 1752 after an agonizing thousand-foot climb up Globe Mountain to what is now Blowing Rock. They were guided by Henry Day, "Gentleman" John Perkins and John Rhodes acting as chain carriers and hunters. They camped at the site of present Boone where Spangenberg said of the natural meadows, "The land is already clear, long grass grows here, and it is all low-land. Three creeks unite in a river." The site was first called Three Forks.

Spangenberg saw crabapple orchards, "Meadow Mountains" and concluded that Three Forks area was good for an "Indian settlement" but not a large Moravian settlement for New River was "very lonesome, not one man lives there, it is truly a Freydeck."[16] Thus the upper New became known as Freydeck.

The French war kept all but the bravest hunters out of the area. When they did come they hunted along Henry Day's Creek named for Spangenberg's guide and along Farenell Creek probably named for Daniel Yarnell (Farnell). Day's Creek later became Howard Creek named for Benjamin Howard of Elkville on the Yadkin, the first to graze cattle on Spangenberg's luxuriant meadows. A cabin built for his herders survived into the twentieth century in front of Appalachian State University Men's Dormitory.[17]

Among Howard's herders was an African named Burrell who said he piloted Daniel Boone across the Blue Ridge to the Howard cabin on New River on the first trip Boone ever took across the mountains.[18]

The exact date of Boone's first arrival on the New River is unknown. **The North Carolina Guide** says that from 1760 he came into the upper New River region on hunting trips and that he used a cabin later called Daniel Boone Cabin whose site is marked with an 18-foot stone monument at the corner of Faculty and Newland Streets in Boone. This was located on Daniel Boone Trail the earliest part of the Wilderness Trail.

Boone's trail up to the Watauga area followed an old Indian trail from the Yadkin along a ridge between Elk and Stony Fork Creeks, across the Blue Ridge at Cook's Gap, then to Three Forks or Howard's Cabin, on through Hodge's Gap, down Brushy Fork Creek, crossing Grave Yard Gap to Dog Skin Creek, along the base of Rich Mountain crossing Silverstone to the gap between Zionville, North Carolina and Trade, Tennessee (basically present Route 421). In Tennessee he followed Roan's Creek through the mountains into the Holston Valley.[19]

Exploring trips following Boone's Trail across the New headwaters were the Cutbirth-Ward party, spring 1767; the Boone-Hall party, autumn 1767; and the Boone-Finley party, May 1769.

Gradually as whites came into the area landmarks took their name. Howard's Knob at Boone where today is the world's most advanced windmill built by NASA was named for Ben Howard. Meat Camp Creek was named for a meat storage cabin that hunters built around 1770. The Moravians traded with these hunters. Near Meat Camp is the Ward cabin site where potsherds and remnants of Moravian manufacture have been found. The Ward site is near Sugar Grove at the confluence of Cove Creek and Watauga River.[20]

Shull's Mills located on a most distant reach of New River and though of later vintage than Howard's Cabin and Meat Camp Creek is of early date. Frederick Shull and wife Charity came from Germany about 1750. He was a weaver and weaving paid for their passage while his wife worked in the fields. They lived first in Lincoln County where Simon Shull was born October 24, 1767. He married Mary Sheiffer of Loudoun County, Virginia and they settled on the New at Shull's Mills.[21]

One outstanding relic of these first days on the upper New exists in the Tatum cabin now relocated and seen on the **Horn of the West** out-door drama grounds at Boone. The Tatem cabin was built in

The Horton Clock came from New Jersey
to North Carolina over the Blue Ridge
to the New.

(Photo by Walter L. Johnson)

Tatum Cabin (1770) on the Upper New, Boone, North Carolina
(Photo by Walter L. Johnson)

1770 at Elk Cross Roads (Todd) where Elk Creek enters South Fork of the New.

Travelers of the 1880's describe the Tatem cabin nearly one hundred years after it was built. Approaching from Tennessee, they traveled to Elk Cross Roads ten miles along a stream with "rhododendrons illuminating the way, gleaming in the forest and reflected in the stream." Arriving at the Tatem cabin the travelers said, "It is a house of logs, with two rooms, a kitchen and a spare room with a low loft access, with a ladder at the side of the chimney."

The chimney was remarkable. "The chimney is a huge construction of stone separating the two parts of the house," said the travelers. "In fact the chimney was built first. Two rooms were then built against it." This gives great insight into how first homes along North Carolina's upper New were built.

In 1880 the cabin had a railed veranda (since removed) where they found Mr. Tatem. "These Southern verandas give an air to the meanest dwelling," said the travelers. "They are much cooler so the family sit here and here are the basin and pail filled from the neighboring springhouse."

Upon departure the travelers related, "We enter almost immediately into fine stretches of forest and rode under the shade of great oaks. The way, which began by the New River, soon led us over the hills to the higher levels of Watauga County. So far on our journey we had been hemmed in by low hills, and without any distant or mountain outlooks."

They traveled on to Boone, remarking, "The guideboards notified us that everything in this region tends toward Boone. The simple ingenuity of the guideboards impressed us. If the traveler was to turn to the right the sign read "To Boone 10 M." If he was to go left it read "M01 Enoog oT". With this we leave the 1880 travelers and return to the New one hundred years earlier.

FOOTNOTES—Chapter XXVII

1. John Preston Arthur, **Western North Carolina A History 1730-1913** (Spartanburg, South Carolina: The Reprint Co., 1973) hereafter cited as Arthur, **Western Carolina**, p. 22; De Vaugondy **Map, 1755**; Fry-Jefferson **Map** 1751; Governor Johnston to the Lords of Trade, **NCCR** IV, xiii. **CS,** II, p. 143; Fries, **Moravian Records,** II, p. 536; Fields-Hughes, **Grayson County,** p. 338; **VMHB,** v. 10, pp. 140, 239 and **VMHB,** v. 24, p. 185. Cummings, **Southeast Maps,** pp. 55-56.

2. Governor Arthur Dobbs to the Board of Trade, August 25, 1755, **NCCR** V, pp. 356-359.

3. Thomas McGimsey, Newsome, **Carolina Counties.**

4. **CS,** II, p. 143. Blevins and Cox vs. Newell and Collett, **Map of Carolina 1770.**

5. Lyman C. Draper, **King's Mountain and Its Heroes. History of the Battle of King's Mountain, October 7, 1780 and the Events Which led to it** 1881 ed. reprint (Spartanburg, South Carolina: The Reprint Company, 1967) hereafter cited as Draper, King's Mountain pp. 430-431.

6. Ibid. p. 249 and **SCIAD,** I, p. 244.

7. Arthur, **Western Carolina,** p. 197 and Fries, Shreiner Journey, p. 331.

8. Arthur, **Western Carolina,** p. 101 and Draper, **Kings' Mountain,** p. 437.

9. Hayes, **Wilkes,** pp. 30, 33, 35, 420-424

10. Arthur, **Western Carolina,** p. 106.

11. Draper, **King's Mountain,** pp. 437-446.

12. Fields-Hughes, **Grayson,** pp. 35-36.

13. Dr. Eric Olson, ASU Appalachia Collection, Conversation with author, April 1981.

14. Anderson-Green, **New Frontier,** p. 423.

15. Blackwell P. Robinson, **The North Carolina Guide,** (Chapel Hill: The University of North Carolina Press, 1955) p. 547.

16. Fries, **Moravian Records,** v. I, p. 47.

17. Arthur, **Western Carolina,** p. 82.

18. Arthur **ibid.** Narrative of Col. James M. Isbell.

19. **The North Carolina Guide,** p. 548 and Thwaites, **Boone,** p. 90.

20. Dr. Eric Olson, letter to author, June 1981.

21. Arthur, **Western Carolina,** pp. 351-352.

22. Charles D. Walker, **On Horseback, A Tour in Virginia, North Carolina and Tennessee** (New York: Houghton Mifflin Company, 1888) pp. 32-36.

Life on the Lower New
(Photo by Gerald Ratliff Governor's Office of E.C.D.)

Chapter XXIII

First Settlement on the
Lower New in West Virginia

The portion of New River in present Mercer, Monroe, Summers, Raleigh and Fayette Counties, West Virginia, between the mouth of East River and the mouth of Gauley, was settled later than the Middle and Upper New. The terrain was rough and inaccessible. The river called "River of Death" was nearer the Ohio Indians whose wanderings in the area were frequent. The presence of the war camp at the mouth of Bluestone made settlers wary of the region. Although the English were not eager to settle the area the French knew enough about it to give the Greenbrier their own French name of Ronceverte. Jesuit Father Bonnecamp's map of 1749 calls the Kanawha-Chinondaichio. From the 1740's on French traders frequented the area around the mouth of Kanawha on the Ohio where in 1750 they planned to settle a thousand families.

The Salling-Howard party went through this country in 1742 and mention no settlers nor did Dr. Thomas Walker when he returned from Kentucky and crossed the New on June 28, 1750, near the mouth of Greenbrier. However it is generally accepted that there had been settlers at the mouth of East River as early as 1742 based on the Mary Porter gravestone later discovered by John Toney when he settled there in 1780. The Absalom Looney family from Looney's Ferry on the James River had settled on Bluestone before 1754. Father Robert Looney sent for them to come home when the Indian troubles began in 1753 or '54.[1] By 1755 the Keeney's cabin-fort at the mouth of Greenbrier was the most western settlement on the New on Fry-Jefferson's Map of Virginia.

Andrew Culbertson, from Chambersburg, Cumberland Valley, Pennsylvania, brought relatives including John Culbertson and established Culbertson's Bottom in 1753. By November 1755 the Culbertsons for fear of Indians had moved "a great distance from the

The inaccessible lower New as seen today at Fayette Station Road Bridge
(Photo by Gerald S. Ratcliffe Governor's Office of E.C.D.)

New." Andrew sold out to Samuel Culbertson. During the war the place appeared deserted although Culbertson claimed he "had done everything to prevent it appearing deserted." After the French war when the Loyal Company resumed selling in 1770 they sold the bottom to Thomas Farley or Farlow who paid the Loyal Company and assigned his right to James Burnsides, a ginseng digger and merchant. Samuel Culbertson hired Andrew Reid to get possession and in 1782 a Court of Commissioners decided for Burnsides but soon reversed itself granting the land to Culbertson. [2]

This second settling and selling of land was called the "second settlement." People came from many places, eastern Virginia and Shenandoah, as well as New Jersey.

The Cooks from the Shenandoah settled at Indian Creek and built Cook's Fort about three miles from New River. The Woods on Rich Creek built Woods Fort near present Peterstown, West Virginia. Hezekiah Sellards from Shenandoah made many trips into the forest beyond New River around the head of Wolf and Walkers Creeks. According to one source Sellards founded a colony at Walker's mountain in the 1760s. The Staffords, Porters and Damrons came with Sellards.

The Capertons possibly of French ancestry were on the lower New in the 1760's. They had settled in Ireland where John Caperton's son killed a man and John left for America. In Pennsylvania he married Irish Polly Thompson moved to Augusta or Rockingham County, where they sold out in 1759 soon appearing on New River. They became part of the second settlement of Monroe County, settling first on Rich Creek then on Hans Creek. All the Capertons later moved west except "New River Hugh" who would serve under Captain John Lewis at Point Pleasant and in Captain Wood's company in present Monroe County. Hugh married Rhoda Stodgill and is the ancestor of the New River and Greenbrier Capertons. [3]

Neighbors of the Capertons on Hans Creek were the Ellisons. James Ellison, born in Sussex County, New Jersey in 1735, migrated to New River's Hans Creek in 1771. The Ellisons were noted spinners with one house which had nothing but loams, spinning wheels, cards, and spindles. One of their looms had 22 treadles necessary for Double Weave coverlets. [4]

There was much interest in the lower New for speculators wanted to know how they could get to the Kanawha Valley and tap its riches. In 1769 London merchant Thomas Walpole petitioned the Crown for the Iroquois lands granted at Fort Stanwix. He planned to establish a colony called Vandalia with its capitol at the mouth of

Kanawha. The junction of the New and Greenbrier was to be one corner of Vandalia or the "Walpole Grant." Petitions from the people settled on Greenbrier were sent to London. They said it would be inconvenient for markets and courts. They feared their land would be "consigned to a group of mercenary proprietors tho' it was to avoid inconveniences of this kind that many of your petitioners took shelter in Virginia. Let our fate be what it will. Virginia is the only place of trade we can have." [5]

George Washington and Andrew Lewis two prominent Virginia land speculators immediately went to the Kanawha Valley where Washington surveyed in 1770 planning a large colony of his own. Lewis claimed the land at the mouth of Kanawha on the Ohio called Point Pleasant. Washington had reached the Kanawha by coming down the Ohio, not by coming along the New. For there was believed an inpenetrable barrier placed on the New by Kanawha Falls two miles below the junction of the New and Gauley.

"This is a very remarkable fall," said Governor Thomas Pownall of New Jersey, "not for its great height, but for coming through a mountain now thought impassable for man or beast, and is itself impassable. But no doubt foot or horse paths will be found when a great number of people make the search."

Pownall said all the people on Holston and the New turned "their commerce into James River." Pownall and Washington, also, wanted to establish a James-Kanawha commercial route giving Virginia a southern waterway to the Ohio.

"The waters of James River and those of Kanawha are no more than four miles distant and Kanawha is navigable. From the James to Kanawha is not more than 40 miles portage," reported Pownall. "But it is not improveable to the Ohio for the Kanawha has an impassable fall (Kanawha Falls) impassable for men or beast. But its opening a passage to the New Virginia is a very great advantage." [6]

However a young British Army Lieutenant was giving a different opinion. The British had at Fort Pitt in 1763 Lieutenant Thomas Hutchins who designed the fort. They assigned him the task of making a map of the territory just won from France. In his boat he went down the Ohio and along the rivers draining into it. Hutchins took notes of what he saw and says, "The falls of the Kanawha had been thought impassable but late discoveries have proven that a wagon road may be made through the mountain which occasions the falls."

"By a portage of a few miles only," said Hutchins, "a way may be had between the waters of Great Kanawha and James River in

Kanawha Falls near Gauley Bridge

(Photo by Gerald S. Ratcliffe Governor's Office of E.C'D')

Virginia."[7] It was in 1764 that Matthew Arbuckle traveled the entire New-Kanawha valley to sell a load of skins at the trading post at the mouth of Kanawha.

In February 1773 Walter Kelly, James Pauley, James Campbell and Peter Shoemaker of the Muddy Creek settlement on Greenbrier came down the New heading for Kanawha. At the Gauley Walter Kelly turned back but the others went on to Campbell's Creek in Kanawha County, West Virginia, where Campbell sowed "a large quantity of appleseed" and made a tomahawk improvement. The same year James Morris cleared a tract opposite Campbell on Napier's Creek. Curtis and John Alderson, Joseph Carroll,William Morris and John Herd set out from Shenandoah country for New River below the falls and went as far as James Burnside's on Greenbrier. Joined by Archibald Taylor, Philip Cooper and Walter Kelly they arrived at New River April 6, 1773, made improvements and started home. At Gauley they met James Campbell, Peter Shoemaker and James Pauley and returned home with them.[8]

While these discoveries were being made on the lower New back on the middle New at the seat of government many things were happening. Fincastle County had been formed and settlers were flooding the valley. This land rage would within the year bring another Indian War, "Dunmore's War". When that was finished the river people would be torn by years of Revolution and near civil war between Patriots and Tories. The New would yet again be a corridor to war well deserving of its Indian name, "The River of Death."

FOOTNOTES—Chapter XXVIII

1. CS, I, p. 497.

2. Wythe, **Chancery Cases,** pp. 49-55; CS, I, p. 71 and CS, II, p. 68; Wayland F. Dunaway, **The Scotch-Irish of Colonial Pennsylvania** (Chapel Hill: The University of North Carolina Press, 1944) p. 107.

3. Johnston, **Middle New River,** p. 36; Connelley, **Harman's Station,** p. 20. Bernard Caperton, **The Caperton Family** (Charlottesville, Virginia: 1973).

4. Hannah Steele Ellison, "The Ellisons of Hans Creek Valley," **Goldenseal** v. 6, p. 56.

5. Great Britain: P.R.O.:C.O. 5:1352/103.

6. Pownall, **Description,** pp. 137, 144.

7. Thomas Hutchins, **A Topographical Description** of Virginia, Pennsylvania Maryland and North Carolina **Reprint from the Original 1778** edition by F.C. Hicks (Cleveland: The Burrows Brothers Company, 1904) p. 94.

8. CS, II, pp. 68-69.

One of the last streams to enter New River, Gauley Mountain
(Photo by Gerald S. Ratcliffe Governor's Office of E.C.D.)

Chapter XXIV

Epilogue

Although beyond the time frame of this book no story of New River would be complete unless mention is made of the recent dramatic battle between the American Power Company and the people over the Blue Ridge Project.

In 1962 the American Power Company, the nation's largest public utility and its subsidiary, Appalachian Power Company, asked for a Federal Power Commission license to build twin pumped-storage dams and reservoirs on the upper New River. Known as the Blue Ridge Project plans called for the dams to be built in Grayson

Proposed site of APCO's Blue Ridge Project
Molly Osborne Shoals, Grayson County, Virginia
(Photo by Walter L. Johnson)

County, Virginia at Molly Osborne Shoals and the reservoirs in that county and in the North Carolina Counties of Ashe, Allegheny and Watauga.

Pumped-storage works on the principal of pumping water stored in a lower reservoir to a higher one then dropping it to produce energy at peak load periods. APCO's Blue Ridge Project would take 4 kilowatt hours to produce 3 kilowatt hours of energy thus making the utility itself an energy consumer. The company justified this by saying the peak load demands for energy made it practical. American Power planned to cover its losses by selling to midwestern power companies during their brownouts. None of the power produced would be sold in North Carolina but would be used to run air-conditioners in mid-western cities. Pumped-storage reservoirs fill with silt in about three decades making the system obsolete and leaving the river a ruin.

In 1962 when APCO first asked for the license it planned to flood 20,000 acres in Virginia where it sells power. North Carolina did not object. In 1966 when the Interior Department decided larger reservoirs were needed thus flooding North Carolina land, North Carolina did object. Thinking in terms of pollution-dilution, Interior said the larger system could periodically be opened to release great quantities of water to wash out the chemical mess in the Kanawha at Charleston. Thus rural people living along an unspoiled North Carolina river would have to give up their land to solve West Virginia's waste problems. The New River from Boone to Gauley Bridge would be forever changed.

The Environmental Protection Agency ruled against this but in 1968 APCO decided to go ahead and build the expanded system. The Federal Power Commission issued a license allowing the entire 26.5 miles of North Carolina's New to be flooded.

By law any power company planning to build dams must make an archaelogical survey of the area. APCO made these but did not make them public. They became publicly known in August 1975 and in October the Court of Appeals ruled the license invalid since APCO had "caused the Federal Power Commission to violate federal statutes pertaining to historical and archaelogical properties." In 1976 an amended license required APCO to pay for all archaelogical work needed before building. Failure to protect archaelogical treasures of the New River was one of the things APCO was faulted for at the May 1976 Senate hearing. APCO then hired Thunderbird Research Corporation (see chapter 4) to study the dam site. Their study from

June to September 1976 unearthed 99 sites in the area showing 8,000 years of habitation. They concluded that the New River Valley has vast archaelogical potential.[1]

Meanwhile, from 1962 to 1976, the people of North Carolina and Virginia whose lands were to be flooded had not been asleep. They were tremendously concerned about what was happening to them.

For some time environmentalists had been pointing out the uniqueness of the New River. In 1974 a bill was introduced in Congress to include the New in the National Wild and Scenic Rivers System. The bill passed the Senate but was stopped in the House by a manuever of APCO and AFL-CIO in the Rules Committee to require a 2/3's vote of the House. The bill failed this vote.

North Carolina then enacted legislation designating the main stem of the New River in North Carolina as a state scenic river and asked the Secretary of the Interior to designate this part of New River a "scenic river area" under the Federal Wild and Scenic Rivers Act, but administrated by the state which does not require congressional action. North Carolina petitioned the U.S. Court of Appeals for the District of Columbia, for a stay of execution of APCO's Federal Power Commission license. The court granted the stay in 1975.

On May 22, 1975 the General Assembly of North Carolina added 22 miles of the South Fork of the New River to the above legislation, for a total of 26.5 miles of river and notified the Secretary of the Interior.

Much support had formed in defense of the New. The National Committee for the New River led by Hamilton Horton and the Izaak Walton League had long been working to protect the river. The Wilderness Society, Sierra Club, American Rivers Conservation Council, the Audubon Society and others lined up to help. Each national TV network featured the fight to save the New. **The Washington Post and Star, The New York Times** and other newspapers took a stand for the New. The sentiments of the river's friends were expressed by **Outdoor America** which said: "If those virgin lands with their pure sparkling streams, these people who trace their ancestors back to the first settlers of their present homeland this only remaining portion of a prehistoric river — are of no significance to American history and culture, then we truly have no history and this project signifies much more than the death of a river."

President Ford promised to sign a bill to save the river and Carter and Reagan, then prospective Presidents, both urged that the river be saved. Senators Robert Byrd and Lee Metcalf, Chairman of the Interior and Insular Affairs Committee, announced support. The West Virginia legislature adopted resolutions opposing the dams. The gubernatorial candidates of that state urged saving the New but Governor Arch Moore Jr. supported APCO. In July 1975 5,000 people met in Ashe County to support the river. Six original ballads composed by area residents were sung telling of the struggle.

Meanwhile American Power and APCO were not idle. On January 9 and 14, 1976 they placed two-page ads in **The New York Times, Wall Street Journal and The Washington Post** defending the Blue Ridge Project. They called North Carolinians who opposed the dams "an affluent few" adding that "privileged elitists" were using a "tricky scheme" to "euchre" the people of North Carolina out of "our gift of 3.900 acres. . .for a lake-front state park. No selfish group which stands in the way can remain unchallenged — be they privileged elitists or a prejudiced press." This was printed although APCO's counsel Dowd admitted that the shoreline of the "lake-front park" would fluctuate daily as the company pumped water back and forth creating constant mud flats along the shore. These ads had the reverse effect of winning many new friends for the river.

Then came a harsh blow. The Court of Appeals on March 24, 1976 upheld the Federal Power Commission license to APCO to build dams!

North Carolina promptly appealed to the Supreme Court. Secretary of the Interior Kleppe came to the aid of the New on April 13, 1976 naming 26.5 miles of the New a National Wild and Scenic River. He asked the Justice Department to join North Carolina's appeal. The National Committee for the New River on May. 6, 1976 put notices in **The New York Times, Philadelphia Enquirer,** and **St. Louis Dispatch** supporting the New.

Questions remained. Could the Secretary of Interior cast aside a license given a power company by the Federal Power Commission, an independent Federal regulatory agency? Could APCO legally dam a National Wild and Scenic River? The only certain protection was through an act of Congress.

Senator Jesse Helms of North Carolina introduced in Congress a bill including the New River in North Carolina in the National Wild and Scenic Rivers System and cancelling APCO's license to build the Blue Ridge Project.

Hearings opened on May 20, 1976 before the Senate Subcommittee on Environment and Land Resources of the Committee on Interior and Insular Affairs. Testifying for APCO were Virginians Senator Harry F. Byrd, Jr., Governor Mills Godwin, Jr., and Attorney-General Andrew P. Miller as well as APCO's Vice-President and their Counsel Dowd. Testifying for the New were North Carolinians Governor James Holshouser Jr., Attorney-General Rufus Edmisten, Representative Stephen Neal, Edmund Adams, R.J. Troutman, Ashe Citizens Committee and Sidney Gambill, Upper New River Valley Association. Representative Ken Hechler of West Virginia testified for the New.

Testimony claimed that 50,000 acres of farmland yielding greater incomes and having a greater tax base than the dams would be flooded. Hundreds of farms tilled for 200 years would be destroyed. Farm to market roads would be blocked by water causing more time to be spent going to market, church and school. Towns such as Mouth of Wilson, 12 cemeteries and 15 U.S. Post Offices would be flooded. Geological formations showing the New to be the continent's oldest river would be destroyed. Archaelogical sites showing human habitation over 8,000 years would be destroyed. Canoeing, white water sports and fishing would be devastated. The New River, an unspoiled, freeflowing, unpolluted river unique in every sense, would be replaced by lakes whose shorelines rise and fall continually leaving mud-flats useful for 30 years.

The House passed the bill on August 10, 1976. It went to the Senate where the New found some surprising friends like Barry Goldwater who had voted to build the Glen Canyon Dam but regretted it and now wanted to save the New.

"Of all the votes I have cast in this body," Goldwater said, "there is one I would change. . .the vote I cast to construct the Glen Canyon Dam. I think of that river as it was when I was a boy and that is the way I would like to see it again." The Senate passed the bill to save the New.

On September 11, 1976 in the White House Rose Garden President Ford signed the bill making 26.5 miles of North Carolina's New a part of the National Wild and Scenic River System. Watching Ford were Governor Holshouser and many others who had fought the fourteen year battle with APCO.

The case of the New vs. APCO is a classic case of what the will of the people can accomplish in protecting resources and environment. When the Department of the Interior canvassed the United States to determine which rivers should be eligible as Wild and Scenic rivers New River was not chosen. Now due entirely to the will of the people the New became the sixteenth river of which portions have been selected for the Wild and Scenic Rivers System.

In 1979 the state of Virginia nominated New River and tributaries for inclusion in Virginia's scenic river systems. The entire New River in Virginia and Big Reed Island Creek in Carroll as well as Cripple Creek in Wythe, Little Stony in Giles and Walker Creek in Giles and Bland were chosen for study.

The loss of its license to build the Blue Ridge Project outraged the power company so it went to the Supreme Court requesting that Congress pay for its lost license. This request was refused by the Supreme Court in May 1980. In the same May hundreds of people gathered on the banks of the New at West Jefferson, North Carolina, to celebrate the New's designation as a Wild and Scenic River. Governor Hunt said, "Of all the things you will participate in during your lifetime you will probably do nothing more lasting than helping save the New River."[1]

Truly, after people, power companies and political systems have vanished the river will remain. It was here from the beginning. It alone will remain.

FOOTNOTE CHAPTER XXIV

1. William M. Gardner et al An Archaeological Survey of the Proposed Dam/Sites Along the Upper New River (Washington: Thunderbird Research Corporation, 1976) pp. 5-6, 28, 70, 135, 138; George Laycock, "New River, Old Problem," Audubon, November 1975; North Carolina General Assembly , 1973, Session Laws, Resolution 170; U.S. Senate Document 158 (1976) pp. 21-47, 54, 175-193, 205-207, 223 - 227;   The Congressional Record, January 21, 1976; The Roanoke Times, May 18, 1980; "Ruckus over a Scenic River," U.S. News and World Report, August 23, 1976; David Vaczek, "New May become part of "Scenic River System", The Blacksburg Sun, January 10, 1978; "Ford Signs Bill to Save New River" The Washington Post, September 12, 1976.

The New today serving the needs of all!
(Photo courtesy of West Virginia Governor's Office of E.C.D.)

Acknowledgements

I vividly remember the first time I saw the New River. I was with my father and we crossed the river on an old ferryboat that no longer runs. I was five years old. I remember driving down to the riverside and looking downstream at the wide channel of water flowing between what in my small world seemed huge mountains. Then we were on the ferry in the middle of the fiercest, wildest most turbulent water I had seen. I believe my desire to tell the river's story was born then. Often in the long years ahead my father talked with me about the old river. Years passed. First I wrote of the people and leaders who settled along the river. Upon this I spent fifteen years of research and writing. Only now have I come to the river itself.

Most of my research for **The New River** has been done at Carol Newman Library of Virginia Polytechnic Institute and State University. I feel fortunate to be able to use the resources of this magnificent library and have the aid of its librarians, especially Dorothy McCombs, Humanities Librarian, Special Collections Librarian Glenn McMullen and Wendell Weisend, Archivist, as well as Donald Daidone and Lane Rasmussen for aid with map research. Also with maps and early roads in the Blue Ridge thanks go to Dr. J. Francis Amos and Judge John P. Alderman. Gratitude goes especially to the Otto Hartenstein family for aid with German translation. From Appalachian State University I received aid from Jill Loucks and Eric Olson with Appalachia materials. At Radford University I was aided by Ann Swain, Archivist, Virginia Room, McConnell Library. Special thanks is due my husband for untiring efforts with photography. Finally the West Virginia Governor's Office of Economic and Community Development is to be commended for their gracious and generous aid in adding to the beauty of this book.

Symbols Used In Annotations

CS	Lyman Chalkley	Chronicles of the Scotch-Irish Settlement in Virginia Extracted from the Original Court Records of Augusta County 1745-1800
CVS	William P. Palmer	Calendar of Virginia State Papers and other manuscripts 1652-1778 preserved in the Capitol at Richmond
DP	R. A. Brock	The Official Records of Robert Dinwiddie
DU	Duke University, Perkins Library	
FP	George Reese	The Official Papers of Francis Fauquier Lieutenant Governor of Virginia 1758-1768

HJ   Journals of the House of Burgesses of Virginia

LC PP   The Preston Family of Virginia Papers

NCCR   North Carolina Colonial Records

PMHB   Pennsylvania Magazine of History and Biography

SCIAD   South Carolina Indian Affairs Documents

THQ   Tyler Historical Quarterly

VEJ   Journals of the Executive Council of Colonial Virginia

VMHB   The Virginia Magazine of History and Biography

VSL   The Virginia State Library, Manuscript Division

WH   The State Historical Society of Wisconsin: The Draper Manuscripts Kentucky Papers, CC; King's Mountain Papers, DD; Draper's Notes, S; Preston Papers, QQ; Virginia Papers, ZZ.

WL, FP   Washington and Lee University, William Fleming Papers

WMQ   The William and Mary College Quarterly Historical Magazine

Index

Adena-Hopewell culture 33,40
Aero Jet Ranger Helicopter 8
Africa 2, 187
Alderson, Curtis and John 203
Aldridges, James 152, 155
Algonquian 35, 40
Allegeni Indians 40
Alleghenies 5, 8, 10, 49, 53, 67, 70, 73, 162
Allegheny County 5, 183, 189, 206
Allegheny River 23, 111
Alsace-Lorraine 2, 73
American Power Company 205
Ammonscossittee 105
Anchor and Hope 77, 79, 95, 163
Anderson family 187
Anderson, John 171
Anderson, Green, Paula 187
Angel, Benjamin 138
Antossity, Usteneeka-Outacite 126-130
Anvil Rock 10
Appalachian Mountains 5, 27, 29, 31, 33, 59
Appalachian Power Company 6, 32
Appalachian State University 2, 193
Appelatinian Mountains 8
Apperson, Joseph 180
Appomattox Town 45,
Appomattox River 42, 45, 58, 59
Arbuckle, Matthew 176, 203
Arbuckle Creek 14
Archaeic Culture 32, 33
Army Corps of Engineers 12
Arthur, Gabriel 55, 56, 57
Asbury, Francis 186
Ash, Harrison, 14
Ashe County 5, 21, 29, 43, 183, 189, 190, 206
Attakulla Kulla (Little Carpenter) 98, 130, 142-144, 162, 168, 171-172
Augusta Boys 171
Augusta Court House 65, 71, 78, 83, 98, 115, 121
Austin, Moses 7
Austinville 7, 32, 166
Ayers, Harvard 32

Babcock State Park 12
Back Creek 70
Bacon's Rebellion 57, 110
Baker, Andrew 185, 192
Baker, John 192
Bargar, Casper 80, 117, 118, 124, 135
Barnwell, John 63
Batts-Fallam Expedition 1, 2, 24, 40, 41, 45, 46, 47, 49, 50, 52, 53, 55, 57, 73, 90
Batts, Nathaniel 45
Batts, Thomas 45, 46, 47, 51, 52, 53, 55
Beaver Dam on Tom's Creek 70, 73
Beissel, Conrad 73, 75, 76, 92, 132-133
Belle-Hampton 179
Belspring 8
Benneville, Dr. George 76
Berkeley, William Governor 55, 56, 57
Bethabara 101, 112, 116, 120, 134, 150, 154, 159, 161, 180
Beverley, Robert 45, 46, 50, 51
Bienville, Le Moyne de 65
Big Falls 8
Big Horseshoe 8
Big Reed Island Creek 210
Big Sandy 45, 61, 129-130, 159
Big Walker Mountain (Cloyd's Mountain) 8
Bingamin's Ferry 108, 173
Bingamin, John 108, 115, 119, 120
Bingamin, Katherine 144, 169
Black, John 79
Blacksburg, Virginia 47, 59, 126
Blackwater and Pigg Rivers 69, 79, 84, 88, 120, 138, 139
Bland, Edward 43, 44
Bledsoe, Abraham 119, 155
Bledsoe, Isaac 154, 155
Bledsoes, Lick 155
Blevins, William 153
Blevins Crossroads 191
Blevins family 152-153
Blowing Rock 4, 5, 100

Blue Ridge Mountains 5, 44, 53, 55, 58, 62, 64, 67, 87, 89, 178, 189
Blue Ridge Project 6, 206
Bluestone Dam and Reservoir 8, 10, 11, 12, 19, 61
Bluestone River 10, 35, 61, 83, 198
Blue Spring Gap 153
Blowing Rock 193
Boiling Springs 179
Bonnecamp, Father 110, 198
Boom Furnace 7
Boone, Daniel 2, 54, 149, 152, 155, 194
Boone-Finley expedition 154, 194
Boone-Hall expedition 194
Boone, North Carolina 39, 102, 154, 196, 206
Boren, Bazel 152, 154,
Botetourt, Governor 175-183
Boundary line plan 86
Bouquet, Henry, Colonel 168-169
Bourne, Rosamond and William 183-184, 187
Box, Robert 106
Braddock, Edward General 115, 120, 123
Brandmueller, John 91-92
Brooks, Castleton 155
Brooks Falls 12
Brooks, Maurice 27
Brown, Jacob 108
Buck Dam 7
Buck Mountain 6
Buchanan, John Colonel 24, 66, 67, 69, 70-71, 73, 75, 77, 78, 79, 97, 113, 123, 163, 170
Buchanan, Jane Sayers 78
Buchanan, Molley 97
Buchanan, Peggy Patton 69-70, 95, 97, 120
Buffalo Wallowing Hole 70-71, 73
Bughsen, Billy 163
Bullitt, Thomas 145
Burgell, Samuel 80, 117
Burk, Thomas 9, 120
Burk, James 83, 95, 129
Burkes Garden 29, 129
Burlington County, New Jersey 187, 193
Burnsides, James 200

Burrell, (African) 2, 194
Butcher's Creek 152, 190
Byllesby Dam 4, 6, 7
Byrd, Robert 208
Byrd, William I 52, 53, 57
Byrd, William II 86
Byrd, William III 130, 141, 142, 143, 165, 166, 172
Caesar's Arch 10
Calhouns, Ezekiel, George, James Patrick, William, Zachariah 77, 78, 79, 83, 86, 95, 121, 141
Callaway 87
Calloway, Charles, Thomas, Richard, Samuel 153, 192
Camp Sayers 144
Campbell, Arthur 176
Campbell, Charles 82
Campbell, James 203
Caperton, John 200
Caperton, New River Hugh 200
Captain Jack 62
Carolina Silverbell 27
Carr, William 153-155
Carrico family 187
Castle, Jacob 80, 83, 87, 111, 129
Castle Rock 9
Catawbas 39, 61, 62, 66
Catawba Creek Road and Valley 40, 62, 70, 91, 120, 125
Catawba rhododendron 27
Cawcasean Mountains 58
Cecil, Samuel 157
Chandler, William 141
Charles I 37, 112
Charles II 1, 52
Charleston, West Virginia 28, 38, 52, 65
Cherokees 34, 39, 40, 50, 61, 63, 64, 83, 98, 105, 111, 116, 124, 155
Cherry Tree Bottom 79
Chester County Pennsylvania 193
Chief Hagler 62
Chief New River 62
Chinodacheta 23, 110, 198
Chiswell, John, Colonel 112, 113, 143, 144, 149, 165-173
Chota 40, 55, 98, 113

Christian, Israel 169, 175-176
Christian, William 161, 169-170, 180
Christiansburg, 179
Chronicon Ephratense 75, 76, 115
Churton, William 86, 189
Clapp family 137, 138
Clark, George Rogers 7
Claytor Lake Park and Dam 7, 8, 19, 138
Clayton, Reverend 49, 53, 57
Clement, Maude 87
Cleveland, Benjamin 190-192
Clinker Lot Right Men 186
Cloyd, Joseph, Colonel 179
Coal River 65
Collett 1770 Map 6, 147, 189
Collins, George 185, 192
Connelly, James and John 76, 87, 106-107
Cook's Fort 200
Cook's Gap 194
Cook, John 115
Cooley, William 154
Cornstalk 158
Cotton Hill Bridge 27
Council, Jesse 192
Cowan family 174
Cowan, Ned 155
Cowdon, Samuel 145
Cox, Charles 153-155
Cox, David 153-155, 185
Cox, John 153-155, 183-189, 190-191
Cox, Mary Rankin 185
Coxe, Daniel 43
Crabtree, William 154-155
Cranberry Creek 185
Cripple Creek 4, 7, 143, 179, 187, 210
Crockett, Joseph 78, 106
Crockett, Anne Agnes 79
Crockett, Esther Thompson 78
Crockett, Robert 155
Crockett, Samuel 78-79
Crump's Bottom 10
Culbertson, Andrew 12, 198
Culbertson's Bottom 108, 170, 176
Cull, James 119

Cumberland County, North Carolina 121
Cumberland Gap 82, 95
Currin family 187
Cutbirth, Benjamin 154, 191
Cutbirth-Ward Party 194
Czechoslovakia 2, 69
Damron family 200
Dan River 34
Davis family, James, Thomas 80, 82, 145, 159
Day, H. 190, 193
De Belestre, Picot, Captain 134
DeCeleron, Captain 110
De l'Isle, Guilaume, Map 63
De Soto, Hernando 40
De Vaugondy, Robert, Map, 6, 23, 110, 190
Deep River Monthly Meeting 193
Delaware Indians 40
Delaware River Valley 186
Detroit 58
Devereaux, Charles, Nancy 165
Dennis, Hannah, Joseph 126, 158, 169
Dickenson family 187
Dickey family 184, 187
Dinwiddie, Robert Governor 88, 105, 107, 111, 113, 116, 123, 124-128, 134
Dobbs, Arthur Governor, 112, 190
Doak, Robert 176
Dog Creek 5
Donald, William, James Trading Company 128, 154
Donegal Ireland 79
Double Shoal Rapids 7
Dowdy Bluff and Creek 14
Draper, Betty Robinson 118, 126
Drake, Joseph 154-155
Draper, George, Eleanor, 79, 80, 106, 117
Draper, John 79
Draper's Meadows 77, 79, 106, 108, 117, 118, 119, 123, 126, 135, 137, 178
Dunglen Hotel 14

Dunkard's Bottom 8, 21, 94, 115, 116, 125-133, 141, 144, 158, 171, 179
Dunkleberry, Abraham 138
Dutton, Philip 180
Dysart, James 155
Eagle Bottom 70-71, 79
Early, Mordicia 66
Eason, Francis 137
East River 63, 198
Eastern Woodland culture
Echols, John 137-139
Eckerlin brothers 73, 75, 76
Eckerlin, Israel 73, 94
Eckerlin, Samuel 73, 84, 94, 133
Eggleston, Elizabethtown, N.J. 126
Elk Creek 183, 191
Eggleston Palisades 9, 10, 21, 32
Elkins, Jesse 153
Elkins, Nathaniel, Ralph, Richard 15 153
Ellison, James 200
Engelmann's adder's tongue fern 28
England 52, 57, 62, 110-111, 119, 172
Ephrata Cloisters 70, 73, 74, 75, 77, 133
Essay, Louissiana and Virginia Improved 59, 134
Essex County, New Jersey 187
Evans, Andrew, Barnabas, Robert 83, 105
Fallam, Robert 45, 40, 47, 50, 52, 53, 55
Farley, (Farlow) Thomas, George 124, 200
Farnell, Creek 190
Fauquier, Francis Governor 140, 150, 157, 128, 154
Fayette County, West Virginia 12, 14, 27
Fayette Station Road 15, 18, 19, 199
Finley, John 83, 154
Fincastle County 183, 203
Flour Gap 161-162
Fontaine, Peter 23, 24, 86, 136
Fort Ancient culture 34, 38

Fort Chiswell 88, 143-149, 153, 154, 175-176
Fort Dobbs 123
Fort Frederick 124-129, 133, 138-139
Fort Harman 158
Fort Henry 42, 56
Fort Hope 158
Fort Lewis 141
Fort Lookout 158
Fort Loudoun 141, 142, 144-145
Fort Mayo 88, 137, 139
Fort Preston 125
Fort Vause 61, 133-134, 145
Forest Hill, West Virginia 63
Foster's Falls 7
France 52, 57-58, 62, 63, 65, 66, 67, 83-84, 110-114, 130, 134, 157, 190
Franklin County, Virginia 86, 87, 88,
Freeman (Freeland), Isaac 116
Frey family 76
Frey, George 180-181
Freydeck' 103, 193
Fries Dam 6, 21
Fry-Jefferson Map of Virginia 1751 6, 23, 24, 36, 110, 189
Fry, Joshua 24, 36, 69, 86, 95, 96
Fulkerson, Frederick 190
Fulcarson River 6, 23, 189
Gahagen, Andrew 69
Galax 6, 21
Gallahur, Patrick 107
Gambill, Martin 192
Gap Mountain 8
Gardner, William, Dr. 32
Garrison, Isaac 184
Gauley, Bridge and River 5, 12, 14, 28, 202, 204, 206
George III 162
German River Baptist 70
Germantown, Pennsylvania 76
Gist, Christopher 90, 94-96, 111, 126, 152
Glen Canyon Dam 209
Glen Lyn 8, 10, 61
Goblingtown 139
Goldenseal 28

Goldman, Jacob 66, 79, 92, 108
Goldman, Jacob Jr. 121
Goldman, John 114
Goldwater, Barry 209
Goodwin, Daniel 170
Goodwin's Ferry 8
Gordon, Thomas 155
Grebils (Greybel) 76
Grandfather Mountain 5, 193
Grandview State Park 12, 13, 27
Granny Beck and Aimy 187
Grayson County, Virginia 5, 32, 183
    183
Greenbrier River 10, 25, 61, 63,
    67, 95, 123, 144, 198
Great Iroquois War Trail 62
Great Kanawha Kahaway 23, 142
Great Lakes 2, 30, 31, 35, 59
Great Trading Path 43
Grand Canyon of the East 1, 13, 14
Green, Nathanael, General 7
Green Park Inn Golf Course 5
Greenville 187
Greyhound Bus Stopper 17, 18
Greer, Benjamin 192
Griffith, Phineas 71
Grubb, Henry 107-108
Gunn, Catherine, Mrs. 161
Gunpowder Springs 126, 158
Hale, Lewis 153, 184
Hale Settlement 184
Hales Ford 120
Halifax County 134-140, 152
Hall, Richard 96, 126, 128, 138
Hall, William 138
Halsey family 186
Hamilton, John 141, 159, 179
Hammond, Francis 44
Hammerer, John Daniel 172, 183
Hanover Rangers 123
Hans Creek 200
Harless, Philip 80, 82, 91, 120
Harman,family 73, 129, 140, 162-
    164
Harman, Heinrich Adam 69, 70-71,
    79, 80, 83, 111, 119, 126, 138,
    163
Harman, Daniel 129, 138
Harman, George 80
Harman, Henry 139-140, 163

Harman, Jacob 69-70, 71, 80, 91-
    92, 107, 120, 155
Harman, Louisa Katrina 69
Harman, Valentine 69, 80, 83, 107,
    129, 164
Harrison, Benjamin 108, 114
Hart, Charles 70-71, 108
Hart, Simon 79
Hartmann, Adam 181
Hashe, Eleanor 186
Hashe, John 185-189
Hashe, Thomas 186
Hashe, William 186
Hauck-Fry Cemetery 181
Haw River, Orange County, N.C.
    80, 117
Hawk's Nest State Park and Dam 7,
    17, 18, 19, 28
Helms, Jesse 208
Helton, Creek 5
Helton, David 190
Henkel, Paul 90
Henry, Patrick 113
Herbert, David 165
Herbert, William 165, 170, 173,
    179
Herd, John 203
Herndon, Joseph 192
Herndon, John Goodwin 78
Herman, see Harman
Hico 18
Hickenbotham, Captain 161
Hinton, West Virginia 12, 21, 63
Hocomawanach 35
Hogan, Humphrey 155
Hoge, James 179
Hogg, Peter 123, 129, 136
Holden, Joseph 154
Holland, C. C. Dr. 32,34
Holshouser 209
Holston, Stephen, 66
Holston River 63, 82, 83, 114, 116,
    120, 123, 124, 134, 148, 157-
    158, 163, 194
Hoopaugh, George 76, 107
Horn of the West 194-195
Horseshoe (Bottom) Meadow 70,
    80, 134
Horton, Hamilton 207

Horton, Nathan 193, 195
Hotchkiss, Jedeiah 24
Howard, Benjamin 193, 194
Howard, John 63-65
Howard Knob 7, 194
Howe, Eleanor 179
Howe, Joseph 179
Howell, William 192
Huff, William 192
Hunt, Governor 210
Huss, John 69
Hutchins, Thomas Lt. 201
Independence, Virginia 6
Indian Creek Junction 10, 61, 160-161
Indian Fields 95
Indian Road 71, 120
Ingles Ferry 63, 145
Ingles, Mary Draper 9, 117, 118, 126-127
Ingles, William 117, 118, 120, 127, 145, 159, 170, 173
Iroquois Confederacy 35, 36, 61, 62, 67, 73, 111, 119
Ivanhoe 7
Izaak Walton League 207
Jackson's Ferry 7
James River 38, 43, 52, 69, 87, 120
Jamestown, Virginia 37, 42
Jefferson, Peter 86, 95
Jefferson, Thomas 143, 149
Jersey Settlement 193
John's Creek, Levisa River 152
Johnston, Gabriel, Governor 86, 110
Jones, Cadwallader 36, 58-61
Jones, Minitree 184
Jones, Peter 58
Jones Creek' 59, 70
Jones Ford 153, 184
Judd, Nathaniel 191-192
Judd family, Rowland 152, 191-192
Kanawha Falls 201, 202
Kanawha River and Valley (Great Kanawha) 5, 12, 14, 23, 30, 31, 38, 39, 40, 45, 55, 61, 62, 63, 96, 126, 158, 170, 198, 200
Kanawha Trail 61
Kelly, Walter 203

Keeney Brothers Rapids 17
Keeney's Creek 12
Keeney Fort 198-199
Kent family 174
Kentucky 2, 14, 49, 54
Kettering, Jacob 108
Kilgore, Thomas 155
Kimberlain Creek 161
Kimberlain, Jacob 161
La Salle, Sieur de 2, 52, 110
Lancaster 64, 75, 80, 181
Lane, John 80
Landes family 76
Lang, Stephen 80
Laurel Creek 5
Lead Mines 7, 161, 165, 174, 175
Leatherwood Creek, Henry County 59
Leeper (Leopard), William 108, 116
Lederer, John 44-45, 57
Lewes, Sussex County, Delaware 78
Lewis, Andrew 116, 127, 134, 148, 159, 167-168, 171-172, 201
Lewis, John 77, 175-176
Lewisburg, West Virginia 61
Lick Creek 47
Lingle, family 116, 120
Linkous Ferry 8
Little, Abraham 59, 90
Little River 8, 21, 43, 47, 59, 62, 84, 88, 90, 159
Little Stony Creek 210
Livesay family 187
Lloyd, Thomas, Dr. 119, 123
Lockhart, Charles 170
Loesch, George 159, 163, 166
Long Canes Creek, South Carolina 141
Long Hunters 2
Looney, Absalom, Robert 129, 198
Looney, Thomas 80
Loudoun County, Virginia 193
Lorton, Israel 70, 80
Lost Provinces 189
Louis Philippe, Duke of Orleans 143
Lowman Ferry 8
Loy, Martin and family 116
Loyal Company 104-105, 108, 163, 176

Lucas, John 141
Lucas, Charles 108
Lutherans 80-82, 91
Lyon, Humberston 76, 77, 80, 87, 98, 107, 112, 144
Lyon, Stephen 114
Lybrook family 117-118, 120, 178
Mack, Alexander 73
Mack, Alexander Jr. 75, 76, 83, 85
Mack, William 70, 75
Mack's Meadow 70
Madison, John 119, 120
Mahanaim 70, 74, 75, 76, 83, 94, 95, 115, 180
Mann Creek 12
Mannheim, Germany 69
Mansker, Kaspar 154
Mansker's Lick 155
Marquette and Joliet 2, 52, 53, 110
Martin's Gazetteer of Virginia 10
Matthews Manor 42
Maynard, Christopher 192
Maynard family 191
McCall, James 83, 95
McCullum, John 161
McCord, Howard, Colonel 36
McFarland, James 115
McFarland, John 87, 95, 105
McGavock, Williamson 78
McGimsey, Thomas 183, 190
Maclin, John, James, William 108
McLain, William 190
McQueen, Samuel 192-193
Meador, Josiah 12
Meadow Creek Fishery 12
Meat Camp Creek 194
Mercer West Virginia 198
Meriwether, David, Thomas 185
Miller, Henry 76, 88, 132-133
Miller, Jacob 76
Miller, John 76, 83, 132-133
Mill Creek Hundred, New Castle, Delaware 70
Mining towns of New River Gorge 14
Mississippi 1, 5, 31, 33, 43, 52, 59, 62, 63, 64, 66, 75, 86, 112, 113, 114, 154

Mitchell, John, Map of the British and French Dominions, 1755, 26, 41, 47, 69, 90, 110, 114
Meat Camp Creek 152
Metcalf, Lee 208
Moll, Herman, Map, 63
Molly Osborne Shoals 6, 32, 205, 206
Momongoseneka 10
Mondongacheta 23, 35
Monroe County, West Virginia 198
Montgomery, Elizabeth 79
Montgomery, John 79, 129, 154
Montgomery, Robert 179
Mooney, James 154
Moravians, 91-92, 100-103, 149, 159
Morgan's Glade 71
Morris, James 203
Morris, Henry 108
Moser, Adren 80, 129
Mount Rogers 29
Mountain Lake 28, 29, 30, 96 (Salt Pond)
Mountain Lake Biological Station 29
Mouth of Wilson 6, 189, 208
Muhlenberg, Henry M. 82
Muhlhofen, Rheinland Phalz 80
Mulberry Fields 152, 192
Mulkey, James 185, 192
Mt. Pleasant-Chestnut Creek Meeting 193
Narrows and Narrows Bridge 10, 21, 40
National Committee for the New River
National Wild and Scenic River 1, 6, 12
Neck Creek 71
Needham, James 55
Neeley, Alexander 154
Nelson, William 67
New Brittaine 25, 43
New Dublin Presbyterian Church 180
New England 2
New Jersey 2, 193, 195
New Kanawha Power Company 18

New Kanawha Valley 28, 38, 39, 45, 49, 55, 58, 110, 126, 203
New River, Chief 63
New River Community College 3, 46, 47, 52
New River, 1-20, 23-29, 57
New River family 63
New River Gorge 12, 14, 31, 32
New River Gorge Bridge 18, 19
New River Gorge National River 12, 27
New Virginia 25
Newell, James 120
Newman, William 153
Nicholson, Francis, Governor 57-59
Noble, John 77
Noble, Mary 77
North Carolina 5, 27, 30, 44, 62, 86, 112, 146, 162, 205-210
North Fork of the New 189
Northumberland County, Pennsylvania
Nuckolls, Charles 187
Nuttall, Lawrence 28
Nyberg, Laurentius T. 91
Occonee Trail 62
Occoneechee Indians 36, 39
Occonnechee Trail 45
Offenbach, Rheinland Pfalz, Germany, 80
Ohio Company 95, 104
Ohio (La Belle Riviera) 5, 32, 35, 38, 43, 52, 56, 48, 59, 73, 84, 96, 110, 114, 126
Oliver, Joseph 98
Orange County, North Carolina 152
Osborne, Alexander 185-189
Osborne, Ephraim 185-189
Osborne, Enoch 185-189, 192
Osborne family 6, 185-189
Otter River, Bedford County 63
Outacite (Antossity Usteneoka) 126- 130, 149, 191
Overhill Cherokee 98, 124
Overton, Samuel 123, 125, 129, 133
Pack, "Hunter" 152, 159
Paint Creek 61
Paleo-Indian culture 32
Pallatia 55-61

Parrot 8, 21
Parsons, West Virginia 61
Pate, Jeremiah 71
Patterson, Erwin 76, 105, 106, 169
Patton, Henry 87, 95, 108
Patton, James 24, 66-68, 73, 77, 82, 83, 98, 104, 109, 111, 113, 115, 117, 118, 119, 120, 123, 137, 163
Patton, Mary Osborne 78
Paul, Audley, Captain 160-161
Pauley, James 203
Peach Bottom 6, 184, 185, 190
Peaked Mountain Settlement 120
Pearis Mountain 126
Pearis, George 126-127, 179
Pearis, Richard 113, 124, 129
Pearisburg 10, 32, 51, 52
Pembroke 21
Pennington Mill 191-192
Pennsylvania 25-26
Pepper, Samuel 179
Peppers Ferry 179
Perecute 45, 46, 50, 52
Perkins, John 193
Perkins, Timothy 192
Peter's Falls 52
Peter's Mountain 10, 52
Peterstown 61, 200
Phelps, John 124
Philadelphia County, Pennsylvania 187
Philips family 187
Pierce, Jeremiah 180
Pine Spur Gap 88, 139
Pipestem State Park 12
Pisgah culture 40
Pitman, William 160
Pittsylvania County 137, 152-153
Point Hope Furnace 184
Point Lookout Mountain 6
Pompey's Pillar 10
Pontiac's War 157-168, 190
Popple, Mary 63, 198
Powell's Valley 155
Pownall, Thomas, Governor 25, 201
Preisch, David and Agnes Hoffman 80

Preston, William 61, 62, 115, 118, 123, 124-129, 158, 163, 170, 17 178
Price, Anna Margaretha 80
Price, Augustine 80, 111, 120
Price, Daniel 80, 120
Price, Henry 80, 120
Price, Michael 80, 119
Price's Fork, Montgomery, Virginia 80
Prince Bridge 12, 14, 27
Quinimont 12
Radford Arsenel 8, 119
Radford University 3
Radford, Virginia 8, 32, 36, 37, 38, 179
Raines, John 155
Rappahannock River Fort 58-59
Ratcliff, Richard 137
Ray, Joseph 141
Ray, William 191
Redd, John 83, 153
Reed Creek settlement 76, 77, 113
Rentfro's Path 88
Rentfro, Peter 66, 69, 79, 88
Report on the Back settlements 36
Reeves, George 185, 192
Rhine River and Valley 2, 69
Rich Creek 61
River of Death 23, 35, 161, 198, 203
Roanoke River 35, 38, 43, 45, 46, 59, 62, 86, 90, 119, 120
Robinson, David 159, 163, 167
Robinson, George 69-70, 78, 82
Robinson, John 165-173
Robinson, William 167
Robinson,Tract 70
Rockford 179
Ronceverte 198
Rosaco, Bob 33
Round Meadows 192
Routledge, Robert 173
Rowan County, North Carolina 123, 137, 189
Sabbatarians 25, 73, 74, 95, 133
Salt Pond Mountain 29
Salling, John Peter 2, 24, 26, 64, 65, 69, 90, 198
Saluda River Settlements 121

Sandbar Falls 10
Sandstone Falls 12, 14
Sault River 23, 63
Sayer's Mill 142
Sayers, Alexander 78, 87, 106, 120, 158, 163, 171
Sayers, David 179
Sayers, William 78, 179
Scaggs, Charles, Henry 152-155
Scaggs, James 76-77, 80
Schaefer, Peter
Schmid, P. 181
Schnell, Leonard 91-92
Schriesheim Germany 70, 76
Sellards, Hezekiah 200
Seneca Trail 61
Senecas 36, 62
Sevier, Valentine 83
Shannon site 38
Shafer, Peter 76, 132
Sharp, George and Henry 116
Shawnee prisoner list 168-169
Shawnees 35, 36, 38, 40, 41, 50-52, 56, 61, 62, 124-130, 134-140, 154-168
Shell, Jacob 120
Shelton, John 82
Shenandoah River and Valley 1, 54, 58, 63, 68, 120
Shoemaker, Peter 203
Shot Tower 7
Shull, Frederick 194
Shull, Simon 194
Shull's Mills 194
Shumate Falls 10
Siebentangers 70
Silverstone 5, 194
Simon the Baptist 180
Sinclair (St. Clair) Charles 64, 82, 87, 106
Sinking Creek 10, 30, 107, 180
Siouan tribes 45, 46
Smith River "Round-About" 153
Smith, Abraham 98, 171
Smith, Henry 155
Smith, John 35, 124, 125, 129, 133-134, 141
Smith, Richard 143
Smith River (Irvine) 44, 159-160
Smithfield 62, 177, 178

Smyth, J.F.D. 73, 88, 89, 139, 162
Snidow Elizabeth 9
Snowville 47
South Fork of the New 5, 6, 30, 189
Sparta 6
Spangenberg, August Gottlieb 100-103
103, 193
Spanish Oak 28
Spotswood, Governor 1, 54
Spratt, Thomas (Kanawha) 62
Springfield (Back Creek) 70, 95,
158, 177
Spruce, Run 8
St. Peter's Lutheran Church 80-81
Starn, Frederick 71, 76, 80, 115,
119
Starn, Katherine 155
Starn, Mary 76
Stafford family 186
Stalnaker, Samuel 71, 73, 76, 78,
79, 83, 95, 98, 105, 115, 124,
134, 146
Staunton 66
Stegg, Thomas 52, 53
Stephen, Adam, Colonel 146, 148
Stogill, Rhoda 200
Stoner, Michael 154
Stuart, John 142
Stuart Dam 4
Sturgill, Francis 183-185
Sturgis family 186
Strouble's Creek 59, 79, 117, 118
Stroud, John 71, 73, 79
Stringer, Reuben 191
Stoner, Michael 153-155
Stone, Uriah 153-155
Stonecliff Bridge 14
Stuart Dam 6
Summers, West Virginia 198
Swope, Hunter 160
Swift, Flower 187
Switzerland 2
Summers, Lewis Preston 43, 44, 124
Sunset Rapids (Double Z) 18
Talbot, Matthew, Colonel 136
Talbot, William, Sir 57
Tatem cabin 194-196
Taylor, Archibald 203
Taylor, John 179
Teays River 1, 23, 27, 29, 31-32

Tennessee 2, 27, 40, 55, 63, 82,
98, 110, 141
Terrell, Obadiah 152, 154
Terry, Mr. 157
Terry, Nathaniel 124
Terry's Fork 139
Three Forks 6, 154
Thompson, John and Esther 78
Thompson, Mary Patton 95
Thompson, William 95, 158, 169-
170, 174, 176, 179
Thorn Spring 70-71
Thunderbird Research Corporation
32
Thurmond 12, 14
Todd (Elk Crossroads) 6, 196
Tomahitans 55, 56
Tom's Creek 8, 59, 70, 79, 80, 118,
119
Toney, Berry 192
Toney, John 198
Tonty, Henri de 58
Toteras 36, 39, 45, 53, 56
Toteras Town 46, 53, 62
Town Fork of Dan (Walnut Cove)
120
Trade, Tennessee 194
Trapper's Meadow 152
Treaty of Lancaster 67, 73-74
Trigg family 180
Turnhole Knob 10
Tyler, James Hoge 179
United States 12
Utley, Brother 181
Undercut Rock Rapids 18
Valley of Contention 77, 78
Fance, John 69, 87, 121
Vascular Flora of New River Gorge
28
Vaughan, Mr. 63
Vause, Ephraim 125
Verdiman, William 137
Viele, Arnold 58
Virginia Polytechnic Institute and
SU 3
Virginia 1, 2, 5, 6, 10, 57-59, 86,
114
Wachovia-Wachau 103
Waddell, Hugh 123, 148

Wade, Robert, Captain 23, 88, 137-139
Waistcoat, Ebnezer 98, 106, 111
Walker, Dr. Thomas 82, 90, 94-95, 98, 109, 144, 146, 157, 175-176, 185, 190, 198
Wall, Adam 80
Wallen family 152-155, 190
Wallen, Elisha 153-155
Wallen, Joseph 153-155
Wallen, Thomas 153-155
Wallen, William 190
Ward, James 191
Walpole Grant 201
Ward, John 152-155, 191
Ward, Nancy (Mrs. Brian) 191
Ward's Gap 44, 191-192, 194
Wart Mountain 88
Warwick Road 62, 86-90, 120-139, 145
Warwick Wharf 87, 113
Washington, George 49, 111, 128-129, 201
Watauga County 5, 32, 34, 39, 40, 100, 183, 189, 193, 194, 206
Watauga Purchase 176
Wates, Mr. 62
Watkins, Beverley 192
Watts, John 105-106
Weason, Jack 45
Weldon, Daniel 189
Wells, Zachariah 192
Welsh Mines See Lead Mines
West Jefferson 5, 210
West Virginia 1, 5, 10, 12, 27, 28
Wheeling, West Virginia 119
Whitehead family 186
Whitethorne 8
Whitetop 5

Wilcoxen, Elizabeth 154
Wilderness Trail 194
Will Jackson Worship Site 39
Williams (Wilhelm), Henry, Michael, Philip 120
Wilkesboro, North Carolina 62
Wilkesboro-Jefferson Turnpike 21
Williamsburg 97-98, 105, 111, 113, 116, 117, 123, 124, 126, 130, 134, 167-168, 170-172
Willis, John and Francis 141
Wiltshire, Nathaniel 87, 98, 115, 119, 168, 179
Wilson, "Surveyor" 189
Wiley, Jennie 126
Withers, Alexander S. 61, 64
Witt, Christopher 76
Wood, Abraham, Major-General 23, 42, 43, 44, 45, 52, 55, 56
Wood, Thomas 23, 45, 53, 57, 58
Woods Fort 200
Woods Gap 43, 44
Wood's River 23, 24, 25, 26, 42, 49, 65, 86, 90, 104, 114, 149
Wood's River Company 80, 97
Wood's River Land Entry Book 24, 25, 68, 69-70
Wright family 186
Wylie Falls 10
Wythe Community College 3
Yadkin 44, 55, 100, 103, 149, 152, 191-194
Yellow Bird and Round O 129
Yarnell, Daniel 192
Young family 186
Zinn, Gerhart and Margaret 94, 115, 116, 132-133, 173
Zinn, Henry 76, 115
Zinn, Valentine 173

Covered bridge built in 1912
Giles County, Virginia on
Sinking Creek of the New
(Photo by Stuart Link)

Dam on Sinking
Creek of the New.
At David Price Mill
built at Newport in
1850's. Dam restored
in 1930 by Hugh P.
Givens.
(Photo by Stuart Link)

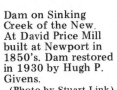

Ingles Ferry Inn on the New built in the 1760's

Covered bridge on Indian Creek on the Seneca Trail
West Virginia's New River Country
(Photo by Walter L. Johnson)

Rhododendron on New River
(Photo by Walter L. Johnson)

James McGavock house Reed Creek of New River
(Photo by W.R. Chitwood)

The New near Stroubles-Lick Creek entrance
Montgomery County, Virginia

(Photo by Frank Shelton)